COUNTRIES, REGIONAL STUDIES, TRADING BLOCKS, UNIONS, WORLD ORGANIZATIONS

MEXICO: BACKGROUND AND ISSUES

COUNTRIES, REGIONAL STUDIES, TRADING BLOCKS, UNIONS, WORLD ORGANIZATIONS

Additional books in this series can be found on Nova's website under the Series tab.

Additional E-books in this series can be found on Nova's website under the E-books tab.

COUNTRIES, REGIONAL STUDIES, TRADING BLOCKS, UNIONS, WORLD ORGANIZATIONS

MEXICO: BACKGROUND AND ISSUES

RICHARD C. BRADLEY
EDITOR

Nova Science Publishers, Inc.
New York

For permission to use material from this book please contact us:
Telephone 631-231-7269; Fax 631-231-8175
Web Site: http://www.novapublishers.com

LIBRARY OF CONGRESS CATALOGING-IN-PUBLICATION DATA
Mexico : background and issues / editor, Richard C. Bradley.
p. cm.
Includes index.
ISBN 978-1-61728-498-4 (hardcover)
1. United States--Foreign relations--Mexico. 2. Mexico--Foreign relations--United States. 3. United States--Foreign economic relations--Mexico. 4. Mexico--Foreign economic relations--United States. 5. Mexico--Economic conditions. 6. Mexico--Strategic aspects. 7. Drug traffic--Mexico. I. Bradley, Richard C.
E183.8.M6M466 2010
327.73072--dc22
2010023784

Published by Nova Science Publishers, Inc. ✦ New York

CONTENTS

PREFACE

The United States and Mexico have a close and complex bilateral relationship, with extensive economic linkages as neighbors and partners under the North American Free Trade Agreement (NAFTA). Bilateral relations are characterized by strong commercial and cultural ties and cooperation on a range of bilateral and international issues. In recent years, security issues have dominated the bilateral agenda, as the United States has supported Mexican President Felipe Calderon's campaign against drug trafficking organizations (DTOs) and organized crime. This new book is an overview on the background, history, economic trends, and current issues facing Mexico today.

Chapter 1 - The United States and Mexico have a close and complex bilateral relationship, with extensive economic linkages as neighbors and partners under the North American Free Trade Agreement (NAFTA). Bilateral relations are characterized by strong commercial and cultural ties and cooperation on a range of bilateral and international issues. In recent years, security issues have dominated the bilateral agenda, as the United States has supported Mexican President Felipe Calderón's campaign against drug trafficking organizations (DTOs) and organized crime.

Halfway through his six-year term, President Calderón of the conservative National Action Party (PAN) is focused on dealing with two major challenges: restarting the Mexican economy, which contracted by 7% in 2009 (largely as a result of the U.S. recession), and combating DTOs. In addition, Calderón submitted a wide-ranging political reform proposal to the Mexican Congress in December 2009, which, if enacted, would introduce run-off presidential elections, permit legislators to run for re-election, and reduce the size of the Congress. As the 2012 presidential elections approach, the Congress, which is now dominated by the Institutional Revolutionary Party (PRI), could be reluctant to give President Calderón any major legislative victories or to take up difficult issues such as reforming the declining oil sector.In recent years, U.S.-Mexican relations have grown stronger as the two countries have worked together to combat drug trafficking and secure their shared border. President Obama met with President Calderón in Mexico on April 16-17, 2009, to discuss counterdrug cooperation, immigration reform, and climate change. The leaders met again in August 2009 alongside Canadian Prime Minister Stephen Harper at the North American Leaders Summit in Guadalajara to discuss how to coordinate their responses to the global economic crisis, climate change, and security issues. They pointed to North America's successful response to the H1N1 "swine flu" outbreak as a model for future collaboration. One challenge for Mexico-U.S. relations has been how to resolve an ongoing dispute involving the implementation of NAFTA trucking provisions. In March 2009, Congress terminated a pilot project for Mexican-registered trucks to operate beyond the border commercial zone, and Mexico responded by imposing import tariffs on more than 90 U.S. agricultural and industrial products.

During its second session, the 111th Congress is likely to maintain an active interest in Mexico with counternarcotics, border, and trade issues dominating the agenda. To date, Congress has appropriated some $1.3 billion in assistance for Mexico under the Mérida Initiative, an anti-crime and counterdrug package first funded in FY2008, including $210.3 million in the FY2010 Consolidated Appropriations Act (P.L. 111-117). Congress is likely to maintain a keen interest in how implementation of the Mérida Initiative and related domestic initiatives to improve border security are proceeding, particularly as it considers the President's FY2011 budget request, which includes at least $341 million in assistance to Mexico, including $310 million in assistance accounts that have funded the Mérida Initiative. Congress may also be interested in how the Obama Administration moves to resolve the current trucking dispute with Mexico now that P.L. 111-117 would permit the resumption of a U.S.-funded pilot program for Mexican trucks. Congress may also consider proposals for comprehensive immigration reform.

Chapter 2 - Mexico has a population of about 110 million people making it the most populous Spanish- speaking country in the world and the third most populous country in the Western Hemisphere. Based on a gross domestic product (GDP) of $1.0 trillion in 2008 (about 7% of U.S. GDP), Mexico has a free market economy with a strong export sector. Economic conditions in Mexico are important to the United States because of the proximity of Mexico to the United States, the close trade and investment interactions, and other social and political issues that are affected by the economic relationship between the two countries.

The United States and Mexico have strong economic ties. An important feature of the relationship is the North American Free Trade Agreement (NAFTA), which has been in effect since 1994. In terms of total trade, Mexico is the United States' third largest trading partner, while the United States ranks first among Mexico's trading partners. In U.S. imports, Mexico ranks third among U.S. trading partners, after China and Canada, while in exports Mexico ranks second, after Canada. The United States is the largest source of foreign direct investment (FDI) in Mexico. These links are critical to many U.S. industries and border communities.

In 2008, about 11% of total U.S. merchandise exports were destined for Mexico and 10% of U.S. merchandise imports came from Mexico. In the same year U.S. exports to Mexico increased almost 10%, while imports from Mexico increased about 3%. For Mexico, the United States is a much more significant trading partner. About 82% of Mexico's exports go to the United States and 50% of Mexico's imports come from the United States. FDI forms another part of the economic relationship between the United States and Mexico. The United States is the largest source of FDI in Mexico. U.S. FDI in Mexico totaled $91.7 billion in 2007. The overall effect of NAFTA on the U.S. economy has been relatively small, primarily because two-way trade with Mexico amounts to less than three percent of U.S. GDP. Major trade issues between Mexico and the United States have involved the access of Mexican trucks to the United States; the access of Mexican sugar and tuna to the U.S. market; and the access of U.S. sweeteners to the Mexican market.

Over the last decade, the economic relationship between the United States and Mexico has strengthened significantly. The two countries continue to cooperate on issues of mutual concern. On March 23, 2005, the leaders of the United States, Canada, and Mexico met to discuss issues related to North American trade, immigration and defense. After the meeting, the three leaders announced the Security and Prosperity Partnership of North America (SPP), an initiative that is intended to increase cooperation and information sharing in an effort to increase and enhance prosperity in the United States, Canada, and Mexico. In April 2008, the North American leaders held a summit to discuss how they might further advance the goals of the SPP. The three leaders decided that their respective ministers should continue to renew and focus their work in the five SPP priority areas.

Chapter 3 - Increasing violence perpetrated by drug trafficking organizations (DTOs) and other criminal groups is threatening citizen security in Mexico and Central America. Drug-related violence claimed more than 6,500 lives in Mexico in 2009, and several Central American countries have among the highest homicide rates in the world. Mexican DTOs dominate the illicit drug market in the United States and are expanding their operations by forming partnerships with U.S. gangs. As a result, some of the drug-related violence in Mexico has spilled over into the United States.

On October 22, 2007, the United States and Mexico announced the Mérida Initiative, a proposed package of U.S. counterdrug and anticrime assistance for Mexico and Central America that would begin in FY2008 and last through FY2010. Congress appropriated roughly $1.3 billion for Mexico and Central America, as well as Haiti and the Dominican Republic, in the FY2008 Supplemental Appropriations Act (P.L. 110-252), FY2009 Omnibus Appropriations Act (P.L. 111-8), and the FY2009 Supplemental Appropriations Act (P.L. 111-32). Each of these Acts contained human rights conditions on 15% of certain law enforcement and military assistance provided.

Throughout 2009, drug-related violence in Mexico and the potential threat of spillover along the Southwest border focused congressional concern on the pace of implementation of the Mérida Initiative. On December 3, 2009, the Government Accountability Office (GAO) issued a preliminary report for Congress on the status of funding for the Mérida Initiative. By the end of September 2009, GAO found that $830 million of the $1.3 billion in Mérida funds appropriated for Mexico and Central America had been obligated by the State Department, but only $26 million of the funds had actually been spent. The pace of implementation has accelerated since that time, particularly in Mexico, but implementation challenges remain.

For FY2010, the Obama Administration requested $450 million in Mérida funding for Mexico and $100 million for Central America. On December 13, 2009, Congress passed the FY2010 Consolidated Appropriations Act (H.R. 3288/P.L. 111-117), which allows for $210.3 million for Mexico and $83 million for Central America under a new Central America Regional Security Initiative (CARSI). These Mexico (Mérida) and Central America (CARSI) funds are subject to the same human rights conditions as those provided in P.L. 111-8. Congress also provided $37 million in P.L. 111-117 for a new Caribbean Basin Security Initiative (CBSI).

During its second session, the 111th Congress is likely to maintain a strong interest in how well U.S. agencies and their foreign counterparts are implementing the Mérida Initiative and the degree to which the nations involved are fulfilling their domestic obligations under Mérida. Congress may also monitor enforcement of Mérida's human rights conditions, particularly with respect to Mexico. Congress is likely to play a role in the design of post-Mérida security cooperation with Mexico, Central America, and the Caribbean Basin during its consideration of the Obama Administration's FY2011 budget request. This chapter provides an overview of the funding provided for the Mérida Initiative, the status of Mérida implementation, and a discussion of some policy issues that Congress may consider as it oversees the Initiative.

Chapter 4 - Drug-related violence in Mexico has spiked in recent years as drug trafficking organizations (DTOs) have competed for control of smuggling routes into the United States. Drug trafficking issues are prominent in Mexico because the country has for at least four decades been among the most important producers and suppliers of heroin, marijuana and (later) methamphetamine to the U.S. market. Today it is the leading source of all three drugs and is now the leading transit country for cocaine coming from South America to the United States. Although previous Mexican governments had accommodated some drug trafficking in the country, when President Felipe Calderón came into office in December 2006 he made battling the Mexican drug trafficking organizations a top priority. He has raised spending on security and sent thousands of troops and federal police to combat the DTOs in states along the U.S.-Mexico border and throughout the country. In response to the government's crackdown, the DTOs have responded with escalating violence.

In recent years, drug trafficking violence in Mexico has claimed thousands of lives and reached a level of intensity and ferocity that has exceeded previous periods of drug-related violence. The government's intensified campaign against the DTOs resulted in changes in the structure of these criminal organizations. The seven major DTOs in Mexico have reconfigured. The fracturing of some of the most powerful drug trafficking syndicates and the reemergence of once powerful DTOs have led to bloody conflict within and among the DTOs. Today a small number of DTOs control the lucrative drug trafficking corridors through which drugs flow north from Mexico into the United States and high-powered firearms and cash flow south fueling the narcotics trade.

President Calderón has demonstrated what has been characterized as an unprecedented willingness to cooperate with the United States on counterdrug measures. In October 2007, both countries announced the Mérida Initiative to combat drug trafficking, gangs and organized crime in Mexico and Central America. To date, the U.S. Congress has appropriated a total of $700 million for Mexico under the Mérida Initiative. The program, which combines counternarcotics equipment and training with rule of law and justice reform efforts, is still in its initial stages of implementation.

The scope of the drug violence and its location—much of it in northern Mexico near the U.S.-Mexico border—has been the subject of intense interest in Congress. The 111th Congress has held more than a dozen hearings dealing with the increased violence in Mexico as well as U.S. foreign assistance and border security efforts. This chapter examines the causes for the escalation of the violence in Mexico. It provides a brief overview of Mexico's counterdrug efforts, a description of the major DTOs, the causes and trends in the violence, the Calderón government's efforts to crackdown on the DTOs, and the objectives and implementation of the Mérida Initiative as a response to the violence in Mexico.

Chapter 5 - Mexico has had a growing commitment to trade integration through the formation of free trade agreements (FTAs) since the 1990s and its trade policy is among the most open in the world. Mexico's pursuit of FTAs with other countries not only provides economic benefits, but could also potentially reduce its economic dependence on the United States. The United States is, by far, Mexico's most significant trading partner. About 80% of Mexico's exports go to the United States and 49% of Mexico's imports come from the United States. Mexico's second largest trading partner is China, accounting for approximately 6% of

Mexico's exports and imports. In an effort to increase trade with other countries, Mexico has a total of 11 trade agreements involving 41 countries. These include agreements with most countries in the Western Hemisphere including the United States and Canada, Chile, Costa Rica, Nicaragua, Guatemala, El Salvador, and Honduras. In addition, Mexico has negotiated FTAs outside of the Western Hemisphere and entered into agreements with Israel and the European Union in July 2000. Mexico also has an FTA with Japan. The large number of trade agreements, however, has not yet been successful in decreasing Mexico's dependence on trade with the United States.

Economic motivations are generally the major driving force for the formation of free trade agreements among countries, but there are other reasons countries enter into FTAs, including political and security factors. One of Mexico's primary motivations for the unilateral trade liberalization efforts of the late 1980s and early 1990s was to improve economic conditions in the country, which policymakers hoped would lead to greater investor confidence and attract more foreign investment. Trade agreements were also expected to improve investor confidence, attract foreign investment, and create jobs. Mexico may have other reasons for entering into FTAs, such as expanding market access and decreasing its reliance on the United States as an export market. The slow progress in multilateral negotiations may also contribute to the increasing interest throughout the world in regional trade blocs. Some countries may see smaller trade arrangements as "building blocks" for multilateral agreements.

Since Mexico began trade liberalization in the early 1990s, its trade with the world has risen rapidly, with exports increasing more rapidly than imports. Mexico's trade balance with all countries went from a deficit of \$13.5 billion in 1993 to surpluses of \$7.1 billion in 1995 and \$6.5 billion in 1996. Since 1998, Mexico's trade balance has remained in deficit, reaching \$17.5 billion in 2008. The trade balance with the United States went from a deficit of \$2.4 billion in 1993 to a surplus of \$82.0 billion in 2008. Exports to the United States increased 447% between 1993 and 2008, from \$42.9 billion to \$292.6 billion. Mexico's imports from the United States increased 237% during the same time period, from \$45.3 billion to \$152.6 billion.

In the 110th Congress, issues of concern related to the trade and economic relationship with Mexico involved mostly economic conditions in Mexico, issues related to the North American Free Trade Agreement (NAFTA), the effect of NAFTA on Mexico, and Mexican migrant workers in the United States. The 111th Congress will likely maintain an active interest concerning Mexico on these issues. This chapter provides an overview of Mexico's free trade agreements, its motivations for trade liberalization and entering into free trade agreements, and some of the issues Mexico faces in addressing its economic challenges.

Chapter 6 - The North American Free Trade Agreement (NAFTA), in effect since January 1994, plays a very strong role in the bilateral economic relationship between Mexico and the United States. The two countries are also closely tied in areas not directly related to trade and investment such as security, environmental, migration, and health issues. The effects of NAFTA on Mexico and the state of the Mexican economy have important impacts on U.S. economic and political interests. As NAFTA approaches its 15th anniversary, a number of policymakers have raised the issue of revisiting NAFTA and renegotiating parts of the agreement. Some important factors in evaluating NAFTA include the effects of the agreement on Mexico and how these relate to U.S.-Mexico economic relations. In the 110th Congress, major issues of concern have been related mostly to economic conditions in

Mexico, the effect of NAFTA on the United States and Mexico, and Mexican migrant workers in the United States.

In 1990, then Mexican President Carlos Salinas de Gortari approached the United States with the idea of forming a free trade agreement (FTA). Mexico's main motivation in pursuing an FTA with the United States was to stabilize the Mexican economy by attracting foreign direct investment. The Mexican economy had experienced many difficulties throughout most of the 1980s with a significant deepening of poverty. The intention of Mexico in entering NAFTA was to increase export diversification by attracting foreign direct investment (FDI), which would help create jobs, increase wage rates, and reduce poverty.

At the time that NAFTA went into effect, the expectation among supporters was that the agreement would improve investor confidence in Mexico, attract investment, and narrow the income differentials between Mexico and the United States and Canada. Measuring the effects of NAFTA on the Mexican economy is difficult because the economy was also affected by other factors, such as economic cycles in the United States (Mexico's largest trading partner) and currency fluctuations. In addition, Mexico's unilateral trade liberalization measures of the 1980s and the currency crisis of 1995 both affected economic growth, per capita gross domestic product (GDP), and real wages.

While NAFTA may have brought economic and social benefits to the Mexican economy as a whole, the benefits have not been evenly distributed throughout the country. Wages and employment tend to be higher in states experiencing higher levels of FDI and trade. The agricultural sector experienced a higher amount of worker displacement after NAFTA because of increased competition from the United States and because of Mexican domestic agricultural reforms. In terms of regional effects, initial conditions in Mexico determined which Mexican states experienced stronger economic growth as a result of NAFTA. States with higher levels of telecommunications and transportation infrastructure gained more benefits than poorer states with lower levels of education, infrastructure, and institutional capacity. Some economists argue that while trade liberalization may narrow income disparities over the long run with other countries, it may indirectly lead to larger disparities in income levels within a country.

Chapter 7 features a profile of Mexico.

Chapter 8 - Mexico is a major non-OPEC oil producer, with one of the world's largest oil companies, Pemex.

In: Mexico: Background and Issues
Editor: Richard C. Bradley
ISBN: 978-1-61728-498-4

Chapter 1

MEXICO-U.S. RELATIONS: ISSUES FOR CONGRESS*

Clare Ribando Seelke, Mark P. Sullivan and June S. Beittel

SUMMARY

The United States and Mexico have a close and complex bilateral relationship, with extensive economic linkages as neighbors and partners under the North American Free Trade Agreement (NAFTA). Bilateral relations are characterized by strong commercial and cultural ties and cooperation on a range of bilateral and international issues. In recent years, security issues have dominated the bilateral agenda, as the United States has supported Mexican President Felipe Calderón's campaign against drug trafficking organizations (DTOs) and organized crime.

Halfway through his six-year term, President Calderón of the conservative National Action Party (PAN) is focused on dealing with two major challenges: restarting the Mexican economy, which contracted by 7% in 2009 (largely as a result of the U.S. recession), and combating DTOs. In addition, Calderón submitted a wide-ranging political reform proposal to the Mexican Congress in December 2009, which, if enacted, would introduce run-off presidential elections, permit legislators to run for re-election, and reduce the size of the Congress. As the 2012 presidential elections approach, the Congress, which is now dominated by the Institutional Revolutionary Party (PRI), could be reluctant to give President Calderón any major legislative victories or to take up difficult issues such as reforming the declining oil sector.In recent years, U.S.-Mexican relations have grown stronger as the two countries have worked together to combat drug trafficking and secure their shared border. President Obama met with President Calderón in Mexico on April 16-17, 2009, to discuss counterdrug cooperation, immigration reform, and climate change. The leaders met again in August 2009 alongside Canadian Prime Minister Stephen Harper at the North American Leaders Summit in Guadalajara to discuss how to coordinate their responses to the global economic crisis, climate change, and security issues. They pointed to North America's successful response to

---

* This is an edited, reformatted and augmented version of a CRS Report for Congress publication dated February 2010.

the H1N1 "swine flu" outbreak as a model for future collaboration. One challenge for Mexico-U.S. relations has been how to resolve an ongoing dispute involving the implementation of NAFTA trucking provisions. In March 2009, Congress terminated a pilot project for Mexican-registered trucks to operate beyond the border commercial zone, and Mexico responded by imposing import tariffs on more than 90 U.S. agricultural and industrial products.

During its second session, the 111th Congress is likely to maintain an active interest in Mexico with counternarcotics, border, and trade issues dominating the agenda. To date, Congress has appropriated some $1.3 billion in assistance for Mexico under the Mérida Initiative, an anti-crime and counterdrug package first funded in FY2008, including $210.3 million in the FY2010 Consolidated Appropriations Act (P.L. 111-117). Congress is likely to maintain a keen interest in how implementation of the Mérida Initiative and related domestic initiatives to improve border security are proceeding, particularly as it considers the President's FY2011 budget request, which includes at least $341 million in assistance to Mexico, including $310 million in assistance accounts that have funded the Mérida Initiative. Congress may also be interested in how the Obama Administration moves to resolve the current trucking dispute with Mexico now that P.L. 111-117 would permit the resumption of a U.S.-funded pilot program for Mexican trucks. Congress may also consider proposals for comprehensive immigration reform.

RECENT DEVELOPMENTS

On February 1, 2010, the Obama Administration submitted its FY2011 budget request to Congress. Although the complete budget request for Mexico will not be available until the State Department releases its FY2011 Congressional Budget Justification for Foreign Operations, it appears that the Administration has requested at least $341 million in assistance to Mexico, including $310 million in assistance accounts that have funded the Mérida Initiative. (see "U.S. Assistance to Mexico")

On January 27, 2010, Mexico's Central Bank announced that remittance inflows fell 15.7% in 2009 to $21 billion.

On January 15, 2010, Mexican officials announced that 2,000 newly trained federal police would take over primary responsibility for securing Ciudad Juarez, Chihuahua, the country's most violent city, from the military forces that had controlled public security efforts in the city since the spring of 2009. A day later, the Mexican military deployed 850 more soldiers to Tijuana, Baja California, a city where violence has spiked in recent months.

On January 12, 2010, the Mexican government arrested Teodoro "el Teo" Simental, a drug trafficker accused of orchestrating at least 300 murders in Baja California.

On January 1, 2010, Mexican authorities found the bodies of an American educator from El Monte, California, Agustin Roberto "Bobby" Salcedo, and five other men who were allegedly kidnapped from a restaurant and then killed by suspected drug traffickers in Durango, Mexico.

On December 30, 2009, Mexican federal police arrested Carlos Beltrán Leyva, the brother of Arturo Beltrán Leyva and himself a major drug trafficker, in Sinaloa.

On December 30, 2009, the Bureau of Alcohol, Tobacco, Firearms, and Explosives announced that it had deployed a bilingual version of its "e-Trace" firearms tracing technology to Mexico.

On December 16, 2009, Mexican marines killed Arturo Beltrán Leyva, one of Mexico's most wanted drug traffickers, during a shootout in Cuernavaca, Morelos. Just prior to the funeral for one of the marines who was killed in the operation against Beltrán Leyva, gunmen entered the marine's home and killed four of his close family members.

On December 16, 2009, Congress appropriated $50 million in funding for counternarcotics communication equipment for Mexico in the FY2010 Department of Defense Appropriations Act (P.L. 111-118).

On December 15, 2009, the U.S. Embassy in Mexico City announced the delivery of five Bell helicopters, valued at $66 million, that had been purchased for Mexico's Secretary of Defense as part of the Mérida Initiative.

On December 15, 2009, President Calderón presented a proposal for comprehensive political reform to the Mexican Congress. Among other things, the reform package seeks to introduce a presidential run-off election in the event that neither candidate wins an outright majority, to allow senators and deputies to be re-elected and to serve for up to 12 years, and to reduce the size of the Mexican Senate and Chamber of Deputies.

On December 13, 2009, Congress passed the FY2010 Consolidated Appropriations Act (P.L. 111-117), which allows for $210.3 million for Mérida funds for Mexico subject to the same human rights conditions as those provided in P.L. 111-8. The Act does not include language that was in P.L. 111-8 prohibiting the Department of Transportation from funding a pilot project for Mexican-registered trucks to operate beyond the border commercial zone.

On December 3, 2009, the Government Accountability Office (GAO) issued a preliminary report for Congress on the status of funding for the Mérida Initiative. By the end of September 2009, GAO found that $830 million of the $1.3 billion in Mérida funds appropriated for Mexico and Central America had been obligated by the State Department, but only $26 million of the funds had actually been spent. The report is available at: http://www.gao.gov/products/GAO-10-253R.

On November 17, 2009, the Mexican Congress gave final approval for the FY2010 budget. While the final bill included an increase in income taxes for the country's top income brackets, a slight increase in the value-added tax, and a tax on beer and cigarettes, it did not include a 2% consumption tax that President Calderón had proposed. On the expenditure side, the budget requires the Calderón Administration to make cutbacks in its operating and personnel budgets, while maintaining spending for social programs, infrastructure, and the agriculture sector. The budget dedicates roughly $6.9 billion for security-related programs.

On October 22-23, 2009, agents from several U.S. federal agencies, as well as state and local police, engaged in a joint operation in 38 U.S. cities against La Familia Michoacana. The raid resulted in 300 arrests.

On October 11, 2009, President Calderón ordered the liquidation of Luz y Fuerza del Centro (LyFC), an ill-performing state-owned electricity company that served Mexico City and several surrounding states. The move sparked massive protests by the 42,000 unionized workers that had enjoyed overly generous benefits from the company.

Source: Map Resources, adapted by CRS.

Figure 1. Map of Mexico, Including States and Border Cities

Background on Mexico

Political Developments

Over the past decade, Mexico has moved from one-party rule by the PRI to multi-party democracy. Current PAN President Felipe Calderón won the July 2006 presidential election in an extremely tight race, defeating Andrés López Obrador of the leftist Democratic Revolution Party (PRD) by less than 234,000 votes. The presidential race was so close that final results were not announced until early September 2006, when the Federal Electoral Tribunal completed adjudication of all the challenges to those results. Calderón was sworn in to a six-year term on December 1, 2006.

In the first half of his term, President Calderón, whose PAN party became the largest party in the Senate and Chamber of Deputies after the 2006 legislative elections, had some success in turning to the PRI for help in advancing his legislative agenda. In 2007, he secured passage of long-awaited fiscal and pension reforms that had stalled under the Fox Administration. In June 2008, President Calderón signed a judicial reform decree after securing the approval of Congress and Mexico's states for an amendment to Mexico's

Constitution. Under the judicial reform, Mexico will have eight years to move from a closed door process based on written arguments to a public trial system with oral arguments and the presumption of innocence. In October 2008, the government secured approval of an energy sector reform intended to improve the transparency and management flexibility of state-oil company, *Petroleos Mexicanos* (PEMEX). Critics maintained that its watered-down provisions, which provide only limited opportunities for private investment in the company, would not do enough to encourage new oil exploration.[1]

In the months leading up to the July 5, 2009 midterm elections, most polls indicated that the PRI, which had fared well in recent state and municipal elections, would fare well as compared to the PAN and the PRD. The PRI performed even better than those polls had suggested, capturing 237 of 500 seats in the Chamber of Deputies, five of six governorships, and several municipalities. Analysts have attributed the PRI's strong performance to growing popular concern about the country's economic downturn, as well as the party's effective use of its still formidable national machinery. Although President Calderón is still popular, the PAN lost seats in the Chamber (from 206 to 147) and two key governorships, with voters expressing frustration with the party's failure to distinguish itself from the PRI. (The PAN still controls the Senate, however.) The PRD fared even worse than the PAN in the mid-term elections, winning just 72 seats in the Chamber, as internal divisions within the party led Andrés Lopez Obrador to throw his support behind left-leaning candidates from smaller parties, many of whom won.[2]

The composition of the new Congress, which was sworn in on September 1, 2009, could complicate President Calderón's agenda in the second half of his term. The PRI, which, combined with the support of the allied Green Ecological Party (PVEM) party, now controls a majority in the Chamber, is likely to try to use its position to gear up for the 2010-2011 gubernatorial elections and the 2012 presidential election. However, many observers maintain that the PRI is unlikely to block any major security or economic stimulus initiatives, given the severity of the drug violence and economic challenges that Mexico is facing. Moreover, the PRI is expected to be more cooperative now than it was after winning a majority in the 2003 elections, for fear of being dismissed by voters in 2012 as obstructionist.[3]

Drug Trafficking and Heightened Violence and Crime in Mexico[4]

Mexico is a major producer and supplier to the U.S. market of heroin, methamphetamine, and marijuana and the major transit country for as much as 90% of the cocaine sold in the United States. A small number of Mexican drug trafficking organizations (DTOs), often erroneously referred to as "drug cartels,"[5] control the most significant drug distribution operations along the Southwest border. The criminal activities of these Mexican DTOs reach well beyond the towns and cities of the border, extending along drug trafficking routes into cities across the United States.[6] In the past few years, the violence and brutality of the Mexican DTOs have escalated as an increasing number of groups have battled each other for control of lucrative drug trafficking routes into the United States.

Since taking office in December 2006, President Calderón has made combating drug trafficking organizations (DTOs) a top priority of his administration. He has called increasing drug violence in Mexico a threat to the Mexican state and has sent thousands of soldiers and police to drug trafficking "hot-spots" in at least 16 states throughout Mexico. Joint deployments of federal military and police officials are just one part of the Calderón government's strategy against the DTOs. That strategy involves (1) deploying the military to restore law and order, (2) law enforcement operations, (3) institutional reform and anti-corruption initiatives[7], (4) recovering social cohesion and trust, and (5) building up international partnerships against drugs and crime (like the Mérida Initiative).[8] President Calderón has also used extradition as a major tool to combat drug traffickers, extraditing 95 individuals in 2008 and a record-breaking 107 individuals in 2009.[9] These efforts, combined with increased collaboration and intelligence-sharing with U.S. law enforcement agencies, have resulted in some significant government victories against the DTOs – including the recent killing of Arturo Beltrán Leyva and capture of Teodoro Garcia Simental.[10]

Despite these victories, the persistent and increasingly brazen violence committed by the drug traffickers, which has occurred partially in response to government pressure, has led to increasing criticism of Calderón's aggressive anti-drug strategy.[11] In 2008 and again in 2009, the government's crackdown and rivalries and turf wars among Mexico's DTOs fueled an escalation in violence throughout the country, including in northern states near the U.S.-Mexico border. In the past two years, conservative estimates indicate that at least 11,740 Mexicans died in drug-related violence, including nearly 535 police and military officers who were killed in 2009.[12] Kidnapping for money, robbery, and extortion have also increased significantly, as some of the DTOs have evolved into what analysts have termed "full-scale mafias."[13]

Some experts assert that, in order to maintain popular support for its security policies, the Calderón government will have to show success in dismantling the DTOs, while also reducing drug-related violence in places like Ciudad Juarez, Sinaloa, Durango, and Baja California.[14] Mexican officials are reportedly revising their military-led strategy in Ciudad Juarez and have just deployed 2,000 newly trained federal police to set up checkpoints and patrol the city. This move may help respond to academics and human rights groups who have argued that Calderón's heavy reliance on military forces to perform public security tasks has resulted in a growing number of human rights violations by security forces.[15] The Mexican government is also reportedly considering an increase in funding for social and economic development programs to address the root causes of violence in Juarez and other border communities.[16]

Economic Crisis and Nascent Recovery[17]

Mexico's economy is strongly dependent on economic conditions in the United States because more than 80% of its exports are destined for the U.S. market and the United States is its primary source of tourism revenues and foreign investment. The Mexican economy grew 3.3% in 2007, the first year of the Calderón government. Slower growth was already anticipated for 2008 due in part to decreasing consumer demand in the United States, declining Mexican oil production, and slow growth in remittances sent by Mexicans abroad. The global financial crisis, which caused a run on the Mexican peso, further reduced GDP growth in 2008 to just 1.4%. For 2009, the Mexican economy contracted by approximately

7%, the worst decline in six decades. Experts do not expect Mexico's real GDP to recover 2008 levels until 2011.[18]

The Calderón government has been struggling to cope with the combined effects of the U.S. and global recessions, a nationwide outbreak of H1N1 "swine" flu, and declining oil production. The U.S. recession has resulted in steep declines in demand for Mexican exports, particularly in the manufacturing sector. Mexico's exports to the United States between the period of January – November of 2009 declined by 22% when compared to the same period of 2008.[19] The economic decline in the United States has also resulted in declining remittance flows to Mexico. In 2008, remittances to Mexico fell to an estimated $25 billion, the lowest level since 2005. According to Mexico's Central Bank, remittance flows through in 2009 totaled just $21.2 billion, 16% lower than last year.[20] These developments were further exacerbated by the outbreak of pandemic H1N1 "swine flu" in April 2009, which prompted the government to close restaurants, schools, and retail establishments for nearly two weeks. The tourism industry, Mexico's third largest foreign exchange earner, was especially hard hit by the outbreak, with a 50% drop in income earned by foreign visitors in May and a 29% drop in June as compared to the year before.[21] Declining oil prices and production have also been major economic setbacks for Mexico, which depends on oil proceeds for over one-third of government revenue.

The Calderón government took a number of measures to attempt to cushion the Mexican economy from the fallout of the global economic crisis and the U.S. recession. The government used billions in its international reserves to shore up the peso, and the Mexican central bank established a temporary reciprocal currency sway line with the U.S. Federal Reserve for up to $30 billion. The government also hedged its oil exports for 2009 at a price of $70 a barrel in an effort to protect the economy from the decline in oil prices. The central government increased liquidity in the banking system, including multiple cuts in the prime policy lending rate. It also increased its credit lines with the World Bank, International Monetary Fund, and Inter-American Development Bank. In 2009, Mexico's fiscal stimulus amounted to 2.5% of GDP and was targeted on infrastructure spending and subsidies for key goods of household budgets, particularly those reducing energy costs. Government programs to support small and medium-sized businesses, worker training, employment generation, and social safety nets were maintained and, in some cases, expanded.[22]

There are signs that the Mexican economy has begun to recover from the economic crisis, but the costs of the government's policy responses to that crisis have placed significant strain on Mexico's public finances. Economic growth picked up in the third and fourth quarters of 2009, and many experts are predicting that the Mexican economy may grow by as much as 3.5% in 2010.[23] However, Mexico's overall fiscal deficit is expected to reach 2.8% for 2010, estimated to be near the maximum that the country can afford. Recent downward revisions of Mexico's credit rating (still investor grade) reflect growing concern over Mexico's financial position in light of weak economic fundamentals and Mexico's recovery relying so heavily on a U.S. economic rebound. As a result, the Calderón government has ended some of the fuel subsidies put into place in January 2009 and garnered legislative approval for a relatively austere budget for 2010.[24]

As elsewhere in Latin America, there are concerns that the economic downturn in Mexico has negatively impacted the country's recent progress in reducing poverty. Mexico, with a population of almost 110 million, is classified by the World Bank as an upper middle income developing country, with a per capita income level of $9,980 (2008). According to officials from the United Nations Economic Commission for Latin America and the Caribbean (ECLAC), the percentage of Mexicans living in poverty fell between 2000 and 2006, but rose again between 2006 and 2008 to include roughly 45% of the population. ECLAC has also estimated that the number of individuals living in extreme poverty in Mexico and Central America increased by 800,000 in 2009.[25]

Mexico's main poverty reduction program is *Oportunidades* (Opportunities). The program, formerly known as *Progresa* (Progress), began under President Ernesto Zedillo (1994-2000) and has since expanded to benefit 5 million Mexican families (25 million individuals). The program seeks not only to alleviate the immediate effects of poverty through cash and in-kind transfers, but to break the cycle of poverty by improving nutrition, health standards, and educational attainment. It provides cash transfers to families in poverty who demonstrate that they regularly attend medical appointments and can certify that children are attending school. While some have praised *Oportunidades* for its positive effects on educational and nutrition outcomes, others have criticized it for creating dependency on government handouts.[26] On April 9, 2009, the World Bank approved a $1.5 billion loan to Mexico to expand the *Oportunidades* program in an effort to relieve the social impact of the economic downturn.

Foreign Policy Challenges

While the bilateral relationship with the United States has continued to dominate Mexican foreign policy, former President Fox (2000-2006) and current President Calderón have pursued more diversified foreign policies than their recent predecessors. The Fox Administration pursued other policy initiatives after the September 2001 terrorist attacks turned U.S. attention away from Mexico and toward the Middle East. Mexico held a temporary seat on the U.N. Security Council in 2002 and 2003 and voted against the U.S. invasion of Iraq, which disappointed the Bush Administration. Fox promoted Plan Puebla-Panama, now called the Mesoamerican Plan, a series of energy, infrastructure, and regional connectivity initiatives with Central America. He attempted to revive the G-3 group trade preferences (Colombia, Venezuela, and Mexico); however, Venezuela formally withdrew from the group in November 2006. Fox also sought better ties with countries in South America. He attempted to expand trade with the European Union under the EU-Mexico free trade agreement (FTA) that went into effect in July 2000, and with Japan under the Mexico-Japan FTA that entered into force in April 2005.[27]

President Calderón has sought to pursue an independent foreign policy with even closer ties to Latin America. Calderón has regularly met with President Álvaro Uribe of Colombia, with whom he has formed a partnership, along with the leaders of Guatemala and Panama, to combat drug trafficking and organized crime. The Colombian government has offered to share training, intelligence, and "best practices" with Mexico that it has gathered through many years of counterdrug operations. In mid-August 2009, President Calderón visited Brazil to discuss the possibility of forming a Brazil-Mexico FTA, as well as developing greater energy cooperation between PEMEX and Petrobras, Brazil's state-owned oil company. Security cooperation between Mexico and the Central American Integration System (SICA) has also expanded under President Calderón. Progress has also continued to advance, albeit slowly, on the Mesoamerican Project mentioned above. The Calderón government attempted to help resolve the political crisis in Honduras after the ouster of former president Manuel Zelaya in June 2009, and has recognized the new government of Porfirio Lobo elected in November 2009. In response to the January 2010 earthquake in Haiti, Mexico pledged $8 million in financial support and sent 10 aircraft, 2 ships (one of which is a hospital ship), 208 experts in search and rescue, and 1,500 tons of humanitarian supplies.[28]

President Calderón has also tried to mend relations with Cuba and Venezuela, which had become tense during the Fox Administration. In September 2007, Mexican and Venezuelan ambassadors presented credentials to the respective governments, restoring full relations for the first time since November 2005. In May 2004, President Fox recalled Mexico's ambassador to Cuba; ambassadors were later restored, but relations between the two countries remained tense through the remainder of the Fox administration. A Cuban ambassador to Mexico also presented his credentials to President Calderón in September 2007. In November 2008, a new Mexico-Cuba agreement intended to help slow the trafficking of undocumented Cubans passing through Mexico to the United States took effect.[29]

MEXICAN-U.S. RELATIONS

Background

Until the early 1980s, Mexico had a closed and statist economy and its independent foreign policy was often at odds with the United States. Those policies began to shift, however, under President Miguel de la Madrid (1982-1988), and changed even more dramatically under President Carlos Salinas de Gortari (1988-1994) and President Ernesto Zedillo (1994-2000). Presidents Salinas opened Mexico's economy to trade and investment, while President Zedillo adopted electoral reforms that leveled the playing field for opposition parties and increased cooperation with the United States on drug control and border issues.

President Fox (2000-2006) encouraged strong relations with the United States, and called for greater cooperation under NAFTA and for a bilateral migration agreement that would regularize the status of undocumented Mexicans in the United States. In the aftermath of the September 2001 terrorist attacks in the United States, the focus of relations shifted to border security issues as the United States became increasingly concerned about homeland security. Relations became strained during the debate on immigration reform in the United States. After President Bush approved the Secure Fence Act of 2006, Mexico, with the support of 27 other nations, denounced the proposed border fence at the Organization of American States.

Under the Calderón government, drug trafficking and violence, border security, and immigration have continued to define the bilateral relationship. Felipe Calderón made his first official visit to the United States as President-elect in early November 2006, after first visiting Canada and several Latin American countries. During his visit, Calderón criticized the authorization of 700 miles of fencing along the U.S.-Mexico border and noted that it complicated U.S.-Mexico relations. He asserted that job creation and increased investment in Mexico would be more effective in reducing illegal migration from Mexico than a border fence. Calderón signaled a shift in Mexican foreign policy when he noted that while immigration is an important issue in the bilateral relationship, it is not the only issue, as trade and economic development are also important.

President Calderón reiterated these concerns during President Bush's March 2007 visit to Mexico. During the visit, President Calderón also called for U.S. assistance in combating drug and weapons trafficking. Specifically, Calderón promised to continue his efforts to combat drug trafficking and called for U.S. efforts to reduced the demand for drugs. Calderón's willingness to increase narcotics cooperation with the United States led to the development of the Mérida Initiative, a multi-year U.S. assistance effort announced in October 2007 to help Mexico and Central America combat drug trafficking and organized crime.

Obama Administration

U.S.-Mexican relations have continued to be close under the Obama Administration, largely focusing on cooperation in combating organized crime and drug trafficking. In mid-January 2009, President Calderón visited then President-elect Obama in Washington D.C. That pre-inaugural meeting, which has become somewhat of a tradition for recent U.S. presidents, demonstrated the importance of strong relations with Mexico.

Secretary of State Hillary Clinton traveled to Mexico City and Monterrey, Mexico, on March 25-26, 2009 to discuss a broad range of bilateral issues, including cooperation under the Mérida Initiative. The Secretary asserted that the U.S. relationship with Mexico "is one of the most important relationships between any two countries in the world" and that both countries "need a strong and sustained partnership, one based on comprehensive engagement, greater balance, shared responsibility, and joint efforts to address hemispheric and global issues."[30] During her visit, Secretary Clinton and Mexican Foreign Minister Patricia Espinosa announced the creation of a new bilateral implementation office in Mexico where Mexican and U.S. officials will work together on efforts to combat drug traffickers and associated violence. Perhaps most significantly, Secretary Clinton criticized the failure of U.S. antidrug policy and acknowledged that an "insatiable demand for illegal drugs" in the United States "fuels the drug trade."[31]

Clinton's visit to Mexico was followed in early April 2009 with trips by Homeland Security Secretary Napolitano and Attorney General Holder where they met with Mexican officials and attended an arms trafficking conference. Both officials emphasized new efforts by their agencies to combat the drug cartels, including the deployment of additional personnel and resources to support anti-gun trafficking and interdiction efforts, as well as law enforcement cooperation.

On April 16-17, 2009, President Barack Obama traveled to Mexico to meet with President Calderón. The two presidents discussed cooperation in the fight against drug-related violence, immigration reform, and a new bilateral framework on clean energy and climate change. During the visit, President Obama acknowledged the U.S. demand for drugs was helping to keep the Mexican drugs cartels in business, and that "more than 90% of the guns recovered in Mexico come from the United States."[32]

At the North American Leaders' Summit in Guadalajara, Mexico in August 2009, President Obama praised Mexico's response to the H1N1 swine flu outbreak and gave his full support for President Calderón's struggle against the drug cartels. Obama stated that he has "great confidence in President Calderón's administration applying the law enforcement techniques that are necessary to curb the power of the cartels, but doing so in a way that's consistent with human rights."[33] During the summit, President Obama, President Calderón, and Canadian Prime Minister Harper pledged to work together to restore economic growth in North America, combat climate change, and prepare for the fall flu season.

U.S. Assistance to Mexico

Mexico, a middle income country, traditionally has not been a major recipient of U.S. foreign assistance, but this changed in FY2008 with congressional approval of the Administration's request for funding to support the Mérida Initiative (see "Mérida Initiative" section below). Because of the Mérida Initiative funding, U.S. assistance to Mexico rose from $65 million in FY2007 to almost $406 million in FY2008. Table 1 provides an overview of recent U.S. assistance to Mexico funded through State Department aid accounts, while Table 2 provides a breakdown of Mérida assistance by account. Aside from Mérida-related funding, Mexico receives development assistance aimed at reducing poverty and inequality and helping the Mexican economy benefit from the North American Free Trade Agreement. Mexico also benefits from military training programs funded through the State Department's International Military Education and Training Account (IMET), as well as counter-terrorism assistance provided through the Non-proliferation, Anti-terrorism and Related Programs (NADR) account.

On February 1, 2010, the Obama Administration submitted its FY2011 budget request to Congress. Although the complete budget request breakdown for Mexico will not be available until the State Department releases its FY2011 Congressional Budget Justification for Foreign Operations, the President's budget request to Congress shows that that the Administration is requesting at least $341 million in total assistance to Mexico. This includes $310 million in assistance accounts that have funded the Mérida Initiative: $292 million in INCLE, $8 million in FMF, and $10 million in ESF.

Bilateral Cooperation on Counternarcotics and Security Efforts

In the 1980s and 1990s, U.S.-Mexican counternarcotics efforts were often marked by mistrust. Beginning in 1986, when the U.S. President was required to certify whether drug-producing countries and drug-transit countries were cooperating fully with the United States, Mexico often was criticized for its lack of efforts, which in turn led to Mexican government criticism of the U.S. assessment. Reforms to the U.S. drug certification process enacted in September 2002 (P.L. 107-228) essentially eliminated the annual drug certification requirement, and instead required the President to designate and withhold assistance from countries that had "failed demonstrably" to make substantial counternarcotics efforts.[34] In the aftermath of these reforms, U.S. bilateral cooperation with Mexico on counternarcotics efforts improved considerably during the Fox administration (2000-2006), and as described above, combating DTOs has become a priority of the current Calderón administration.

Table 1. U.S. Assistance to Mexico by Account, FY2007-FY2010
U.S. $ millions

Account	FY2007	FY2008[a]	FY2009 Regular (Est.)[a]	FY2009 Supp.	FY2009 Total	FY2010 (est.)[b]
CSH[c]	3.7	2.7	2.9	—	2.9	n/a
DA	12.3	8.2	11.2	—	11.2	10.0
ESF	11.4	34.7	15.0	—	15.0	15.0
FMF	0.0	116.5	39.0	260.0	299.0	5.3
IMET	0.1	0.4	0.8	—	0.8	n/a
INCLE	36.7	242.1	294.0	160.0	454.0	190.0
NADR	1.3	1.4	3.9	—	3.9	n/a
TOTAL	65.4	405.9	366.88	420.0	786.8	n/a

Sources: U.S. Department of State, Congressional Budget Justification for Foreign Operations FY2008-FY2010, Joint Explanatory Statement to Division F, FY2010 Consolidated Appropriations Act (H.R. 3288/P.L. 111-117).

Notes: CSH= Child Survival and Health; DA=Development Assistance; ESF=Economic Support Fund; FMF=Foreign Military Financing; IMET=International Military Education and Training; INCLE=International Narcotics Control and Law Enforcement; NADR=Non-proliferation, Anti-terrorism and Related Programs.

a. FY2008 assistance includes funding from the Supplemental Appropriations Act, 2008 (P.L. 110-252). FY2009 assistance includes FY2009 bridge funding from the Supplemental Appropriations Act, 2008 (P.L. 110-252).

b. FY2010 appropriations levels will not be available until the U.S. Department of State's FY2011Congressional Budget Justification for Foreign Operations is released.

c. Beginning with the FY2010 request, the Child Survival and Health Account became known as Global Health and Child Survival—USAID.

Until 2006, Mexico refused to extradite criminals facing the possibility of life without parole to the United States. However, two decisions by the Mexican Supreme Court facilitated extraditions to the United States. In November 2005, in a partial reversal of its October 2001 ruling, the Court found that life imprisonment without the possibility of parole is not cruel and unusual punishment. Then the Court ruled in January 2006 that U.S. extradition requests only need to meet the requirements of the 1978 bilateral extradition treaty, not Mexico's general law on international extradition that was promulgated in 1975.[35] That decision made the extradition process easier. President Calderón has used extradition as a major tool to combat drug traffickers. Extraditions from Mexico rose from 41 in 2005 to a record 107 in 2009.

The State Department's 2009 INCSR maintains that the degree of U.S.-Mexican cooperation on counternarcotics and law enforcement under the Calderón Administration is unprecedented, and characterizes President Calderón's efforts to deal with increased violence stemming from the drug cartels as courageous. In 2008, Mexican law enforcement seized over 19 metric tons (mt) of cocaine, down from 48 mt in 2007, while seizures of cannabis, and heroin were also down significantly. In the report, U.S. law enforcement agencies attribute the recent reductions in seizures to better Mexican enforcement, which has forced traffickers to seek alternative routes. The decline in methamphetamine seizures is attributed to the government's actions to restrict the importation of precursor chemicals used for the production of the drug.

Table 2. FY2008 – FY2010 Mérida Funding for Mexico by Aid Account and Appropriations Measure ($ in millions)

Account	FY2008 Supp. (P.L. 110-252)	FY2009 Bridge (P.L. 110-252)	FY2009 (P.L. 111-8)	FY2009 Supp. (P.L. 111-32)	FY2010 P.L. 111-117)	Account Totals
ESF	20.0	0.0	15.0	0.0	15.0	50.0
INCLE	215.5	48.0	246.0	160.0	190.0	859.5
FMF	116.5	0.0	39.0	260.0	5.3	420.8
Total	**352.0**	**48.0**	**300.0**	**420.0**	**210.3**	**1,330.3**

Sources: U.S. Department of State, FY2008 Supplemental Appropriations Spending Plan; FY2009 Appropriations Spending Plan, and FY2009 Supplemental Spending Plan; FY2010 Consolidated Appropriations Act (P.L. 111-117).

Notes: ESF=Economic Support Fund; FMF=Foreign Military Financing; INCLE=International Narcotics Control and Law Enforcement.

Mérida Initiative[36]

The United States and Mexico issued a joint statement on October 22, 2007, announcing a multi-year plan for $1.4 billion in U.S. assistance to Mexico and Central America to combat drug trafficking and other criminal organizations. The Mérida Initiative, named for the location of a March 2007 meeting between Presidents Bush and Calderón, expands bilateral and regional cooperation to combat organized crime, DTOs, and criminal gangs. The stated objective of the Mérida Initiative, according to the U.S. and Mexican government joint statement, is to maximize the effectiveness of efforts against drug, human, and weapons trafficking.[37] The Bush Administration first requested funds for Mérida, $500 million for Mexico and $50 million for Central America, in its FY2008 supplemental appropriations request.

To date, Congress has appropriated a total of $1.1 billion for Mexico under the Mérida Initiative. Legislative action on Mérida appropriations has included the following:

- In June 2008, the 110th Congress appropriated $352 million in FY2008 supplemental assistance and $48 million in FY2009 bridge fund supplemental assistance for Mexico in P.L. 110-252, the FY2008 Supplemental Appropriations Act. Congress divided the funding for Mexico in P.L. 110-252 between the International Narcotics Control and Law Enforcement (INCLE), Foreign Military Financing (FMF), and Economic Support Fund (ESF) aid accounts. Congress limited the amount of FMF and INCLE available to provide equipment to the Mexican military and made 15% of FMF and IMET contingent on meeting certain human rights conditions.[38] Congress also earmarked $73.5 million for judicial reform, institution building, rule of law, and anti-corruption activities.
- In March 2009, the 111th Congress passed the Omnibus Appropriations Act, (P.L. 111-8) providing $300 million for Mexico within the INCLE, ESF, and FMF accounts with not less than $75 million for judicial reform, institution building, anti-corruption, and rule of law activities. The measure continues human rights conditions similar to those set forth in P.L. 110-252.[39]

- In June 2009, the 111th Congress passed the FY2009 supplemental appropriations measure, P.L. 111-32, which includes $160 million in INCLE assistance and $260 million in FMF for Mexico, $354 million more than the Administration's request. The $160 million in INCLE funds can be used to supply the Mexican federal police with items such as fixed and rotary wing aircraft (including three requested Blackhawk helicopters). The $260 million in FMF funding is for expedited aviation assistance to the Mexican Navy (SEMAR) to enhance air transport ability and aerial surveillance. While the INCLE funds provided by P.L. 111-32 are subject to the same human rights conditions as in P.L. 111-8, the FMF funds provided are not subject to human rights conditions.
- On December 13, 2009, Congress passed the FY2010 Consolidated Appropriations Act (H.R. 3288/P.L. 111-117), which allows for $210.3 million for Mexico in the INCLE, ESF, and FMF accounts subject to the same human rights conditions as P.L. 111-8. While Congress provided less funding for Mérida-related programs in Mexico and Central America than the Administration's FY2010 request, Congress had appropriated significantly more for Mexico than requested in the FY2009 supplemental spending measure, and considered $254 million of this as forward funding of FY2010.[40]

The August 2009 submission of the State Department's human rights progress report for Mexico met the statutory requirement for the release of the FY2008 supplemental and FY2009 regular FMF and IMET funds that had been on hold. Those funds totaled roughly $88.5 million.

Congress has expressed concerns about the slow implementation of the Mérida Initiative. On December 3, 2009, the Government Accountability Office (GAO) issued a preliminary report for Congress on the status of funding for the Mérida Initiative. By the end of September 2009, GAO found that $830 million of the $1.3 billion in Mérida funds appropriated for Mexico and Central America had been obligated by the State Department, but only $26 million of the funds had actually been spent.[41]

State Department officials in Mexico City have reported significant progress in Mérida implementation since the GAO reporting period ended. According to an equipment report provided by State Department officials, roughly $77.2 million worth of equipment was delivered to Mexico by the end of December 2009, including 30 ion scanners and five Bell helicopters for the Mexican Army. Another $135.5 million in equipment is scheduled to be delivered by June 2010, including a $50 million CASA surveillance aircraft for the Mexican Navy and three UH-60 helicopters for the SSP. With respect to Mérida-funded training programs, 42% of training projects were reported to have achieved "significant progress" in implementation by mid-November 2009, including those involving police professionalization and continuing education, prison reform, prosecutorial capacity building, and human rights training programs.[42]

Department of Defense Assistance to Mexico

Apart from the Mérida Initiative, the U.S. Department of Defense (DOD) provided a $13 million counterterrorism training and equipment package to the Mexican military in FY2008.[43] In addition, while DOD only provided some $3.1 million in CN training assistance to Mexico in FY2008, DOD assistance expanded to roughly $28.2 million in FY2009 in order to complement Mérida programs.[44] On December 16, 2009, Congress appropriated an additional $50 million in funding for counternarcotics communication equipment for Mexico in the FY2010 Department of Defense Appropriations Act (H.R. 3326/P.L. 111-118).[45]

Related Security Cooperation with Mexico

In March 2009, Secretary of Homeland Security Janet Napolitano announced a set of Southwest border initiatives aimed at (1) guarding against violent crime spillover into the United States; (2) supporting Mexico's crackdown campaign against drug cartels in Mexico; and (3) reducing the movement of contraband in both directions across the border.[46]

Components of the Department of Homeland Security are providing significant assistance to advance those aims. Immigration and Customs Enforcement (ICE) has created a dozen Border Enforcement Security Taskforces (BESTs) since 2006, including eight on the U.S. southwest border. The taskforces serve as platforms for cooperation among local, state, and federal agencies as well as a point of cooperation with Mexico's Secretary of Public Security (SSP). ICE has also coordinated the establishment of Special Investigative Units in Mexico that work with ICE special agents on criminal investigations and prosecutions in such areas as money laundering, human trafficking, and alien smuggling. DHS components such as ICE, Customs and Border Protection (CBP), and the U.S. Coast Guard have longstanding relationships with their Mexican counterparts to jointly disrupt the activities of drug trafficking organizations.

In late March 2009, the Department of Justice (DOJ) announced increased efforts to combat Mexican drug cartels in the United States and to help Mexican law enforcement battle the cartels in their own country. Deputy Attorney General David Ogden is leading a Mexican Cartel Strategy that uses federal prosecutor-led task forces that bring together all law enforcement components to identify and dismantle the cartels through investigation, prosecution, and extradition of their key leaders and facilitators. Department of Justice components involved in the increased efforts include the FBI, Drug Enforcement Administration (DEA), Bureau of Alcohol, Tobacco, Firearms, and Explosives (ATF), U.S. Marshals Service (USM), and the Department's Criminal Division and the Office of Justice Programs.[47] On August 20, 2009, U.S. Attorney General Holder announced indictments against 43 Mexican drug dealers accused of exporting narcotics into the United States and distributing them in U.S. cities. He praised Mexico-U.S. cooperation in the investigations that led to those indictments. On October 22-23, 2009, agents from several U.S. federal agencies, as well as state and local police, engaged in a joint operation in 38 U.S. cities against La Familia Michoacana. The raid resulted in 300 arrests.

ATF has begun a new intelligence-driven effort known as Gunrunner Impact Teams (GRITs), deployed eTrace firearms tracking technology to Mexico, and beefed up its Project Gunrunner program as a part of its efforts to stop the flow of guns into Mexico. (For more see "Weapons Trafficking"" section below).

DEA has worked with the Mexican government for decades and has 11 offices in the country. The agency is increasing its agents allocated to the Southwest border field divisions and is forming mobile teams to target Mexican methamphetamine trafficking operations. DEA's cooperation with Mexico has included Project Reckoning targeting the Gulf Cartel and Operation Xcellerator targeting the Sinaloa Cartel. DEA also is the lead agency at the El

Paso Intelligence Center (EPIC), a national tactical intelligence center that emphasizes law enforcement efforts on the Southwest border.

In July 2009, the U.S. Treasury Department designated four drug cartel leaders of the Gulf Cartel and Los Zetas as Specially Designated Narcotics Traffickers pursuant to the Foreign Narcotics Kingpin Designation Act (Kingpin Act), thereby imposing U.S. economic sanctions on those individuals.

Money Laundering and Bulk Cash Smuggling

Interrupting the flow of money from drug sales in the United States to Mexico, estimated to range from $15 billion to $25 billion annually,[48] may be one of the most effective ways to disrupt the activities of the Mexican DTOs. A portion of this money is used to buy weapons in the United States to arm the DTOs and their drug enforcers. Other drug proceeds are used to corrupt law enforcement and public officials, enabling the DTOs to continue to operate with impunity. Some analysts suggest that the U.S. Treasury is doing a good job of making it difficult to launder money within financial institutions. Therefore, the preferred mode to transfer drug proceeds by the Mexican DTOs is through shipments of bulk cash.[49]

In order to address the problem of bulk cash smuggling, the DEA has carried out bulk cash seizures with the FBI, ICE, and Customs and Border Protection (CBP). In 2005, ICE and CBP launched a program known as "Operation Firewall," which resulted in increased operations against bulk cash smuggling in the U.S.-Mexico border region. Since 2005, Operation Firewall has resulted in 583 arrests and the seizure of more than $282 million.[50] Many operations have been carried out in coordination with Mexican customs and the Mexican money laundering vetted unit. In 2008, ICE created a Trade Transparency Unit (TTU) in Mexico. Mexican TTU representatives are receiving training and technical support from ICE officials in how to identify cross-border trade anomalies that could be indicative of bulk cash smuggling.

Precursor Chemicals

Reducing the trafficking of chemicals necessary for drug manufacture is addressed in the Mérida Initiative joint statement. The recent NDIC report of the U.S. Department of Justice credits Mexico's recently established import restrictions on products containing methamphetamine precursors with reducing Mexican methamphetamine shipments to the United States in 2007 and 2008.[51] Strong bilateral cooperation between the United States and Mexico has resulted in large drug seizures including the shutting down of five "super" methamphetamine laboratories in Mexico in 2008 according to the Department of State's 2009 International Narcotics Control Strategy Report.

Weapons Trafficking[52]

In recent years, Mexican drug traffickers and enforcer gangs have increasingly relied on military-style firearms, a large percentage of which are purchased in the United States. The cartels often obtain their weapons through "straw purchases," whereby people who are legally qualified buy the weapons from licensed gun dealers or at gun shows in border states and sell them to smugglers who take them across the border. In November 2008, the Mexican government made the largest seizure of drug-cartel weapons in Mexican history when it found a cache of 540 rifles, 15 grenades, 500,000 rounds of ammunition, and 14 sticks of TNT at a house in the border town of Reynosa, Mexico.[53]

In FY2004, ATF began a Southwest border initiative dubbed Project Gunrunner that aims to deny firearms to criminal organizations in Mexico, and to combat firearms-related violence affecting communities on both sides of the border. [54] The number of ATF personnel dedicated to Project Gunrunner has increased from around 100 special agents and 25 industry operations investigators in FY2007, to some 148 special agents and 59 industry operations investigators in March 2009.[55] From FY2004 through June 2009, ATF referred 415 cases of firearms trafficking for prosecution involving more than 1,135 defendants and almost 13,382 guns.[56] The 111th Congress has appropriated additional funding to support Project Gunrunner: $10 million in the American Recovery and Reinvestment Act of 2009 (P.L. 111-5), $5 million in the FY2009 Omnibus Appropriations Act (P.L. 111-8), and $6 million in the FY2009 Supplemental Appropriations Act (P.L. 111-32).

In addition to these efforts in the United States, under the Mérida Initiative, ATF received $4.5 million for the deployment of eTrace technology to U.S. Consulates in Mexico to combat arms trafficking.[57] In FY2008, Mexico submitted more than 7,500 recovered guns for tracing, showing that most originated in Texas, Arizona, and California. Roughly 93% of those firearms were either made in, or imported to, the United States.[58]

The Department of Homeland Security (DHS), especially ICE and CBP are also involved in taking action to stop the southbound flow of weapons to Mexico. Both ICE and CBP have the authority to enforce export provisions of the Arms Exports Control Act. In collaboration with Mexican law enforcement authorities, ICE launched a new bilateral program against weapons smuggling in June 2008 known as Operation *Armas Cruzadas*. Among other activities, the program involves intelligence sharing and joint law enforcement efforts with vetted Mexican units. As DHS reported in March 2009, the operation has resulted in more than 100 criminal arrests, 42 convictions, and the seizure of more than 400 weapons.[59]

On June 18, 2009, the Government Accountability Office (GAO) released a report identifying some problems that exist in the information-gathering and coordination efforts of U.S. agencies charged with combating arms trafficking to Mexico, namely ATF within DOJ and ICE within DHS.[60] The two agencies have since signed an updated agreement on how to coordinate their Southwest border gun trafficking programs. Further, on August 13, 2009, DHS and DOJ, along with Mexico, signed a letter of intent to develop a coordinated, bilateral arms trafficking strategy, another recommendation suggested in the GAO report.

Mexico, for its part, began a pilot program in February 2009 to screen incoming traffic to look for guns, bulk cash, and other contraband, and is expanding the program across the entire border. On August 16, 2009, the Mexican government replaced all of the customs inspectors posted at the country's airports and border crossings with 1,454 new, better-trained inspectors. Those inspectors are now using non-intrusive inspection equipment provided through the Merida Initiative to check vehicles entering Mexico for arms and cash smuggled from the United States.

In light of intensified U.S. efforts to curb weapons trafficking to Mexico, some advocates have called for the U.S. Senate to act on a pending treaty, the Inter-American Convention Against the Illicit Manufacturing of and Trafficking in Firearms, Ammunition, Explosives, and Other Related Materials (CIFTA).[61] The treaty, which was signed by the United States in 1997 entered into force in July 1998, was submitted to the Senate for its advice and consent in

June 1998.[62] President Obama called for congressional action on CIFTA while in Mexico in April 2009.

Human Smuggling

The Operation Against Smuggling Initiative on Safety and Security (OASISS) is a bilateral effort begun in August 2005 to combat human smuggling. The program, spearheaded by ICE and several Mexican agencies, was initially limited to the area between San Diego, California and Yuma, Arizona, but was extended to El Paso, Texas in April 2006. In August 2007, the United States and Mexico agreed to extend the program to the Mexican state of Coahuila and the area between El Paso and Eagle Pass, Texas. The program assists both the Mexican and U.S. governments in the prosecution of alien smugglers and human traffickers along the southwest border. According to DHS, with funding from the Mérida Initiative, Mexico intends to implement the program across the entire United States-Mexico border.[63]

Human Rights Issues

According to the State Department's human rights report covering 2008, the Mexican government generally respected human rights at the national level by investigating, prosecuting, and sentencing public officials and members of the security forces accused of abuses, but serious problems remained. These included unlawful killing by security forces; kidnappings; physical abuse; poor and overcrowded prison conditions; arbitrary arrests and detention; corruption, inefficiency and lack of transparency in the judicial system; confessions coerced through torture; criminal intimidation of journalists leading to self-censorship; impunity and corruption at all levels of government; domestic violence against women; trafficking in persons; social and economic discrimination against some members of the indigenous population; and child labor.

The State Department report maintained that neither the government nor its forces commited any politically motivated killings, but that there were reports that security forces killed several people during the year in various cases. The report asserted that cruel treatment and physical abuse of security forces, especially at the state and local level, remained a serious problem. Corruption was reported to be a major problem, particularly at the state and local level, with police involved in kidnapping, extortion, or providing protection for organized crime and drug traffickers. Impunity was pervasive, according to the report, and was a reason that many victims were reluctant to file complaints.

In the case of the American journalist Bradley Will, who was shot and killed while covering a protest in Oaxaca in 2006, the State Department report noted that Mexico's National Human Rights Commission (CNDH) issued a report in September 2008 criticizing the federal and Oaxacan state investigations into the killing and implicating Oaxacan state officials. In October 2008, the government arrested Juan Manuel Martínez, an antigovernment protestor, for the killing, maintaining that Will was shot at close range. Human rights groups and the CNDH maintain that Will was shot at a distance.[64] Human rights lawyers are arguing for Mr. Martínez's release, asserting that the Attorney General lacks evidence against him.[65]

On August 9, 2009, Mexico's Supreme Court rejected an appeal by a human rights organization challenging the Mexican military's assertion of jurisdiction in cases involving allegations of human rights abuses committed by soldiers against civilians. In its 2010 human rights report, the New York-based Human Rights Watch highlighted human rights abuses by military forces and impunity in the military justice system as major issues that have yet to be addressed by the Calderón government. In early December 2009, Amnesty International released a new report on alleged cases of human rights abuses committed by Mexican military forces engaged in counterdrug efforts that occurred between October 2008 and August 2009.[66]

Compliance with Human Rights Conditions in the Mérida Initiative

Human rights organizations generally lauded the inclusion of human rights conditions in Mérida Initiative appropriations legislation. More recently, however, there have been concerns that Mexico has not been fulfilling the conditions set forth in the legislation. In particular, Mexican and international human rights groups have criticized the Mexican government for failing to hold military and police officials accountable for past abuses.[67] On July 13, 2009, Human Rights Watch issued a statement asserting that "Mexican military courts ... have not convicted a single member of the military accused of committing a serious human rights violation."[68] The head of the Mexican military's human rights office held a press conference on July 23, 2009, to dispute those assertions, but reportedly did not provide details on particular cases that had been successfully prosecuted in the military justice system.[69] In late July, a coalition of U.S. and Mexican human rights groups sent a letter to the State Department urging it not to issue a favorable report on the Mexican government's human rights record.[70]

On August 13, 2009, the State Department submitted its human rights progress report for Mexico to Congress, thereby meeting the statutory requirements for FY2008 supplemental and FY2009 regular funds that had been on hold to be released. While acknowledging that serious problems remain, the report outlines steps that the Mexican government has made to improve police transparency and accountability, consult with Mexican human rights organizations and civil society on the Mérida Initiative, investigate and prosecute allegations of human rights abuses by security forces, and prohibit the use of torture. The report acknowledges that human rights complaints against the Mexican military have "increased almost six-fold" since the beginning of the Calderón government. It also states that "the opaqueness of the [Mexican] military court system makes it difficult to analyze the nature and type of complaints filed, the status of cases against members of the military alleged to have violated human rights, or the results of the military prosecution."[71] Human rights groups have criticized the State Department report, and the release of Mérida funds that were on hold. [72]

Accountability for Abuses Committed during the "Dirty War" Period

During his administration, President Fox pledged to investigate and prosecute those responsible for past human rights violations, including the "Dirty War" period from the 1960s to 1980s. The CNDH presented a report to President Fox in November 2001 that documented human rights abuses and disappearances of persons in the 1970s and early 1980s, and President Fox named legal scholar Ignacio Carrillo in January 2002 as a Special Prosecutor to investigate these and other cases. In November 2006, Ignacio Carrillo presented his final report on the repressive era from the late 1960s to 1982. The report found that the repression was a matter of state policy and led to the summary execution of over 700 Mexicans, torture, and the razing of villages.

The report was praised by some as an acknowledgment of state responsibility. Others remain critical since no one has been convicted of charges relating to these alleged crimes. Only one of the three presidents from this period, Luis Echeverria (1970-1976), is still alive. President Echeverria faced genocide charges for his role in the repression of a 1968 student protest that left dozens dead when he was interior minister. Echeverria tried to evade prosecution by claiming the 30-year statute of limitations had expired. A judge rejected this argument and reinstated the arrest order in November 2006 after he determined that the statute of limitations did not go into effect until Echeverria left public office in December 1976. In July 2007, the Criminal Tribunal absolved Echeverria of any responsibility for the 1968 killings. This ruling was upheld by a Mexican federal court in March 2009, and was criticized by human rights organizations. Amnesty International maintains that the Mexican government is effectively condoning the abuses of the past by not effectively prosecuting past human rights cases.[73]

Migration

Widely cited demographers at the Pew Hispanic Center estimate that there were 7 million undocumented Mexican migrants residing in the United States as of March 2008, accounting for almost 59% of the total estimated illegal alien population of 11.9 million.[74] Mexico takes the view that the migrants are "undocumented workers," making the point that since the U.S. market attracts and provides employment for the migrants, it bears some responsibility. Mexico regularly voices concern about alleged abuses suffered by Mexican workers in the United States, and for the loss of life and hardships suffered by Mexican migrants as they utilize increasingly dangerous routes and methods to circumvent tighter border controls. However, Mexico benefits from illegal migration in at least two ways: (1) it is a "safety valve" that dissipates the political discontent that could arise from higher unemployment in Mexico, and (2) it is a source of remittances by workers in the United States to families in Mexico.

In February 2006, the Mexican Congress approved a concurrent resolution on migration and border security calling for the development of a guest worker program in the United States under the principle of shared responsibility. The resolution commits Mexico to enforcing legal emigration "if a guest country offers a sufficient number of appropriate visas."[75] In the resolution, Mexico also accepts the need to revisit its migration policies to consider enforcement of its northern and southern borders, enforcement of Mexican immigration laws that respect the human rights of migrants, and the need to combat human trafficking. The Mexican government further acknowledges that Mexican workers will continue to emigrate until there are more opportunities in Mexico. The February 2006 resolution remains the most detailed explanation to date of the major principles behind Mexico's policy on immigration.

The U.S. Congress last enacted major immigration reform in 1986 and 1996. Main provisions of the Immigration Reform and Control Act of 1986 (P.L. 99-603) included civil and criminal penalties for U.S. employers who knowingly hire undocumented workers;

increased border control and enforcement measures; anti-discrimination safeguards; provision for legalization of illegal aliens who resided continuously in the United States before 1982; and a special legalization for farm workers previously employed on American farms. In 1996, two laws relating to immigration were enacted, the Illegal Immigration Reform and Immigrant Responsibility Act of 1996 (IIRIRA, P.L. 104-208) and the Personal Responsibility and Work Opportunity Reconciliation Act of 1996 (P.L. 104-193). The first measure sought to control illegal immigration by adding 1,000 Border Patrol agents per year for five years (FY1997-FY2001), along with additional personnel, equipment, and procedures. The IIRIRA increased penalties for unlawful presence and created the expedited removal program.[76] Individuals who depart the United States after more than 180 days of unlawful presence now face either a three or 10-year bar to admission to the United States, depending on the total period of unlawful presence.

In the 110th Congress, the U.S. Senate voted against cloture on the Comprehensive Immigration Reform Act of 2007 (S. 1348) in June 2007, and the measure was not considered after that vote. The bill would have improved border security, established a temporary worker program, and normalized the status of most illegal immigrants in the United States. Mexico has long lobbied for such reforms. Immigration reform legislation also was introduced in the House of Representatives in March 2007. The House measure, the Security Through Regularized Immigration and Vibrant Economy Act of 2007 (H.R. 1645), would have set border and document security benchmarks to be met before normalizing the status of illegal immigrant or the creation of a guest worker program. A variety of other migration-related legislative initiatives were introduced in the 110th Congress, but none were enacted.[77]

It is unclear whether comprehensive immigration legislation will be considered in the 111th Congress.[78] During Secretary of State Clinton's March 2009 visit to Mexico, she maintained that "President Obama remains committed to comprehensive immigration reform" and that immigration reform "is and will be a high priority for him and his presidency." On June 25, 2009, President Obama and officials in his Administration met with Members of Congress from both parties on comprehensive immigration reform. During that meeting, he announced the formation of a high-level working group headed by DHS Secretary Napolitano to work with Members from the relevant House and Senate committees that will be drafting immigration legislation.[79] At the North American Leaders Summit in early August, President Obama acknowledged that since several of his other major legislative initiatives were still pending, immigration reform was unlikely to occur until early 2010.[80] A bill to enact comprehensive immigration reform was introduced on December 15, 2009, but few observers are predicting that it will be taken up prior to the 2010 mid-term elections.[81]

Cooperation in the Aftermath of the 2009 H1N1 "Swine Flu" Outbreak

On April 24, 2009, Mexico's Health Ministry announced that a new strain of influenza—subsequently dubbed pandemic H1N1 by the World Health Organization (WHO)—was affecting the country with just over 1,000 suspected cases and 20 deaths.[82] In addition to closing all schools and public events through May 6, 2009, the Calderón government also ordered a May 1-5 work-stoppage around the country, with the exception of banks, hotels, supermarkets, and the government's emergency services. Although there were some inaccuracies in its initial reporting of the number of cases involved in the outbreak, the Mexican government has been praised for acting "swiftly, transparently, and efficaciously" to prevent the spread of H1N1.[83] In particular, the government has been recognized for its willingness to share information and work collaboratively with other countries (including the United States) to prevent and treat cases of H1N1, for launching a high-profile public awareness campaign about the virus, and for using isolation and quarantine to mitigate its spread.

In response to the outbreak in Mexico, the Centers for Disease Control and Prevention (CDC) issued a travel health warning, the agency's highest advisory level, on April 27, 2009 recommending that U.S. citizens avoid all nonessential travel to Mexico. By May 15, however, the CDC downgraded the advisory to a travel health precaution that removed the recommendation that travel to Mexico be avoided.

The U.S. government responded to the H1N1 outbreak in Mexico by providing at least $16 million in assistance, including a $5 million donation to the WHO and PAHO. On April 29, 2009, Health and Human Services Secretary Kathleen Sebelius announced that her department had begun to move 400,000 antiviral drug treatment courses to Mexico—valued at $10 million—to help slow the spread of the virus.[84] On May 2, 2009, the U.S. Agency for International Development (USAID) provided about $1 million in emergency relief supplies to the government of Mexico. These supplies were in addition to a previous donation of $1 million in emergency supplies provided by the U.S. military.[85] With international help from the CDC and others, Mexico was able to build a laboratory within record time that was able to process hundreds of tests for H1N1 daily.[86]

Trade Issues[87]

Trade between Mexico and the United States has grown dramatically since the North American Free Trade Agreement (NAFTA) between the United States, Mexico, and Canada entered into force in 1994.[88] Total U.S. trade with Mexico more than quadrupled from $82 billion in 1993 to $367 billion in 2008, but the balance of U.S. trade with Mexico has shifted from a surplus of $1.3 billion in 1994 to a deficit of $64.4 billion in 2008 (U.S. exports of $151.5 billion; U.S. imports of $215.9 billion).[89]

The United States is Mexico's most important customer by far, receiving about 80% of Mexico's exports, including petroleum, automobiles, auto parts, and winter vegetables, and providing about 50% of Mexico's imports. The United States is the source of over 60% of foreign investment in Mexico, and the primary source of important tourism earnings. Mexico is also the leading country in Latin America in terms of U.S. investment, with the total stock of U.S. investment reaching more than $120 billion in 2008.[90]

While NAFTA has increased Mexican trade with the United States and contributed to rising foreign investment in the country, it has also increased Mexico's dependence on the U.S. economy. In 2009, declining U.S. demand for Mexican exports, combined with a drop in tourism revenues and a record drop in remittances from Mexican workers in the United States, caused a dramatic downturn in the Mexican economy. Mexico's economy was among the poorest performing in Latin America this year, as the country's GDP contracted by almost 7%. Some have attributed the severity of the current crisis in Mexico to a lack of diversification in the country's export markets.[91]

Functioning of NAFTA Institutions

Several NAFTA institutions mandated by the agreements have been functioning since 1994. The tripartite Commission on Environmental Cooperation (CEC) was established in Montreal, Canada; and the Commission for Labor Cooperation (CLC) was established in Dallas, Texas. In addition, the bilateral Border Environment Cooperation Commission (BECC), located in Ciudad Juarez, Mexico; and the North American Development Bank (NADBank), headquartered in San Antonio, Texas, were created to promote and finance environment projects along the U.S.-Mexico border. Following up on a March 2002 agreement by Presidents Bush and Fox in Monterrey, Mexico, to broaden the mandate of the NADBank, Congress agreed in March 2004 to permit the NADBank to make grants and nonmarket rate loans for environmental infrastructure along the border. The NAFTA institutions have operated to encourage cooperation on trade, environmental and labor issues, and to consider nongovernmental petitions under the labor and environmental side agreements.

Trade Disputes

Outstanding trade disputes between the countries include access for Mexican trucks to operate in the United States and access for Mexican tuna to the U.S. market. A longstanding dispute involving sugar and high fructose corn syrup was resolved in 2006.[92]

Trucking[93]

Since 1995, the implementation of NAFTA trucking provisions has been in dispute. In March 2009, Congress included a provision in P.L. 111-8, the FY2009 Omnibus Appropriations Act, to terminate a pilot program that had allowed Mexican-registered trucks to operate beyond the 25-mile border commercial zone inside the United States. This move prompted retaliation from Mexico, which argued that the U.S. action was protectionist. Mexico imposed tariffs on over 90 U.S. agricultural and industrial products. The goods accounted for a value of $2.4 billion in U.S. exports to Mexico in 2007, and most will now face Mexican import duties of between 10-20% of their value, although in the case of fresh grapes, a 45% duty was imposed.[94]

Obama Administration officials have repeatedly expressed confidence that a resolution to the current trucking dispute can be found that will satisfy congressional concerns about the safety of Mexican trucks, but still fulfill U.S. market access obligations under NAFTA. In March 2009, Secretary of State Clinton acknowledged that Mexico had the right to use remedies under NAFTA to impose tariffs on U.S. products, but maintained that neither the U.S. congressional action on Mexican trucking nor Mexico's retaliation were in the best interests of either country.[95] Transportation Secretary Ray LaHood submitted a set of principles on how to resolve the issue to the White House in May 2009. President Obama reiterated his commitment to resolving the issue to President Calderón at their August 9, 2009 meeting in Guadalajara, Mexico, but did not present a proposal.

While some Members of Congress favor the creation of a new pilot program with Mexico, others, though concerned about the effects of Mexican retaliatory tariffs on U.S. businesses, remain opposed to allowing Mexican trucks to operate in the United States.[96] In late July 2009, the Senate Appropriations Committee issued a report (S.Rept. 111-69) to the FY2010 Department of Transportation, Housing and Urban Development, and Related

Agencies Appropriations measure (H.R. 3288) that includes non-binding language urging the Obama Administration to develop a cross-border trucking program that meets U.S. safety standards. The FY2010 Consolidated Appropriations Act (P.L. 111-117), signed into law on December 16, 2009, does not include language that was in P.L. 111-8 prohibiting the Department of Transportation from funding a pilot project for Mexican-registered trucks to operate beyond the border commercial zone.

Tuna

On tuna issues, the Clinton Administration lifted the embargo on Mexican tuna in April 2000 under relaxed standards for a dolphin-safe label in accordance with internationally agreed procedures and U.S. legislation passed in 1997 that encouraged the unharmed release of dolphins from nets. However, a federal judge in San Francisco ruled that the standards of the law had not been met, and the Federal Appeals Court in San Francisco sustained the ruling in July 2001.

Under the Bush Administration, the Commerce Department ruled on December 31, 2002, that the dolphin-safe label may be applied if qualified observers certify that no dolphins were killed or seriously injured in the netting process, but Earth Island Institute and other environmental groups filed suit to block the modification. On April 10, 2003, the U.S. District Court for the Northern District of California enjoined the Commerce Department from modifying the standards for the dolphin-safe label. On August 9, 2004, the federal district court ruled against the Bush Administration's modification of the dolphin-safe standards, and reinstated the original standards in the 1990 Dolphin Protection Consumer Information Act. That decision was appealed to the U.S. Ninth Circuit Court of Appeals, which ruled against the Administration in April 2007, finding that the Department of Commerce did not base its determination on scientific studies of the effects of Mexican tuna fishing on dolphins.

In late October 2008, Mexico initiated World Trade Organization (WTO) dispute proceedings against the United States, maintaining that U.S. requirements for Mexican tuna exporters prevents them from using the U.S. "dolphin-safe" label for its products.[97] In April 2009, the WTO agreed to set up a dispute panel to rule on Mexico's complaint. The United States prefers that the dispute should be handled by a NAFTA dispute panel instead of a WTO panel. On November 5, 2009, the U.S. government announced that it had requested formal dispute settlement consultations under NAFTA.[98]

North American Cooperation on Security and Economic Issues

In addition to the increased U.S.-Mexican bilateral cooperation that has occurred during the past two decades, trilateral cooperation between the United States, Mexico, and Canada has also increased, particularly since NAFTA took effect. During the second George W. Bush Administration, annual meetings between the North American leaders and their ministers took place within the framework of the Security and Prosperity Partnership (SPP) of North America, established in March of 2005. [99] Through the SPP, which consisted of expanded cooperation and harmonization of policies, the three governments sought to advance the common security and prosperity of their countries. To make this partnership operational, the leaders established ministerial-led working groups to develop measurable and achievable goals in priority areas: competitiveness, smart and secure borders, energy security and environmental protection, food and product safety, and emergency response. Beginning in June 2005, the SPP working groups provided annual reports to the three North American leaders on their work and key accomplishments, with the last SPP report submitted prior to the April 2008 North American Leaders' Summit.

Although President Obama and his counterparts in Mexico and Canada no longer refer to trilateral cooperation as occurring under the SPP initiative, North American cooperation continues to occur on a wide range of economic and security issues. As previously discussed, the most recent North American Leaders' Summit took place in Guadalajara, Mexico on August 9-10, 2009. In addition to important discussions that occurred with respect to combating drug trafficking and preparing for the fall flu season, the leaders produced, among other things, a list of energy deliverables aimed at reducing carbon emissions in North America.[100] The leaders also committed to meet again in Canada in 2010.

LEGISLATION IN THE 111TH CONGRESS

Enacted and Considered Legislation

P.L. 111-5 (H.R. 1), American Recovery and Reinvestment Act of 2009. Signed into law February 17, 2009, the measure provides $220 million for construction for the water quantity program of the International Boundary and Water Commission, United States and Mexico. The measure also provides $40 million in Department of Justice state and local law enforcement assistance for competitive grants to provide assistance and equipment along the southern border and in high-intensity drug trafficking areas to combat criminal narcotics activity, of which $10 million is to be transferred to ATF for Project Gunrunner.

P.L. 111-8 (H.R. 1105), Omnibus Appropriations Act, 2009. Signed into law March 11, 2009. In Division H, the measure appropriates $300 million for Mexico as a second installment under the Mérida Initiative. Human rights conditions similar to those included in the FY2008 Supplemental Appropriations Act (P.L. 110-252) apply to 15% of the total funds provided, not including assistance for judicial reform, institution building, anti-corruption, and rule of law activities. In Division I, Section 136, the measure prohibits funds in the Act from being used for a pilot program granting certain Mexican trucks access to U.S. highways beyond the commercial zone. In the joint explanatory statement for Division B, not less than $5 million is provided for Project Gunrunner and other firearms trafficking efforts targeting Mexico and the border region.

P.L. 111-32 (H.R. 2346), Supplemental Appropriations Act, 2009. Signed into law June 24, 2009, the measure appropriates $420 million in Mérida Initiative funding for Mexico: $160 million in INCLE assistance and $260 million in FMF assistance. Of the $420 million in FY2009 supplemental assistance to Mexico, 15% of the $160 million in INCLE assistance is subject to the same human rights conditions set forth in P.L. 111-8, section 7045(e) of Division H. However, the FMF funds appropriated are not subject to human rights conditions. According to the conference report (H.Rept. 111-151), the supplemental measure requires a report from the Secretary of State within 45 days of enactment of the measure detailing actions by the government of Mexico since June 30, 2008, to investigate and prosecute human rights violations by members of the Mexican federal police and military forces. The report also calls for a "thorough, independent, and credible investigation" of the murder of Bradley Will, an American journalist killed while covering a protest in Oaxaca in 2006.

P.L. 111-84 (H.R. 2647), National Defense Authorization Act for FY2010. Signed into law October 28, 2009, the measure contains a provision that allows for the Department of Defense to continue providing support for counter-drug activities in Mexico.

P.L. 111-117 (H.R. 3288), Consolidated Appropriations Act, FY2010, Signed into law December 16, 2009. In Division F, the measure appropriates up to $210.3 million in Mérida Initiative funding for Mexico: $190 million in INCLE assistance, $15 million in ESF, and $5.25 million in FMF assistance. Human rights conditions apply to 15% of the total funds provided, not including assistance for judicial reform, institution building, anti-corruption, and rule of law activities. In the Joint Explanatory Statement to P.L. 111-117, the conferees direct the Secretary of State to submit a report to within 90 days of the enactment of the Act addressing how prior Mérida funds have been used, progress to date, any planned adjustments in the uses of funds, and post-Merida plans. Apart from the Mérida Initiative, the measure includes $10 million in DA assistance for Mexico. The measure does not include language prohibiting funds appropriated in the Act from being used for a pilot program granting certain Mexican trucks access to U.S. highways beyond the commercial zone.

P.L. 111-118 (H.R. 3326), Defense Appropriations Act, FY2010, Signed into law December 19, 2009, the measure appropriates $50 million in funding for counternarcotics communication equipment for Mexico.

H.R. 2410 (Berman) Foreign Relations Authorization Act, FY2010 and FY2011. Introduced May 14, 2009; House Committee on Foreign Affairs held markup and ordered the bill reported (H.Rept. 111-136). House approved June 22, 2009. Title IX, Subtitle A of the bill, as introduced, consists of actions to enhance the Mérida Initiative, including the designation of a high-level coordinator within the Department of State to implement the program; the addition of Caribbean Community (CARICOM) countries to the Mérida Initiative; the establishment and implementation of a program to assess the effectiveness of assistance provided under the Mérida Initiative; within 180 days and not later than December 1 of each year thereafter, a reporting requirement regarding the programs and activities carried out under the Mérida Initiative. Title IX, Subtitle B of the bill would require the President to establish an inter-agency task force on the prevention of illicit small arms trafficking in the Western Hemisphere; increase penalties for illicit trafficking in small arms and light weapons; and express congressional support for the ratification by the United States of the Inter-American Convention Against the Illicit Manufacturing of and Trafficking in Firearms, Ammunition, Explosives, and Other Related Materials (CIFTA). H.Amdt. 201 (King) to H.R. 2410, introduced and agreed to on June 10, 2009, provides that the Secretary of State shall report to Congress on the flow of people, goods, and services across the borders shared by the United States, Canada, Mexico, Bermuda, and the Caribbean nations.

Additional Legislative Initiatives

H.Res. 258 (Giffords)/S.Res. 72 (Menendez). H.Res. 258 introduced March 18, 2009; referred to Committee on Foreign Affairs. S.Res. 72 introduced March 10, 2009; referred to Committee on Foreign Relations. The identical resolutions would express full support for Mexico's efforts to confront drug trafficking organizations, apprehend their members, and bring them to justice. The resolutions would also call on the Department of State to ensure the prompt delivery of Mérida Initiative equipment and training; to continue to support the Mexican government's efforts to strengthen institutions and the rule of law, root out corruption, and protect human rights; and to ensure full accountability for all assistance and equipment provided by the United States to Mexico.

H.Res. 1032 (Chu). Introduced January 21, 2010; referred to Committee on Foreign Affairs. The resolution would express support for continued U.S. assistance to the Mexican government for fighting drug traffickers and curbing the violence they commit against Mexican and U.S. citizens.

H.R. 495 (Rodriguez)/S. 205 (Bingaman), Southwest Border Violence Reduction Act of 2009. H.R. 495 introduced January 14, 2009; referred to Committee on the Judiciary and Committee on Foreign Affairs. S. 205 introduced January 12, 2009; referred to Committee on the Judiciary. Both bills would direct the Attorney General to expand the resources provided for ATF's Project Gunrunner initiative to identify, investigate, and prosecute individuals involved in the trafficking of firearms across the international border between the United States and Mexico. The bills would authorize $15 million for each of FY2010 and FY2011 for Project Gunrunner in the United States, and $9.5 million for each of FY2010 and FY2011 for the Attorney General, in cooperation with the Secretary of State, to assign ATF agents to the U.S. mission in Mexico, provide equipment to support ATF efforts, and provide training for Mexican law enforcement.

H.R. 937 (Filner), Visitors Interested in Strengthening America (VISA) Act of 2009. Introduced February 10, 2009; referred to Committee on the Judiciary. The bill would waive certain entry documentary requirements for a non-immigrant child (unmarried and under the age of 16) who is a citizen or national of Mexico and accompanying parent or adult chaperone in instances of medical visits, student groups, and/or special community events.

H.R. 1437 (Cuellar), Southern Border Security Task Force Act of 2009. Introduced March 11, 2009; referred to Committees on Homeland Security and the Judiciary. Would establish a task force to coordinate the efforts of federal, state, and local border law enforcement officials and task forces to protect U.S. border cites and communities from violence associated with drug trafficking, gunrunning, illegal alien smuggling, violence, and kidnapping along and across the international border between the United States and Mexico.

H.R. 1448 (Rodriguez), Border Reinforcement and Violence Reduction Act of 2009. Introduced March 11, 2009; referred to Committees on the Judiciary, Homeland Security, and Foreign Affairs. The bill would authorize the Secretary of Homeland Security and the Attorney General to increase resources to identify and eliminate illicit sources of firearms smuggled into Mexico for use by violent drug trafficking organizations and for other unlawful activities by providing for border security grants to local law enforcement agencies and reinforcing Federal resources on the border. It would authorize: $150 million for FY2010 and each succeeding fiscal year to the Secretary of Homeland Security for a border relief grant program; $9.5 million for each of FY2010 and FY2011 for Project Gunrunner (an ATF program) and $15 million for each of FY2010 and FY2011 for Operation Armas Cruzadas (an ICE program) to deter the trafficking of firearms across the international border between the United States and Mexico.

H.R. 1611 (Flake). Introduced March 19, 2009; referred to Committee on Transportation and Infrastructure. The bill would repeal a provision in the Omnibus Appropriations Act, 2009 (P.L. 111-8, Division I, Section 136) that prohibits the use of funds for a cross-border motor carrier demonstration program to allow Mexican-domiciled motor carriers to operate beyond the commercial zones along the international border between the United States and Mexico.

H.R. 1867 (Kirkpatrick), Border Violence Prevention Act of 2009. Introduced April 2, 2009; referred to Committee on Homeland Security. The bill would authorize additional resources to enhance security activities along the international border with Mexico.

H.R. 1900 (Jackson-Lee), Border Security, Cooperation, and Act Now Drug War Prevention Act. Introduced April 2, 2009; referred to Committees on Homeland Security and the Judiciary. Among its provisions, the bill would authorize emergency deployments of U.S. Border Patrol, DEA, and ATF agents along the border with Mexico; and would authorize $150 million in FY2010 and each subsequent fiscal year for a border relief grant program.

H.R. 2076 (Grijalva), Border Security and Responsibility Act 2009. Introduced April 23, 2009; referred to Committees on Homeland Security, Armed Services, and Agriculture. The bill would require the Secretary of Homeland Security, in consultation with other federal, state and local authorities, to submit a new border protection strategy to Congress that, among other measures, would not involve the construction of border fencing.

H.R. 2083 (Hunter), Border Sovereignty and Protection Act. Introduced April 23, 2009; referred to Committees on the Judiciary, Homeland Security, and Education and Labor. The bill would require the completion of at least 350 miles of reinforced fencing along the southwest border within one year of the enactment of the measure.

H.R. 3239 (Kirkpatrick) Introduced July 16, 2009; referred to Committees on Homeland Security and Foreign Affairs. House Committee on Homeland Security held markup and ordered the bill reported November 17, 2009. The bill would require the Secretary of Homeland Security, in consultation with the Secretary of State, to submit a report on the effects of the Mérida Initiative on the border security of the United States.

H.R. 3252 (Hinojosa). Introduced July 17, 2009; referred to Committee on Financial Services. The bill would authorize the President to agree to an amendment to the agreement between the U.S. and Mexican governments to expand the purposes and functions of the

Border Environment Cooperation Commission and the North American Development Bank to allow the Commission to certify, and the Bank to finance, any type of border infrastructure project.

H.R. 3308 (Schuler)/S. 1505 (Pryor), Secure America Through Enforcement and Verification Act of 2009 or SAVE Act of 2009. Introduced July 23, 2009; referred to Committees on Homeland Security, the Judiciary, Ways and Means, Education and Labor, Oversight and Government Reform, Armed Services, Agriculture, and Natural Resources. The bill sets forth a wide range of border security and enforcement provisions.

H.R. 4321 (Ortiz) Comprehensive Immigration Reform for America's Security and Prosperity Act of 2009, CIR ASAP Act of 2009. Introduced December 15, 2009; referred to Committees on the Judiciary, Homeland Security, Armed Services, Foreign Affairs, Natural Resources, Ways and Means, Education and Labor, Oversight and Government Reform, and Administration. The bill contains both border enforcement and legalization provisions and would attempt to address visa backlogs in the current immigration system.

S. 91 (Vitter). Introduced January 6, 2009; referred to Committee on Foreign Relations. The bill would reduce the amount of financial assistance provided to the government of Mexico in response to the illegal border crossing from Mexico into the United States.

S. 339 (Bingaman), Border Law Enforcement Relief Act of 2009. Introduced January 28, 2009; referred to Committee on the Judiciary. The bill would provide financial aid to local law enforcement officials along the nation's borders. It would authorize $100 million for each of FY2010 through FY2014 for a border relief grant program run by the Attorney General.

S. 1190 (Bingaman), Border Law Enforcement Anti-Drug Trafficking Act of 2009. Introduced June 4, 2009; referred to Committee on the Judiciary. The bill, related to S. 339, would authorize the Attorney General to award competitive grants to local law enforcement agencies and institutions of higher education for combating drug-related criminal activity.

End Notes

[1] Alexandra Olson, "Mexico Approves Oil Reform Bill in General Terms, Experts Call it Disappointment for Investors," *AP*, October 28, 2008.

[2] Andrew Selee and Katie Putnam, "Mexico's 2009 Midterm Elections: Winners and Losers," Woodrow Wilson Center, July 2009; George W. Grayson, "The PRI Makes a Comeback in Mexico," Foreign Policy Research Institute, July 2009.

[3] "Country Report: Mexico," *Economist Intelligence Unit*, January 2010.

[4] For more on DTOs and drug-related violence in Mexico, see CRS Report R40582, *Mexico's Drug-Related Violence* , by June S. Beittel.

[5] The term drug cartel remains the term used colloquially and in the press, but some experts disagree with this because "cartel" often refers to price-setting groups and it is not clear that Mexican drug cartels are setting illicit drug prices.

[6] The U.S. Justice Department's *National Drug Threat Assessment 2009*, published in December 2008, identified Mexican DTOs as the greatest drug trafficking threat to the United States. The current dominance of the Mexican DTOs over the U.S. drug market arose with the closing of the Caribbean route through which drugs, and particularly cocaine from Colombia, was channeled into the United States. With increased U.S. efforts to interdict narcotic smugglers in the Caribbean and Florida in the late 1980s and 1990s, the Colombian drug

cartels began subcontracting with Mexican DTOs to smuggle cocaine into the United States across the Southwest border. By the late 1990s, Mexican DTOs had pushed aside the Colombians and gained greater control and market share of cocaine trafficking into the United States.

[7] In August 2009, for example, the Mexican government replaced all of the customs inspectors posted at the country's airports and border crossings with 1,454 new, better-trained inspectors.

[8] Embassy of Mexico, Washington, DC. "Mexico and the Fight Against Drug Trafficking and Organized Crime: Setting the Record Straight," June 2009, p. ii.

[9] Email from Mexican Embassy in Washington D.C., January 12, 2010.

[10] Elliot Spagat, "Mexico-U.S. Cooperation Cited in 2nd Drug Lord Arrest," *Associated Press*, January 12, 2010.

[11] José de Cordoba and Joel Millman, "Mexico Ramps up Drug War With a Surge on Rio Grande," *Wall Street Journal*, December 22, 2009; Jorge C. Castañeda, "What's Spanish for Quagmire?" *Foreign Policy*, January/February 2010.

[12] Figures for 2008 and 2009 are drawn from David Shirk, "Drug Violence in Mexico: Data and Analysis from 2001-2009," Trans-Border Institute (TBI), January 2010, citing data gathered by *Reforma* newspaper. For a description as to why *Reforma* data are used instead of other sources, see p. 2-3 of the TBI report, available at: http://www.justiceinmexico.org/resources/pdf/drug-violence.pdf.

[13] Mark Stevenson, "Mexican Cartels go From Drugs to Full-Scale Mafias," *AP*, August 16, 2009.

[14] Shirk, January 2010.

[15] Jorge Rocha Quintero, "Public Security and Human Rights," in *Police and Public Security in Mexico*, edited by Robert A. Donnelly and David A. Shirk. San Diego, CA: University Readers, 2009.

[16] William Booth and Steve Fainaru, "Mexico Questions its Drug Strategy; Violence in Juarez Prompts Officials to Admit Military Failure," *Washington Post*, December 27, 2009.

[17] For background on the Mexican economy and U.S.-Mexican economic relations, see CRS Report RL32934, *U.S.-Mexico Economic Relations: Trends, Issues, and Implications*, by M. Angeles Villarreal.

[18] "Country Report: Mexico," *EIU*, January 2010.

[19] Based on data from the United States International Trade Commission (USITC) dataweb.

[20] "Mexico's Record Drop in Remittances," *Latinnews Daily*, January 28, 2010.

[21] "Mexico Foreign Tourism Income Sinks 29% in June," *Reuters*, August 10, 2009.

[22] ECLAC. *The Reactions of the Governments of the Americas to the International Crisis: An Overview of Policy Measures up to 31 March 2009.* April 2009.

[23] "Mexico (Country Intelligence)," *IHS Global Insight*, January 28, 2010.

[24] "Mexico Economy: Budget Passed, What Next?" *EIU Viewswire*, November 18, 2009; "President Felipe Calderón Eliminates Fuel Subsidies, Contributing to Increase in Price of Basic Goods," *SourceMex Economic News & Analysis on Mexico*, January 13, 2010.

[25] U.N. Economic Commission for Latin America and the Caribbean, *Statistical Yearbook for Latin America and the Caribbean 2008*; "ECLAC: Extreme Poverty Up in 2009 in Mexico, Central America," *Latin American Herald Tribune*, January 23, 2010.

[26] Santiago Levy, *Good Intentions, Bad Outcomes – Social Policy, Informality and Economic Growth in Mexico*. Washington D.C.: Brookings Institution, April 2008.

[27] For more information, see CRS Report R40784, *Mexico's Free Trade Agreements*, by M. Angeles Villarreal.

[28] Organization of American States (OAS), "Update on OAS Efforts in Support of Haiti," January 21, 2010.

[29] "Cuban Envoy to Mexico Says Migration Agreement to Halt People Trafficking," *BBC Monitoring Americas*, November 20, 2008.

[30] U.S. Department of State, Secretary of State Hillary Rodham Clinton, "Remarks with Mexican Foreign Secretary Patricia Espinosa After Their Meeting," Mexico City, Mexico, March 25, 2009.

[31] Mark Lander, "Clinton Says Demand for Illegal Drugs in the U.S. 'Fuels the Drug Trade' in Mexico," *New York Times*, March 26, 2009.

[32] "President Obama and Mexican President Felipe Calderón Hold News Conference," *CQ Newsmaker Transcripts*, April 16, 2009.

[33] U.S. Department of State, "Press Release: North American Leaders Discuss Trade, H1N1 Flu, Climate Change," August 10, 2009.

[34] See CRS Report 98-174, *Mexican Drug Certification Issues: U.S. Congressional Action, 1986-2002*, by K. Larry Storrs.

[35] Jesus Aranda, "Allana la Corte el Camino para Extraditar a Connacionales a EU," *La Jornada*, February 1, 2006; "Mexico: Court Clears Way for Faster Extraditions to U.S.," *Latin American Weekly Report*, February 7, 2006; and, U.S. Department of State, *INCSR 2006*.

[36] For more information, see CRS Report RS22837, *Mérida Initiative: U.S. Anticrime and Counterdrug Assistance for Mexico and Central America*, by Clare Ribando Seelke.

[37] U.S. Department of State and Government of Mexico, "Joint Statement on the Mérida Initiative," October 22, 2007.

[38] Human rights conditions for Mexico in P.L. 110-252 include (1) improving transparency and accountability of federal police forces; (2) establishing a mechanism to conduct regular consultations among relevant Mexican

government authorities, Mexican human rights organizations, and other relevant Mexican civil society organizations, to make consultations concerning implementation of the Mérida Initiative in accordance with Mexican and international law; (3) ensuring that civilian prosecutors and judicial authorities are investigating and prosecuting, in accordance with Mexican and international law, members of the federal police and military forces who have been credibly alleged to have committed violations of human rights, and the federal police and military forces are fully cooperating with the investigations; and (4) enforcing the prohibition, in accordance with Mexican and international law, on the use of testimony obtained through torture or other ill-treatment.

[39] P.L. 111-8 also has a provision requiring that prior to the procurement or lease of aircraft, that the Director of the Defense Security Cooperation Agency, in consultation with the Secretary of State, shall submit to the Committees on Appropriations an analysis of alternatives for the acquisition of all aircraft for the Merida Initiative.

[40] In the Joint Explanatory Statement to P.L. 111-117, the conferees direct the Secretary of State to submit a report to within 90 days of the enactment of the Act addressing how prior Mérida funds have been used, progress to date, any planned adjustments in the uses of funds, and post-Merida plans.

[41] U.S. Government Accountability Office (GAO), "Status of Funds for the Mérida Initiative," December 3, 2009, GAO 10-253R, available at: http://www.gao.gov/products/GAO-10-253R.

[42] Government of Mexico, Technical Secretariat of the National Security Council, Implementation Tracking System of Merida Initiative Projects, November 20, 2009.

[43] In the FY2006-FY2008 annual Department of Defense (DOD) authorization bills, Congress provided DOD with authority to train and equip foreign military forces to perform counterterrorism operations. This "Section 1206" authority, as it is known, enables DOD to use defense funds to conduct or support train and equip programs such as those usually provided under State Department security assistance authorities and budgets. U.S. Department of Defense, "Section 1206 Programs Fact Sheet." July 29, 2009.

[44] Section 1022 of the National Defense Authorization Act for Fiscal Year 2008 (P.L. 110-181) extends Section 1033(b) of the National Defense Authorization Act for Fiscal Year 1998 to make available train and equip authorities to Mexico. Estimates of DOD CN support to Mexico for FY2008 and FY2009 are from U.S. Department of Defense, "Fact Sheet: Current DOD CN Support to Mexico," July 2009.

[45] Funding for this equipment is listed as "Digital Communications Equipment" on p.352 of the Joint Explanatory Statement for the FY2010 Defense Appropriations Act (H.R. 3326/P.L.-111-118).

[46] U.S. Department of Homeland Security, "Press Release: Secretary Napolitano Announces Major Southwest Border Security Initiative," March 24, 2009.

[47] U.S. Department of Justice, "Department of Justice Announces Resources for Fight against Mexican Drug Cartels," Fact Sheet, March 24, 2009; and "Fact Sheet: Department of Justice Efforts to Combat Mexican Drug Cartels," *US Fed News*, April 4, 2009.

[48] Woodrow Wilson International Center for Scholars Mexico Institute, *The United States and Mexico: Towards a Strategic Partnership*, January 2009.

[49] Testimony of Andrew Selee, Director of the Mexico Institute, Woodrow Wilson Center before the House Subcommittee on National Security and Foreign Affairs of the Committee on Oversight and Government Reform, March 12, 2009.

[50] U.S. Department of Homeland Security, Statement of John T. Morton, Assistant Secretary, ICE, before the House Appropriations Subcommittee on Homeland Security, November 19, 2009.

[51] National Drug Intelligence Center, *National Drug Threat Assessment 2009*, U.S. Department of Justice, Product 2008-Q0317-005, December 2008.

[52] For more information, see CRS Report R40733, *Gun Trafficking and the Southwest Border*, by Vivian S. Chu and William J. Krouse.

[53] "Mexico: Army Seizes Huge Weapons Cache," *Los Angeles Times*, November 8, 2008.

[54] For background on ATF funding and Project Gunrunner, see CRS Report RL34514, *The Bureau of Alcohol, Tobacco, Firearms and Explosives (ATF): Budget and Operations*, by William J. Krouse.

[55] U.S. Embassy, Mexico, "Border and Law Enforcement, Project Gunrunner," ATF Factsheet, available at http://www.usembassy-mexico.gov/eng/texts/et080116eTrace.html; and Department of Justice, Statement of William Hoover, Assistant Director for Field Operations, ATF, and Anthony P. Placido, Assistant Administrator for Intelligence Division, DEA, before Senate Committee on the Judiciary, Subcommittee on Crime and Drugs, March 17, 2009.

[56] DOJ, Statement of Anthony P. Placido, Assistant Administrator for Intelligence Division, DEA, and Bill McMahon, Deputy Assistant Director, ATF, before the House Homeland Security Committee, Subcommittee on Border, Maritime, and Global Counterterrorism, July 16, 2009.

[57] U.S. Department of Justice, "Statement of Joseph M. Arabit, Special Agent in Charge, El Paso Division, Drug Enforcement Administration, and William McMahon, Deputy Assistant Director, Field Operations, ATF," before the Senate Committee on Foreign Relations, March 30, 2009.

[58] U.S. Department of Justice, "Department of Justice Announces Resources for Fight against Mexican Drug Cartels," Fact Sheet, March 24, 2009.

[59] U.S. Department of Homeland Security, "Statement of Mark Koumans, Deputy Assistant Secretary, Office of International Affairs," before House Committee on Appropriations, Subcommittee on Homeland Security, March 10, 2009.
[60] U.S. GAO, "U.S. Efforts to Combat Arms Trafficking to Mexico Face Planning and Coordination Challenges," GAO-09-709, June 2009.
[61] Peter DeShazo and Johnna Mendelson Forman, "A treaty that can help stem drug violence in Mexico," *Washington Times*, February 24, 2009.
[62] U.S. Department of State, The Inter-American Convention Against the Illicit Manufacturing of and Trafficking in Firearms, Ammunition, Explosives, and Other Related Materials," Fact Sheet, March 25, 2009
[63] House Committee on Appropriations, Subcommittee on Homeland Security, Statement of Mark Koumans, Deputy y Assistant Secretary, Office of International Affairs, at hearing on "DHS Security Response to Violence on the Border with Mexico," March 10, 2009.
[64] Elisabeth Malkin, "Mexico Says U.S. Journalist Was Killed by a Protester," New York Times, October 18, 2008.
[65] Their concerns are summarized in: Physicians for Human Rights, "México Presenta Teoría Inconsistente en la Muerte de Periodista Norteamericano," February 4, 2009.
[66] Amnesty International, "Mexico: New Reports of Human Rights Violations by Military," December 2009.
[67] See, for example, Human Rights Watch, "Uniform Impunity, Mexico's Misuse of Military Justice to Prosecute Abuses in Counternarcotics and Public Security Operations," April 2009, available at http://www.hrw.org/en/news/ 2009/04/29/mexico-hold-military-account-rights-abuses.
[68] Human Rights Watch, "Mexico: U.S. Should Withhold Military Aid: Rights Conditions in Merida Initiative Remain Unmet," July 13, 1009, available at: http://www.hrw.org/en/news/2009/07/13/mexico-us-should-withhold-military-aid.
[69] Booth and Fainaru, August 5, 2009.
[70] Letter from Amnesty International and Other Human Rights Groups to Secretary of State Hillary Clinton, "Human Rights Concerns to Inform the U.S. Department of State's Merida Initiative Reporting on Mexico, July 24, 2009.
[71] U.S. Department of State, "Mexico- Merida Initiative Report," August 2009.
[72] Fundar et al., "Obama Administration's Alleged Release of Mérida Funds: A Violation of U.S. Law That Will Encourage Serious Human Rights Violations in Mexico," August 2009.
[73] "Mexico: Hopes of Justice Vanish," Amnesty International, March 27, 2009.
[74] Pew Hispanic Center, *Trends in Undocumented Immigration: Undocumented Inflow Now Trails Legal Inflow,* by Jeffrey Passel and D'Vera Cohn, October 2, 2008.
[75] "Mexico-U.S.: Migration and Border Security," Embassy of Mexico, February 2006.
[76] For more information on expedited removal, see CRS Report RL33109, *Immigration Policy on Expedited Removal of Aliens*, by Alison Siskin and Ruth Ellen Wasem.
[77] For a brief history of U.S.-Mexican migration policies, see: Marc R. Rosenblum, "U.S.-Mexican Migration Cooperation: Obstacles and Opportunities," in *Migration, Trade and Development: Conference Proceedings*, Hollifield et al, eds., Federal Reserve Bank of Dallas, 2007.
[78] For more information, see: CRS Report R40501, *Immigration Reform Issues in the 111th Congress*, by Ruth Ellen Wasem.
[79] The White House, Office of the Press Secretary, "Remarks by the President After Meeting with Members of Congress to Discuss Immigration," June 25, 2009.
[80] Karoun Demirjian, "Obama Says Immigration Overhaul Will Slide Until 2010," *CQ Today*, August 11, 2009.
[81] Seth Stern, "Immigration Advocates Push for Overhaul as a Step to Economic Recovery," *CQ*, January 26, 2010.
[82] Secretaría de Salud (Mexico), "Conferencia de prensa," Número 2009-133c, April 24, 2009.
[83] Alexandra Stern and Howard Markel, "What Mexico Taught the World About Pandemic Influenza Preparedness and Community Mitigation Strategies," *Journal of the American Medical Association*, Vol. 32, No. 11, September 16, 2009.
[84] U.S. Department of Health and Human Services, "HHS Deploys SNS Antivirals to Mexico, and Buys More," Press Release, April 29, 2009.
[85] Email from the U.S. Agency for International Development Mission in Mexico, August 28, 2009.
[86] William Booth and Joshua Partlow, "Mexico Raced to Build Flu Testing Laboratory; Lack of Tools Hindered Initial Response," *Washington Post*, May 8, 2009.
[87] For more information, see CRS Report RL32934, *U.S.-Mexico Economic Relations: Trends, Issues, and Implications*, by M. Angeles Villarreal.
[88] The NAFTA agreement was negotiated in 1991 and 1992, and side agreements on labor and environmental matters were completed in 1993. The agreements were approved by the respective legislatures in late 1993 and went into force on January 1, 1994. Under the agreements, trade and investment restrictions were eliminated over a 15-year period, with most restrictions eliminated in the early years of the agreement.
[89] U.S. Department of Commerce statistics, as presented by World Trade Atlas.
[90] U.S. Embassy in Mexico City, Mexico, "U.S.-Mexico at a Glance: Foreign Direct Investment," June 2009.
[91] "Mexico: No Help From NAFTA," *EIU – Business Latin America,* August 17, 2009.

[92] For more information on recent trade disputes, see CRS Report RL32934, *U.S.-Mexico Economic Relations: Trends, Issues, and Implications*, by M. Angeles Villarreal.

[93] For further information, see CRS Report RL31738, *North American Free Trade Agreement (NAFTA) Implementation: The Future of Commercial Trucking Across the Mexican Border*, by John Frittelli

[94] Christopher Conkey, Jose de Cordoba, and Jim Carlton, "Mexico Issues Tariff List in U.S. Trucking Dispute," *Wall Street Journal*, March 19, 2009.

[95] U.S. Department of State, "Press Availability at TecMilenio University," March 26, 2009.

[96] For the opposing point of view, see: "Kirk Agrees to Work to Minimize Effects of Mexican Trucking Dispute," *Inside U.S. Trade*, August 14, 2009.

[97] "Mexico Initiates WTO Dispute Proceeding Against U.S. 'Dolphin-Safe' Label for Tuna," *International Trade Reporter*, October 30, 2008.

[98] "U.S. Seeks NAFTA Consultations In Tuna Labeling Dispute With Mexico," *Inside U.S. Trade*, November 13, 2009.

[99] For more information, see CRS Report RS22701, *Security and Prosperity Partnership of North America: An Overview and Selected Issues*, by M. Angeles Villarreal and Jennifer E. Lake; also see the website of the SPP, available at http://www.spp.gov/

[100] The White House, Office of the Press Secretary, "North American Leaders' Declaration on Climate Change and Clean Energy," August 10, 2009.

In: Mexico: Background and Issues
Editor: Richard C. Bradley

ISBN: 978-1-61728-498-4

Chapter 2

U.S.-Mexico Economic Relations: Trends, Issues, and Implications*

M. Angeles Villarreal

Summary

Mexico has a population of about 110 million people making it the most populous Spanish- speaking country in the world and the third most populous country in the Western Hemisphere. Based on a gross domestic product (GDP) of $1.0 trillion in 2008 (about 7% of U.S. GDP), Mexico has a free market economy with a strong export sector. Economic conditions in Mexico are important to the United States because of the proximity of Mexico to the United States, the close trade and investment interactions, and other social and political issues that are affected by the economic relationship between the two countries.

The United States and Mexico have strong economic ties. An important feature of the relationship is the North American Free Trade Agreement (NAFTA), which has been in effect since 1994. In terms of total trade, Mexico is the United States' third largest trading partner, while the United States ranks first among Mexico's trading partners. In U.S. imports, Mexico ranks third among U.S. trading partners, after China and Canada, while in exports Mexico ranks second, after Canada. The United States is the largest source of foreign direct investment (FDI) in Mexico. These links are critical to many U.S. industries and border communities.

In 2008, about 11% of total U.S. merchandise exports were destined for Mexico and 10% of U.S. merchandise imports came from Mexico. In the same year U.S. exports to Mexico increased almost 10%, while imports from Mexico increased about 3%. For Mexico, the United States is a much more significant trading partner. About 82% of Mexico's exports go to the United States and 50% of Mexico's imports come from the United States. FDI forms another part of the economic relationship between the United States and Mexico. The United States is the largest source of FDI in Mexico. U.S. FDI in Mexico totaled $91.7 billion in

---

* This is an edited, reformatted and augmented version of a CRS Report for Congress publication dated April 2009.

2007. The overall effect of NAFTA on the U.S. economy has been relatively small, primarily because two-way trade with Mexico amounts to less than three percent of U.S. GDP. Major trade issues between Mexico and the United States have involved the access of Mexican trucks to the United States; the access of Mexican sugar and tuna to the U.S. market; and the access of U.S. sweeteners to the Mexican market.

Over the last decade, the economic relationship between the United States and Mexico has strengthened significantly. The two countries continue to cooperate on issues of mutual concern. On March 23, 2005, the leaders of the United States, Canada, and Mexico met to discuss issues related to North American trade, immigration and defense. After the meeting, the three leaders announced the Security and Prosperity Partnership of North America (SPP), an initiative that is intended to increase cooperation and information sharing in an effort to increase and enhance prosperity in the United States, Canada, and Mexico. In April 2008, the North American leaders held a summit to discuss how they might further advance the goals of the SPP. The three leaders decided that their respective ministers should continue to renew and focus their work in the five SPP priority areas.

INTRODUCTION

Mexico has a population of approximately 110 million people making it the most populous Spanish-speaking country in the world and the third most populous country in the Western Hemisphere (after the United States and Brazil). The bilateral economic relationship with Mexico is among the most important for the United States because of Mexico's proximity and because of the large amount of trade and investment interactions. The most significant feature of the relationship is the North American Free Trade Agreement (NAFTA), through which the United States, Mexico, and Canada form the world's largest free trade area, with about one-third the world's total gross domestic product (GDP).

The United States and Mexico share common interests and are closely tied in areas not directly related to trade and investment. The two countries share a 2,000 mile border and have extensive interconnections through the Gulf of Mexico. There are links through migration and tourism, environment and health concerns, and family and cultural relationships.[1] The economic relationship with Mexico is important to U.S. national interests and to the U.S. Congress for many reasons. As the United States considers free trade initiatives with other Latin American countries, the effects of NAFTA may provide policymakers some indication of how these initiatives might affect conditions in the overall U.S. economy. The 111th Congress will likely maintain an active interest in Mexico on issues related to counternarcotics, migration, trade, and border issues. Comprehensive immigration reform was debated early in the 110th Congress, but the issue was put aside following a failed cloture motion in the Senate on the Comprehensive Immigration Reform Act of 2007 (S. 1348). Immigration reform efforts could be considered once again in the 111th Congress.

This chapter provides an overview of U.S.-Mexico economic trends, background information on the Mexican economy, the effects of NAFTA on the U.S.-Mexico economic relationship, and major trade issues between the United States and Mexico.

U.S.-Mexico Economic Trends

The United States and Mexico have strong economic ties. The United States is, by far, Mexico's most important partner in trade and investment, while Mexico is the United States third largest trade partner after China and Canada. Many economists have focused much attention on the ongoing transformation of Mexico into a manufacturing-for-export nation since the late 1980s and the importance of exports to its economy. Exports represent 31% of Mexico's GDP, up from 10% twenty years ago. After oil and gas, most of Mexico's exports are manufactured goods. Over 80% of Mexico's exports are headed to the United States. Mexico's reliance on the United States as a trade partner appears to be diminishing, although slightly. Between 2004 and 2007, the U.S. share of Mexico's total imports decreased from 56% to 50%, while the share of total Mexican exports going to the United States decreased from 89% to 82%. Although Mexican exports to the United States are steadily increasing, Mexico's share of the U.S. market has lost ground since 2002. In 2003, China surpassed Mexico as a supplier of U.S. imports, and Mexico now ranks third, after China and Canada, as a source of U.S. imports. Because over 80% of Mexico's exports are destined for the United States, any change in U.S. demand can have strong economic consequences in Mexican industrial sectors.

The immigration issue has received much attention by political leaders in recent years and it is one that can be linked to the economic situation in Mexico, although it has social and political aspects as well. In March 2008, there were approximately 12 million unauthorized immigrants living in the United States, with 59% from Mexico.[2] Economic conditions in Mexico and other countries, such as poverty and unemployment, are a major factor related to the migration issue. These workers often send money to their families in Mexico to help provide food and shelter. Worker remittances to Mexico increased from $13.4 billion in 2003 to $24billion in 2007. While Mexico receives the largest amount of remittances in Latin America, remittances comprise a comparatively small share of Mexican national income, accounting for about 3% of Mexico's gross domestic product (GDP) in 2007. The rate of remittance growth slowed to just 1% in 2007, far less than the average annual increase of 19% from 2003 through 2006.[3]

U.S.-Mexico Merchandise Trade

Mexico ranks second among U.S. export markets and is the United States' third largest trading partner in terms of total trade. In 2008, about 11% of total U.S. merchandise exports were destined for Mexico and 10% of U.S. merchandise imports came from Mexico. In the same year U.S. exports to Mexico increased 10.2% while imports from Mexico increased by 7.6%. For Mexico, the United States is a much more significant trading partner. About 82% of Mexico's exports go to the United States and 50% of Mexico's imports come from the United States. Mexico's second largest trading partner is China, accounting for approximately 6% of Mexico's exports and imports.[4]

Table 1. Key Economic Indicators for Mexico and the United States
Click here and type the subtitle, or delete this paragraph

	Mexico		United States	
	1998	**2008**[a]	**1998**	**2008**[a]
Population (millions)	97	110	276	304
Nominal GDP ($US billions) [b]	456	1,035	8,747	14,265
GDP, PPP[c] Basis ($US billions)	917	1,530	8,747	14,265
Per Capita GDP ($US)	4,681	9,410	31,679	46,950
Per Capita GDP in $PPPs	9,426	13,920	31,679	46,950
Total Merchandise Exports (US$ billions)	118	292	682	1,300
Exports as % of GDP[d]	28%	31%	11%	13%
Total Merchandise Imports (US$ billions)	125	309	912	2,100
Imports as % of GDP[d]	30%	33%	13%	18%
Public Debt/GDP	35%	18%	n.a.	n.a.

Source: Compiled by CRS based on data from Economist Intelligence Unit (EIU) on-line database.

Notes: Click here and type the notes, or delete this paragraph

[a] Some figures for 2008 are estimates.

[b] Nominal GDP is calculated by EIU based on figures from World Bank and World Development Indicators.

[c] PPP refers to purchasing power parity, which reflects the purchasing power of foreign currencies in U.S. dollars.

[d] Exports and Imports as % of GDP derived by EIU.

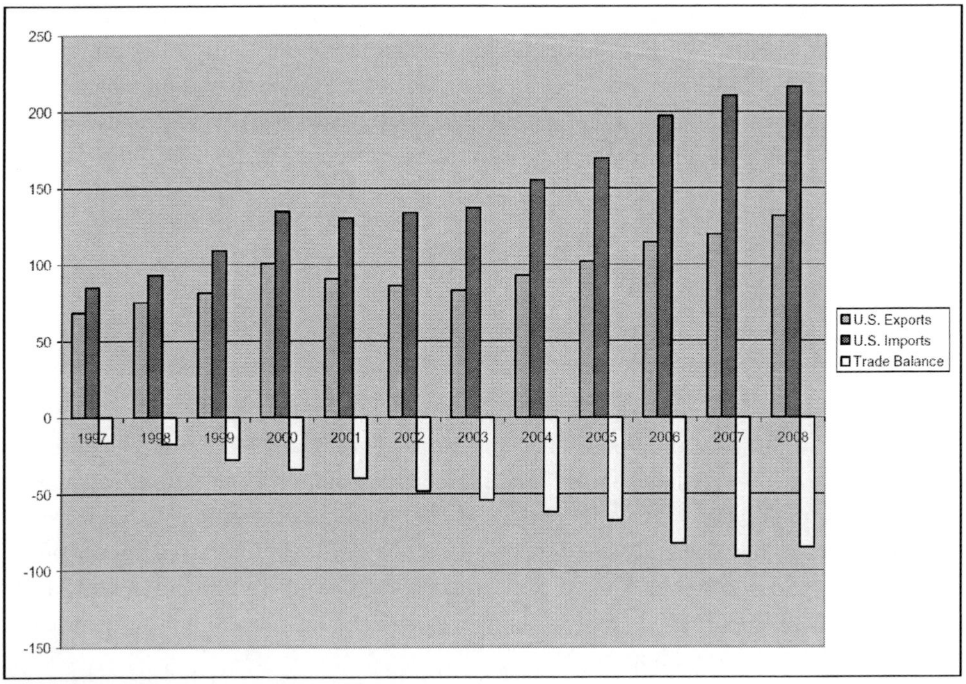

Source: United States International Trade Commission, Interactive Tariff and Trade Data Web. Compiled by CRS.

Figure 1. U.S. Merchandise Trade with Mexico

U.S. merchandise trade with Mexico has grown considerably over the last ten years (see Figure 1). Although some of the increase in trade could be attributable to NAFTA, there are other variables that affect trade, such as exchange rates and economic conditions. Mexico's currency crisis of 1995 limited the purchasing power of the Mexican people in the following years and also made products from Mexico less expensive for the U.S. market. Economic factors such as these played a role in the increasing U.S. trade deficit with Mexico which went from a $1.4 billion surplus in 1994 to a $84.8 billion deficit in 2008. U.S. imports from Mexico increased from $85.0 billion in 1997 to $216.3 billion in 2008, while U.S. exports to Mexico increased from $68.4 billion in 1997 to $131.5 billion in 2007 (see Table 2).

Several studies between 2003 and 2004 on the effects of NAFTA found that trade deficits were largely driven by macroeconomic trends, and, in the case of U.S.-Mexico trade, caused by the respective business cycles in Mexico and the United States.[5] Strong U.S. growth in the 1990s combined with Mexico's deep recession in 1995 were the main factors cited for the large deficits. None of the studies attributed the peso crisis to NAFTA, but to structural misalignments in the Mexican economy combined with political events.[6]

The leading U.S. import item from Mexico in 2007 was oil and gas, which amounted to $37.93 billion, or 17.5% of total U.S. imports from Mexico (see Table 2). The next leading import items were motor vehicles ($22.02 billion or 10.1% of total); motor vehicle parts ($20.58 or 9.51% of total); audio and video equipment ($17.84 billion or 8.2% of total); and communications equipment ($12.99 billion or 6.0% of total). The leading U.S. export item to Mexico in 2008 was motor vehicle parts, which amounted to $10.06 billion, or 7.6% of total exports to Mexico (see Table 3). The next leading export items were petroleum and coal products ($9.63 billion or 7.3% of total); basic chemicals ($7.16 billion or 5.4% of total); resin, synthetic rubber and products ($5.95 billion or 4.5% of total); and oilseeds and grains ($5.94 billion or 4.5% of total). The U.S. industry with the highest volume of trade (imports and exports) with Mexico is the automotive industry.

Table 2. U.S. Imports from Mexico: 2002-2008 (US$ in billions)

Leading Items (NAIC 4-digit)	2002	2003	2004	2005	2006	2007	2008	% Change 2007 - 2008
Oil and Gas	10.70	13.67	17.23	22.48	29.38	30.27	37.93	25.3%
Motor Vehicles	20.74	19.03	18.77	18.36	23.24	23.08	22.02	-4.6%
Motor Vehicle Parts	15.14	15.99	17.82	19.33	20.81	22.65	20.58	-9.2%
Audio/Video Equipment	7.45	6.91	8.18	9.87	13.89	17.06	17.84	4.5%
Communications Equipment	5.70	5.98	7.45	7.34	8.73	13.06	12.99	-0.6%
Other	74.39	75.62	85.51	91.84	101.01	104.04	104.97	3.9%
Total	134.12	137.20	154.96	169.22	197.06	210.16	216.33	2.9%

Source: Compiled by CRS using USITC Interactive Tariff and Trade DataWeb at http://dataweb.usitc.gov: NAIC4-digit level.

Note: Nominal U.S. dollars.

Table 3. U.S. Exports to Mexico: 2002-2008 (U.S. $ in millions)

Leading Items (NAIC 4-digit)	2002	2003	2004	2005	2006	2007	2008	% Change 2007 - 2008
Motor Vehicle Parts	8.14	7.11	7.55	7.39	8.60	9.40	10.06	7.0%
Petroleum and Coal Products	2.36	2.31	2.78	4.73	4.98	5.66	9.63	70.1%
Basic Chemicals	2.85	3.35	4.43	5.01	5.74	6.50	7.16	10.2%
Resin, Synthetic Rubber & Related Products	2.62	2.94	3.57	4.51	5.37	5.43	5.95	9.6%
Oilseeds and Grains	2.46	2.61	2.58	2.52	3.05	3.97	5.94	49.6%
Other	67.65	64.79	72.11	77.51	86.82	88.42	92.77	4.9%
Total	86.08	83.11	93.02	101.67	114.56	119.38	131.51	10.2%

Source: Compiled by CRS using USITC Interactive Tariff and Trade DataWeb at http://dataweb.usitc.gov: NAIC4-digit level

Note: Nominal U.S. dollars.

Mexico-U.S. Bilateral Foreign Direct Investment

Foreign direct investment (FDI) forms another part of the economic relationship between the United States and Mexico. FDI consists of investments in real estate, manufacturing plants, and retail facilities, in which the foreign investor owns 10% or more of the entity. The United States is the largest source of FDI in Mexico. U.S. FDI on a historical cost basis in Mexico increased from $17 billion in 1994 to $91.7 billion in 2007, nearly a 400% increase (see Table 4).

Mexican FDI in the United States is much lower than U.S. investment in Mexico, with levels of Mexican FDI fluctuating over the last ten years. In 2005, Mexican FDI in the United States totaled $8.7 billion, representing an increase of 440% since 1994, as shown in Table 4.

The sharp rise in U.S. investment in Mexico since NAFTA implementation is also a result of the liberalization of Mexico's restrictions on foreign investment in the late 1980s and the early 1990s. Prior to the mid-1980s, Mexico had a very protective policy that restricted foreign investment and controlled the exchange rate to encourage domestic growth, affecting the entire industrial sector. Mexico's trade liberalization measures and economic reform in the late 1980s represented a sharp shift in policy and helped bring in a steady increase of FDI flows into Mexico. NAFTA provisions on foreign investment helped to lock in the reforms and increase investor confidence. Under NAFTA, Mexico gave U.S. and Canadian investors nondiscriminatory treatment of their investments in Mexico as well as investor protection. NAFTA may have encouraged U.S. FDI in Mexico by increasing investor confidence, but much of the growth may have occurred anyway because Mexico likely would have continued to liberalize its foreign investment laws with or without NAFTA.

Table 4. U.S.- Mexican Foreign Direct Investment Positions: 1994-2007 Historical Cost Basis (U.S. $ in millions)

Year	Mexican FDI in the U.S.	U.S. FDI in Mexico
1994	2,069	16,968
1995	1,850	16,873
1996	1,641	19,351
1997	3,100	24,050
1998	2,055	26,657
1999	1,999	37,151
2000	7,462	39,352
2001	6,645	52,544
2002	7,483	55,724
2003	6,680	61,526
2004	8,167	63,502
2005	8,653	71,423
2006	6,075	84,699
2007	5,954	91,663

Source: U.S. Department of Commerce, Bureau of Economic Analysis.

Nearly half of total FDI investment in Mexico is in the manufacturing industry of which the maquiladora industry forms a major part. (See "Mexico's Export-Oriented Assembly Plants.") Mexico's maquiladora industry is important to the economic relationship of the United States and Mexico in several ways. In Mexico, the industry has helped attract investment from countries such as the United States that have a relatively large amount of capital. Therefore, Mexico is able to attract some of the foreign direct investment it was seeking when it liberalized trade and investment barriers. For the United States, the industry is important because U.S. companies are able to locate their labor-intensive operations in Mexico and lower their labor costs in the overall production process. Many economists believe that maquiladoras are an important part of U.S. corporate strategy in achieving competitively priced goods in the world marketplace.[7] Other analysts are concerned that the industry has caused U.S. companies to move their manufacturing facilities to Mexico at the expense of U.S. workers.

Mexico's Export-Oriented Assembly Plants[8]

Mexico's export-oriented assembly plants are closely linked to U.S.-Mexico trade in various labor-intensive industries such as auto parts and electronic goods. These export-oriented plants generate a large amount of trade with the United States and a majority of the plants have U.S. parent companies. Foreign-owned assembly plants, commonly called *maquiladoras,* account for a substantial share of Mexico's imports and about half of its exports. The largest maquiladora operation, Delphi Automotive Systems, headquartered in the United States, had 51 plants with 66,000 employees in Mexico in 2006.[9] Most maquiladora plants are located along the U.S.- Mexico border. The Mexican metropolitan areas with the highest maquiladora activity as of December 2006 (the latest year for which maquiladora statistics are available) were the Mexican border cities of Tijuana, Baja California, 568 maquiladoras with 164,900 employees, and Cd. Juárez, Chihuahua, 279 maquiladoras with 283,300 employees.[10] Recent changes in Mexican regulations on export-oriented industries merged the maquiladora industry and Mexican domestic assembly-for-export plants into one program called the maquiladora Manufacturing Industry and Export Services (IMMEX).

Private industry groups have stated that these operations help U.S. companies remain competitive in the world marketplace by producing goods at competitive prices. In addition, the proximity of Mexico to the United States allows production to have a high degree of U.S. content in the final product, which could help sustain jobs in the United States. Critics of these types of operations argue that they have a negative effect on the economy because they take jobs from the United States and help depress the wages of low-skilled U.S. workers.

After NAFTA, Mexico's regulations governing the maquiladora industry changed significantly. Beginning in 2001, the North American rules of origin determined the duty-free status for a given import and replace the previous special tariff provisions that applied only to maquiladora operations. The initial program ceased to exist and the same trade rules applied to all assembly operations in Mexico and not just those in the maquiladora program.[11] NAFTA rules for the maquiladora industry were implemented in two phases, with the first phase covering the period 1994-2000, and the second phase starting in 2001. During the initial phase, NAFTA regulations continued to allow the maquiladora industry to import products duty-free into Mexico, regardless of the country of origin of the products. This phase also allowed maquiladora operations to increase maquiladora sales into the domestic market. Phase II made a significant change to the industry in that the new North American rules of origin determined duty-free status for U.S. and Canadian products exported to Mexico for maquiladoras. The elimination of duty-free imports by maquiladoras from non-NAFTA countries under NAFTA caused some initial uncertainty for the companies with maquiladora operations. Maquiladoras that were importing from third countries, such as Japan or China, would have to pay applicable tariffs on those goods under the new rules.

Mexico had another program for export-oriented assembly plants called the Program for Temporary Imports to Promote Exports (PITEX) that was established in 1990 to allow qualifying domestic producers to compete with maquiladoras. PITEX plants are usually in areas located in central and southern Mexico while maquiladoras are more common in states along the U.S.- Mexico border. In recent years, the differences in the customs status of maquiladoras and PITEX plants diminished and the Mexican government decided to merge the two export-oriented programs. In 2007, the Mexican government announced a new set of regulations on export- oriented industries. These new rules merge the maquiladora industry and PITEX plants into the Maquiladora Manufacturing Industry and Export Services, or IMMEX. In 2008, maquiladora industry data will be included in Mexican manufacturing reports, without a distinction for maquiladora plants.[12] Prior to NAFTA, a maquiladora was limited to selling up to 50% of the previous year's export production to the domestic market. By 2000, maquiladoras were allowed to sell up to 85% of the previous year's export production to the Mexican market. Most maquiladoras, however, continue to export the majority of their production to the U.S. market.

The maquiladora industry expanded rapidly in the 1990s. The number of plants grew from 1,920 at the end of 1990 to 3,590 in 2000. After 2000, the number of maquiladoras fell to 2,860 in 2003. Since 2004, the number of plants has stayed at approximately the same levels, totaling 2,819 in 2007.[13] Some observers believe that the correlation in maquiladora growth after 1993 is directly due to NAFTA, but in reality it is a combination of factors that has contributed to growth in this sector. Trade liberalization, wages, and economic conditions, both in the United States and Mexico, have all contributed to the growth of Mexican export-oriented assembly plants. Although some provisions in NAFTA may have encouraged maquiladora growth in certain sectors, maquiladora activity is more influenced by the strength of the U.S. economy and relative wages in Mexico. Maquiladora operations usually increase during periods of economic expansion in the United States. A drop in Mexican wages may also be an incentive for U.S. companies to shift production to Mexico.

Between 1993 and 1996, relative wages in Mexico fell considerably due to the peso devaluation. Since 1997, however, Mexican labor costs have risen, and some manufacturers have closed their Mexican plants and shifted production to other low-wage countries. In 2001, maquiladora employment levels fell for the first time since 1982. Between 2000 and 2004, maquiladora employment levels fell from 1.30 million workers to 1.12 million workers. Approximately 176,000 jobs were lost and 780 plants were shut down nationwide during this time. Employment rose to about 1.23 million in 2006.[14]

Worker Remittances to Mexico

Remittances from workers abroad play a strong role in the Mexican economy and form an important aspect of the U.S.-Mexico economic relationship.[15] Worker remittances account for about 3% of Mexico's GDP and are the second-largest source of foreign currency inflows behind oil exports. Mexico was one of the top three recipients of remittances worldwide in 2007. After high levels of growth rates since 2002, the rate of growth of remittances to Mexico has dropped markedly in the past two years. In 2004, Mexico received a record $16.6 billion in remittances, representing a 24% increase over 2003.[16] Remittances from the United States to Mexico reached a peak of $6.2 billion in mid-2006 and have been decreasing since. In 2007, remittances grew by only 1%, after years of high growth. In January 2008, remittances to Mexico were down nearly 6%, the biggest drop in 13 years.[17] The decline in the level of remittances is due to a combination of factors. The slowdown in the U.S. economy, the weakening job market in the construction sector, tighter border controls, and increased anti-immigration sentiment in the United States may all be factors in the reduced number of seasonal migrants in the United States and their ability to send remittances to Mexico.[18]

Worker remittance flows to Mexico have an important impact on the Mexican economy, in some regions more than others. Some studies on remittance flows to Mexico report that in southern Mexican states, remittances mostly or completely cover general consumption and/or housing. One study estimates that 80% of the money received by households goes for food, clothing, health care, and other household expenses. Another study estimates that remittances in Mexico are responsible for about 27%, and up to 40% in some cases, of the capital invested in microenterprises throughout urban Mexico.[19] The economic impact of remittance flows is concentrated in the poorer states of Mexico. The government has sponsored programs to channel the funds directly to infrastructure and investment rather than consumption.[20]

Security and Prosperity Partnership of North America

The Security and Prosperity Partnership of North America (SPP) is a trilateral initiative, launched in March 2005, that is intended to increase cooperation and information sharing in an effort to increase and enhance prosperity in the United States, Canada, and Mexico. The SPP is a government initiative that was endorsed by the leaders of the three countries, but it is not a signed agreement or treaty and, therefore, contains no legally binding commitments or obligations. It can, at best, be characterized as an endeavor by the three countries to facilitate communication and cooperation across several key policy areas of mutual interest. Although the SPP builds upon the existing trade and economic relationship of the three countries, it is not a free trade agreement and is distinct from the existing North American Free Trade Agreement (NAFTA). Some key issues for Congress regarding the SPP concern possible implications related to national sovereignty, transportation corridors, cargo security, and border security. These issues are discussed in various sections of the report.

Since 2005, the SPP working groups have made annual recommendations to the North American leaders on how to accomplish the goals of the SPP. In 2008, the working groups agreed to continue to advance the agenda of the SPP by identifying and focusing on a set of high priority initiatives. They decided to: 1) increase the competitiveness of North American businesses and economies through more compatible regulations; 2) make borders smarter and more secure by coordinating long-term infrastructure plans, enhancing services, and reducing bottlenecks and congestion at major border crossings; 3) strengthen energy security and protect the environment by developing a framework for harmonization of energy efficiency standards and sharing technical information; 4) improve access to safe food, and health and consumer products by increasing cooperation and information sharing on the safety of food and products; and 5) improve North American response to emergencies by updating bilateral agreements to enable government authorities from the three countries help each other more quickly and efficiently during times of crisis.[21]

Goals of the SPP in the area of prosperity are to increase cooperation and sharing of information in order to improve productivity, reduce the costs of trade, and enhance the quality of life. Leaders from the three countries have highlighted the need to enhance North American competitiveness through compatible regulations and standards that would help the three countries protect health, safety and the environment, as well as to facilitate trade in goods and services across their borders. In the 2008 joint statement, the leaders highlighted the need for the three countries to implement compatible fuel efficiency regimes and high safety standards to protect human health and the environment, and to reduce the costs of producing cars and trucks for the North American market. They also emphasized their efforts to advance intellectual property rights protection in North America through the Intellectual Property Action Strategy.

The SPP is not a form of economic integration, and goes only as far as leading to some measure of regulatory harmonization among the United States, Canada, and Mexico. The SPP working groups are not contemplating further market integration in North America. Such a move would require a government approval process within each of the three countries. In the United States, such an agreement would require the approval of the U.S. Congress.

Some observers state that the SPP is an important step forward in the relationship of the United States with Mexico, and also Canada, in view of the distancing that occurred after the terrorist attacks of September 11, 2001.[22] However, other analysts believe that the SPP and any subsequent trade-facilitating measures may fall short of any grander vision of further economic integration.[23] Critics of the SPP contend that it may ultimately lead to a so-called "NAFTA Superhighway" that would link the United States, Canada, and Mexico with a 'super-corridor'.[24] However, if the United States were to potentially consider the formation of a customs union or common market with its North American neighbors, it would require approval by the U.S. Congress.

The Mexican Economy

Mexico has a free market economy with a strong export sector, but this has not always been the case. The transformation of Mexico into an export-based economy began in the late 1980s when the government started to liberalize its trade policy and adopt economic reform measures. One of the more distinctive aspects of the Mexican economy is its strong ties to the economic cycle of the United States, making it very sensitive to economic developments in the United States. The state of the Mexican economy is important to the United States because of the close trade and investment ties between the two countries, and because of other social and political issues that could be affected by economic conditions, particularly those related to immigration.

Economic Reform and the 1995 Currency Crisis

In the late 1980s and early into the 1990s, the Mexican government implemented a series of measures to restructure the economy that included steps toward trade liberalization. For many years, Mexico had protectionist trade policies to encourage industrial growth in the domestic economy. The 1980s were marked by inflation and a declining standard of living. Repercussions of the 1982 debt crisis in which the Mexican government was unable to meet its foreign debt obligations were a primary cause of the economic challenges the country faced in the early to mid-1980's. Much of the government's effort in addressing the challenges was placed on privatizing state industries and moving toward trade liberalization. Efforts included privatization of sea ports, railroads, telecommunications, electricity, natural gas distribution and airports. The negotiation and implementation of NAFTA played a major role in Mexico's changing economic policy in the early 1990s.

Mexico's economic reforms initially attracted a large amount of private foreign investment, but by 1993 the inflow of foreign capital began to slow down. The combination of macroeconomic policies at the time, which led to an overvalued exchange rate, and domestic political uncertainty helped drive down the flow of capital into the country. The decrease in capital inflows and the low levels of international reserves held by the Mexican government led to a peso devaluation in March 1994. Later that year, foreign exchange reserves continued to fall, domestic government debt increased, and the Mexican central bank had limited dollar reserves to support the current peso rate.

By the end of 1994, Mexico faced a currency crisis, putting pressure on the government to abandon its previous fixed exchange rate policy and adopt a floating exchange rate regime. As a result, Mexico's currency plunged by around 50% within six months, sending the country into a deep recession.[25] Several factors influenced the decision to float the peso: overspending in the economy had generated a significant current account deficit; the Mexican government had accumulated large levels of debt with insufficient reserves; and the banking system was facing a crisis due to overexposure.[26] Mexico's finance minister at the time, Guillermo Ortiz, stated later that Mexico had "no choice" but to float the peso because the government had run out of reserves.[27]

In the aftermath of the 1994 devaluation, Mexican President Ernesto Zedillo took several steps to restructure the economy and lessen the impact of the currency crisis among the more disadvantaged sectors of the economy. The goal was to create conditions for economic activity so that the economy could adjust in the shortest time possible. The United States and the IMF assisted the Mexican government by putting together an emergency financial support package of up to $50 billion, with most of the money coming from the U.S. Treasury. The Zedillo Administration wanted to demonstrate its commitment to fulfill all its financial obligations without a default on its debt by adopting tight monetary and fiscal policies to reduce inflation and absorb some of the costs of the banking sector crisis. The austerity plan included an increase in the value-added tax, budget cuts, increases in electricity and gasoline prices to decrease demand and government subsidies, and tighter monetary policy.[28]

Following the lead of former President Ernesto Zedillo, former President Vicente Fox continued efforts to liberalize trade, privatize government enterprises, and deregulate the economy. Through tighter monetary and fiscal policies, the Fox Administration was able to decrease the fiscal deficit, control inflation, and help economic growth.

The peso steadily depreciated through the end of the 1990s, which led to greater exports and helped the country's exporting industries. However, the peso devaluation also resulted in a decline in real income, hurting the poorest segments of the population and also the newly emerging middle class. NAFTA and the change in the Mexican economy to an export-based economy helped to soften the impact of the currency devaluation.

After a real decline in GDP of 6.22% in 1995, the Mexican economy managed to grow 5%-6% in each of the three years to 1998. The combination of a stronger peso and the slowdown in the U.S. economy in 2001, which worsened after the September 11 terrorist attacks, hit Mexico's economy hard. Real GDP growth dropped from 6.2% in 2000 to -0.16% in 2001. Improving economic conditions in the United States helped Mexico's economy improve as well. Real GDP growth in 2004 was 4.37%, up from 1.41% in 2003 and 0.81% in 2002 (see Figure 2). In 2006, real GDP growth was 4.8%, decreasing to 3.3% in 2007 and 1.4% in 2008.

Current Economic Conditions

The global economic crisis is having a significant effect on the Mexican economy. Real GDP growth in Mexico in 2008 was 1.4%, down from 3.3% in 2007. The economy is forecast to contract by 2.6% in 2009.[29] The expected decline in the Mexican economy in 2009 may be the sharpest decline since the 1995 currency crisis. The decline in U.S. demand for imports from Mexico resulting from the U.S. economic slowdown will have an impact on the Mexican economy because of its dependence on the United States as an export market. Job losses in Mexico have increased in recent months, with a possibilities of further job losses in export-oriented assembly plants as they cut capacity due to the downturn in demand.[30] After weakening by an estimated 5% in 2004 and 13% in 2003, the Mexican peso strengthened in 2005 and 2006. The peso remained relatively stable in 2007, but weakened again in 2008. The peso is expected to weaken further in 2009 due to low oil prices, the downturn in U.S. demand, and heightened risk aversion.[31] President Calderón of Mexico has taken a number of measures to attempt to cushion the Mexican economy from the fallout of the global economic crisis and the onset of recession in the United States. Mexico's dependence on exports and on the economic cycle in the United States is reflected in the economic cycles of the two countries depicted in Figure 2.

Poverty is one of the more serious and pressing economic problems facing Mexico. According to a 2004 World Bank Study,[32] the Mexican government had made progress in its poverty reduction efforts, but poverty continues to be a basic challenge for the country's development. The authors of the study note that poverty is often associated with social exclusion, especially of indigenous groups of people who comprise 20% of those who live in extreme poverty.[33] In 2002, over half of the population lived in poverty. According to World Bank estimates, the percentage of people living in extreme poverty, or on less than $1 per day, fell from 24.2% of the population in 2000, to 20.3% in 2002, and 18% in 2005. Those living in moderate poverty, or on about $10 a day, fell from 53.7% in 2000 to 51.7% of the population in 2002 and 45% in 2005. Mexico's continuing problem of poverty is especially widespread in rural areas and remains at the Latin American average.[34]

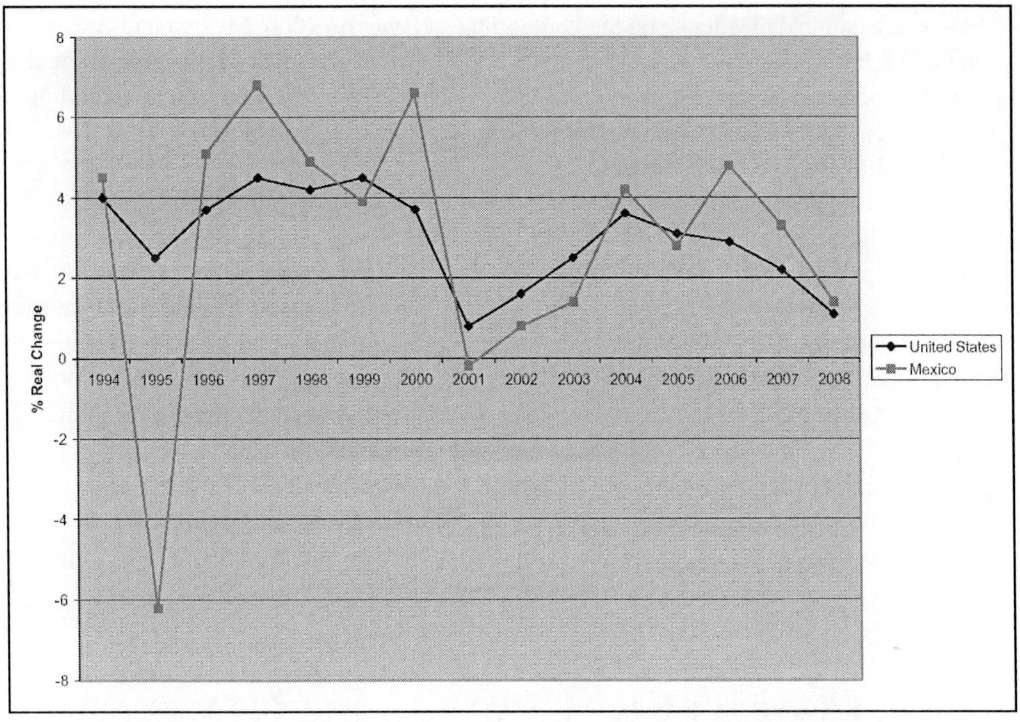

Source: Economist Intelligence Unit.

Figure 2. GDP Growth Rates for the United States and Mexico

Former President Fox considered the problem of poverty one of Mexico's principal challenges and stated that the highest priority of his administration was to combat poverty.[35] Mexico's main program to reduce the effects of poverty is the *Oportunidades* program (formerly known as Progresa). The program began under former President Zedillo and expanded under former President Fox to benefit five million families throughout Mexico. The program seeks to not only alleviate the immediate effects of poverty through cash and in-kind transfers, but to break the cycle of poverty by improving nutrition and health standards among poor families and increasing educational attainment. This program provides cash transfers to families in poverty who demonstrate that they regularly attend medical appointments and can certify that children are attending school. The government provides educational cash transfers to participating families. The program also provides nutrition support to pregnant and nursing woman and malnourished children. Monthly benefits are a minimum of $15 with a cap of about $150. The majority of households receiving *Oportunidades* benefits are in Mexico's six poorest states: Chiapas, Mexico State, Puebla, Veracruz, Oaxaca, and Guerrero.[36]

Mexico's Regional Free Trade Agreements

Since the early 1990s, Mexico has had a growing commitment to trade liberalization and its trade policy is among the most open in the world. Mexico has pursued free trade agreements (FTAs) with other countries as a way to bring benefits to the economy and also to reduce its economic dependence on the United States. By early 2006, Mexico had entered into a total of 12 FTAs involving 42 countries. The Mexican government has negotiated bilateral or multilateral trade agreements with most countries in the Western Hemisphere including the United States and Canada, Chile, Bolivia, Costa Rica, Nicaragua, Uruguay, Colombia, Guatemala, El Salvador, and Honduras.[37]

Mexico has ventured out of the hemisphere in negotiating FTAs, and, in July 2000, entered into agreements with Israel and the European Union. Mexico became the first Latin American country to have preferred access to these two markets. Mexico has also completed an FTA with the European Free Trade Association (EFTA) of Iceland, Liechtenstein, Norway, and Switzerland. The Mexican government has continued to look for potential free trade partners, and expanded its outreach to Asia in 2000 by entering into negotiations with Singapore, Korea and Japan.[38] In 2004, Japan and Mexico signed an Economic Partnership Agreement. It was the first comprehensive trade agreement that Japan signed with any country.[39] Mexico's negotiations on FTAs with Korea and Singapore are stalled.

In addition to the bilateral and multilateral free trade agreements, Mexico is a member of the WTO,[40] the Asia-Pacific Economic Cooperation forum, and the OECD.[41] In September 2003, Mexico hosted the WTO Ministerial Meeting in Cancun.

NAFTA and the U.S.-Mexico Economic Relationship

The North American Free Trade Agreement (NAFTA) has been in effect since January 1994. There are numerous indications that NAFTA has achieved many of the intended trade and economic benefits as well as incurred adjustment costs. This has been in keeping with what most economists maintain, that trade liberalization promotes overall economic growth among trading partners, but that there are significant adjustment costs.

Most of the trade effects in the United States related to NAFTA are due to changes in U.S. trade and investment patterns with Mexico. At the time of NAFTA implementation, the U.S.-Canada Free Trade Agreement already had been in effect for five years, and some industries in the United States and Canada were already highly integrated. Mexico, on the other hand, had followed an aggressive import-substitution policy for many years prior to NAFTA in which it had sought to develop certain domestic industries through trade protection. One example is the Mexican automotive industry which had been regulated by a series of five decrees issued by the Mexican government between 1962 and 1989. The decrees established import tariffs as high as 25% on automotive goods and had high restrictions on foreign auto production in Mexico. Under NAFTA, Mexico agreed to eliminate these restrictive trade policies.

Not all changes in trade and investment patterns between the United States and Mexico since 1994 can be attributed to NAFTA because trade was also affected by other unrelated economic factors such as economic growth in the United States and Mexico, and currency fluctuations. Also, trade-related job gains and losses since NAFTA may have accelerated trends that were ongoing prior to NAFTA and may not be totally attributable to the trade agreement. Overall, Mexico has experienced a slight shift in the composition of trade with the United States since the late 1980s from oil to non-oil exports. In 1987, crude oil and natural gas comprised 17% of Mexico's exports to the United States. The percentage of oil and natural gas exports had declined to 10.6% in 2004, but increased to 14.4% in 2007 due to higher oil prices.

Effects on the U.S. Economy

The overall effect of NAFTA on the U.S. economy has been relatively small, primarily because two-way trade with Mexico amounts to less than three percent of U.S. GDP. Thus, any changes in trade patterns with Mexico would not be expected to be significant in relation to the overall U.S. economy. In some sectors, however, trade-related effects could be more significant, especially in those industries that were more exposed to the removal of tariff and non-tariff trade barriers, such as the textile and apparel, and automotive industries.

Since NAFTA, the automotive, textile, and apparel industries have experienced some of the more noteworthy changes in trading patterns, which may also have affected U.S. employment in these industries. U.S. trade with Mexico has increased considerably more than U.S. trade with other countries, and Mexico has become a more significant trading partner with the United States since NAFTA implementation.

In the automotive industry, the industry comprising the most U.S. trade with Mexico, NAFTA provisions consisted of a phased elimination of tariffs, the gradual removal of many non-tariff barriers to trade including rules of origin provisions, enhanced protection of intellectual property rights, less restrictive government procurement practices, and the elimination of performance requirements on investors from other NAFTA countries. These provisions may have accelerated the on-going trade patterns between the United States and Mexico. Because the United States and Canada were already highly integrated, most of the trade impacts on the U.S. automotive industry relate to trade liberalization with Mexico. Prior to NAFTA Mexico had a series of government decrees protecting the domestic auto sector by reserving the domestic automobile market for domestically produced parts and vehicles. NAFTA established the removal of Mexico's restrictive trade and investment policies and the elimination of U.S. tariffs on autos and auto parts. By 2006, the automotive industry has had the highest dollar increase ($41 billion) in total U.S. trade with Mexico since NAFTA passage.

The main NAFTA provisions related to textiles and apparel consisted of eliminating tariffs and quotas for goods coming from Mexico and eliminating Mexican tariffs on U.S. textile and apparel products. To benefit from the free trade provision, goods were required to meet the rules of origin provision which assured that apparel products that were traded among the three NAFTA partners were made of yarn and fabric made within the free trade area. The strict rules of origin provisions were meant to ensure that U.S. textiles producers would continue to supply U.S. apparel companies that moved to Mexico. Without a rules of origin provision, apparel companies would have been able to import low-cost fabrics from countries such as China and export the final product to the United States under the free trade provision.[42]

While some U.S. industries may have benefitted from increased demand for U.S. products in Mexico, creating new jobs, other industries have experienced job losses. Data on the effects of trade liberalization with Mexico are limited and the effect on specific sectors of the U.S. economy is difficult to quantify. Trade-related job gains and losses since NAFTA may have accelerated trends that were ongoing prior to NAFTA and may not be totally attributable to the trade agreement.[43] Quantifying these effects is challenging because of the other economic factors that influence trade and employment levels. The devaluation of the Mexican peso in 1995 resulted in lower Mexican wages, which likely provided an incentive for U.S. companies to move to lower their production costs. Trade-related employment effects following NAFTA could have also resulted from the lowering of trade barriers, and from the economic conditions in Mexico and the United States influencing investment decisions and the demand for goods.

Effects on the Mexican Economy

While a number of studies have found that NAFTA has brought economic and social benefits to the Mexican economy as a whole, the benefits have not been evenly distributed throughout the country. Most studies after NAFTA have found that the effects on the Mexican economy tended to be modest at most.[44] While there have been periods of positive growth and negative growth in Mexico after the agreement was implemented, much of the increase in trade began in the late 1980s when the country began trade liberalization measures. Though its net economic effects may have been positive, NAFTA itself has not been enough to lower income disparities within Mexico, or between Mexico and the United States or Canada.

A 2005 World Bank study assessing some of the economic impacts from NAFTA on Mexico concluded that NAFTA helped Mexico get closer to the levels of development in the United States and Canada. The study states that NAFTA helped Mexican manufacturers to adopt to U.S. technological innovations more quickly and likely had positive impacts on the number and quality of jobs. Another finding was that since NAFTA went into effect, the overall macroeconomic volatility, or wide variations in the GDP growth rate, has declined in Mexico. Business cycles in Mexico, the United States, and Canada have had higher levels of synchronicity since NAFTA, and NAFTA has reinforced the high sensitivity of Mexican economic sectors to economic developments in the United States.[45]

Several economists have noted that it is likely that NAFTA contributed to Mexico's economic recovery directly and indirectly after the 1995 currency crisis. Mexico responded to the crisis by implementing a strong economic adjustment program but also by fully adhering to its NAFTA obligations to liberalize trade with the United States and Canada. NAFTA may have supported the resolve of the Mexican government to continue with the course of market-based economic reforms, resulting in increasing investor confidence in Mexico. The World Bank study estimates that FDI in Mexico would have been approximately 40% lower without NAFTA.[46]

One of the main arguments in favor of NAFTA at the time it was being proposed by policymakers was that the agreement would improve economic conditions in Mexico and narrow the income gap between Mexico and the United States. Studies that have addressed the issue of economic convergence[47] have noted that economic convergence in North America might not materialize under free trade as long as "fundamental differences" in initial conditions persist over time. One study argues that NAFTA is not enough to help narrow the disparities in economic conditions between Mexico and the United States and that Mexico needs to invest more in education; innovation and infrastructure; and in the quality of national institutions. The study states that income convergence between a Latin American country and the United States is limited by the wide differences in the quality of domestic institutions, in the innovation dynamics of domestic firms, and in the skills of the labor force.[48] Another study also notes that the ability of Mexico to improve economic conditions depends on its capacity to improve its national institutions, adding that Mexican institutions did not improve significantly more than those of other Latin American countries during the post-NAFTA period.[49]

Mexican wages rose steadily from the early 1980s until the mid-1990s, when the currency crisis hit. After a drop in average real wages in 1996 of 15.5%, real wages increased steadily until 2000, when the average rate of growth was 11.8%. Since then the average rate of growth has only varied slightly (see Figure 2). Mexico's trade liberalization measures may have affected the ratio between skilled and non-skilled workers in Mexico. In 1988, the real average wage of skilled workers in Mexico's manufacturing industry was 2.25 times larger than that of non-skilled workers. This ratio increased until 1996, when it was about 2.9, but then remained stable until 2000.[50] The World Bank study found that NAFTA brought economic and social benefits to the Mexican economy, but that the agreement in itself was not sufficient to ensure a narrowing of the wage gap between Mexico and the United States. The study states that NAFTA had a positive effect on wages and employment in some Mexican states, but that the wage differential within the country increased as a result of trade liberalization.[51]

MAJOR ISSUES IN U.S.-MEXICO TRADE RELATIONS

Major trade disputes between Mexico and the United States involve the access of Mexican trucks to the United States; the access of Mexican sugar and tuna to the U.S. market; and the access of U.S. sweeteners to the Mexican market. [52]

Trucking

A major U.S.-Mexico trade issue relates to the implementation of NAFTA trucking provisions. Under NAFTA, Mexican commercial trucks were to have been given full access to four U.S. border states in 1995 and full access throughout the United States in 2000. Citing safety concerns, however, the United States refused implementation of NAFTA's trucking provisions and the Mexican government objected. A NAFTA dispute resolution panel supported Mexico's position in February 2001. President Bush indicated a willingness to implement the provision, but the U.S. Congress required additional safety provisions in the FY2002 Department of Transportation Appropriations Act (P.L. 107-87). On November 27, 2002, with safety inspectors and procedures in place, the Administration announced that it would begin the process that will open U.S. highways to Mexican truckers and buses, but environmental and labor groups went to court in early December to block the action. On January 16, 2003, the U.S. Court of Appeals for the Ninth Circuit ruled that full environmental impact statements were required before Mexican trucks would be allowed to operate on U.S. highways, but the U.S. Supreme Court reversed that decision on June 7, 2004.

Since the ruling, the U.S. and Mexican Administrations worked on resolving the trucking issues, and the two countries engaged in talks regarding a number of safety and operational issues that needed to be resolved before Mexican commercial trucks were granted authority to operate in the United States. In February 2007, the Bush Administration announced a pilot project to grant Mexican trucks from 100 transportation companies full access to U.S. highways. The Administration announced a delay in the program in April 2007, likely in response to critics who contended that Mexican trucks do not meet U.S. standards. The Iraq War Supplemental (P.L. 110- 28), enacted May 25, 2007, mandated that any pilot program to give Mexican trucks access beyond the border region could not begin until U.S. trucks had similar access to Mexico. In addition, the DOT needed to meet certain reporting and public notice requirements before any pilot program could begin. The DOT's Inspector General needed to prepare a report to Congress to verify that the DOT had established mechanisms to ensure that Mexican truck comply with U.S. federal motor carrier safety laws. The report also needed to verify that Mexican trucks meet the safety provisions of P.L. 107-87, mentioned above.

By September 2007, the Department of Transportation launched the one-year pilot program to allow approved Mexican carriers beyond the 25-mile commercial zone, with a similar program allowing U.S. trucks to travel beyond Mexico's commercial zone. As of early January 2008, 57 trucks from 10 Mexican companies had received permission to operate in the United States and 41 trucks from 4 U.S. companies received permission to operate in Mexico. Department of Transportation data reportedly shows that U.S. carriers have made twice as many trips to Mexico as Mexican carriers have to the United States from the time the program was launched until early January 2008.

In the FY2008 Consolidated Appropriations Act (P.L. 110-161), signed into law in December 2007, Congress included a provision prohibiting the use of FY2008 funding for the establishment of a pilot program. The Department of Transportation determined that it could continue with the pilot program because it had already been established. In February 2008, a coalition of unions and environmental groups filed suit in the 9th Circuit Court of Appeals to end the pilot program, but a decision is still pending.[53]

In March 2008, the DOT issued an interim report on the cross-border trucking demonstration project to the Senate Committee on Commerce, Science, and Transportation. The report made three key observations: 1) The Federal Motor Carrier Safety Administration (FMCSA) plans to check every participating truck each time it crosses the border to ensure that it meets safety standards; 2) There is less participation in the project than was expected; and 3) The FMCSA has implemented methods to assess possible adverse safety impacts of the project and to enforce and monitor safety guidelines.[54]

In early August 2008, the Department of Transportation announced that it would be extending the pilot program for an additional two years. On September 9, 2008, the House approved (by a vote of 396 to 128) H.R. 6630, a bill that would prohibit the Department of Transportation from granting Mexican trucks access to U.S. highways beyond the border and commercial zone. The bill would also prohibit the Department of Transportation from renewing such a program unless expressly authorized by Congress. No action was taken by the Senate on the measure.

In the recently enacted FY2009 Omnibus Appropriations Act (P.L. 111-8), the U.S. Congress terminated a pilot program begun in September 2007 that allowed Mexican-registered trucks to operate beyond the 25-mile border commercial zone inside the United States. In response to the abrupt end of the pilot program, the Mexican government announced that it would retaliate by increasing duties on 90 U.S. products with an import value of $2.4 billion. The tariffs, effective as of March 19, 2009, range from 10% to 45% and cover a range of products that include fruit, vegetables, home appliances, consumer products, and paper.[55] During Secretary of State Hillary Clinton's recent trip to Mexico, she pledged to resolve the dispute over Mexican-registered trucks. "We are working to resolve it," she said and added that she anticipated Congress would be responsive to the Administration's plans.[56]

Other Trade Issues

The United States and Mexico resolved a long-standing trade dispute in 2006 involving sugar and high fructose corn syrup. Mexico argued that the sugar side letter negotiated under NAFTA entitled it to ship net sugar surplus to the United States duty-free under NAFTA, while the United States argued that the sugar side letter limited Mexican shipments of sugar. Mexico also complained that imports of high fructose corn syrup (HFCS) sweeteners from the United States constituted dumping, and it imposed anti-dumping duties for some time, until NAFTA and WTO dispute resolution panels upheld U.S. claims that the Mexican government colluded with the Mexican sugar and sweetener industries to restrict HFCS imports from the United States.

In late 2001, the Mexican Congress imposed a 20% tax on soft drinks made with corn syrup sweeteners to aid the ailing domestic cane sugar industry, and subsequently extended the tax annually despite U.S. objections. In 2004, the United States Trade Representative (USTR) initiated WTO dispute settlement proceedings against Mexico's HFCS tax, and following interim decisions, the WTO panel issued a final decision on October 7, 2005, essentially supporting the U.S. position. Mexico appealed this decision, and in March 2006, the WTO Appellate Body upheld its October 2005 ruling. In July 2006, the United States and Mexico agreed that Mexico would eliminate its tax on soft drinks made with corn sweeteners no later than January 31, 2007. The tax was repealed, effective January 1, 2007.

The United States and Mexico reached a sweetener agreement in August 2006. Under the agreement, Mexico can export 500,000 metric tons of sugar duty-free to the United States from October 1, 2006, to December 31, 2007. The United States can export the same amount of HFCS duty-free to Mexico during that time. NAFTA provides for the free trade of sweeteners beginning January 1, 2008. The House and Senate sugar caucuses expressed objections to the agreement, questioning the Bush Administration's determination that Mexico is a net-surplus sugar producer to allow Mexican sugar duty-free access to the U.S. market.[57]

On tuna issues, the Clinton Administration lifted the embargo on Mexican tuna in April 2000 under relaxed standards for a dolphin-safe label in accordance with internationally agreed procedures, and U.S. legislation passed in 1997 that encouraged the unharmed release of dolphins from nets. However, a federal judge in San Francisco ruled that the standards of the law had not been met, and the Federal Appeals Court in San Francisco sustained the ruling in July 2001. Under the Bush Administration, the Commerce Department ruled on December 31, 2002, that the dolphin-safe label may be applied if qualified observers certify that no dolphins were killed or seriously injured in the netting process, but Earth Island Institute and other environmental groups filed suit to block the modification. On April 10, 2003, the U.S. District Court for the Northern District of California enjoined the Commerce Department from modifying the standards for the dolphin-safe label. On August 9, 2004, the federal district court ruled against the Bush Administration's modification of the dolphin-safe standards and reinstated the original standards in the 1990 Dolphin Protection Consumer Information Act. That decision was appealed to the U.S. Ninth Circuit Court of Appeals, which ruled against the Administration in April 2007, finding that the Department of Commerce did not base its determination on scientific studies of the effects of Mexican tuna fishing on dolphins. In late October 2008, Mexico initiated World Trade Organization dispute proceedings against the United States, maintaining that U.S. requirements for Mexican tuna exporters prevents them from using the U.S. "dolphin-safe" label for its products.[58]

On other issues, in early October 2002, the U.S.-Mexico working group on agriculture dealt with major agricultural issues, including Mexico's anti-dumping decisions on apples, rice, swine, and beef, and safeguard actions on potatoes. In January 2003, the countries agreed to permit Mexican safeguard measures against U.S. imports of chicken legs and thighs, and in July 2003, these safeguard measures were extended until 2008, with tariffs declining each year. In September 2006, Mexico revoked anti-dumping duties imposed on U.S. rice imports in 2002 following rulings by the WTO and WTO Appellate Body in 2005, which found that the duties were contrary to WTO rules. Mexico banned beef imports from the United States in December 2003 following the discovery of one cow infected with mad cow disease in Washington State. Mexico resumed importation of boneless beef in early

March 2004, and bone-in beef in February 2006, in response to improved beef cattle screening.

POLICY ISSUES

The United States economic relationship with Mexico has strengthened significantly over the last decade and is of mutual importance. Up to this point, the discussion in the report has focused on the background and surrounding issues of the economic relationship, which leads to the issue of policy considerations. First, there is the question of whether to further economic integration with Mexico in view of the increasing trends in regional trade agreements throughout the world. The close economic relationship between the United States and Mexico that was strengthened by NAFTA is likely to continue but there may be challenges in coming years as the influence of China and other low-wage countries increases. According to a recent study on economic integration in North America, a major shift is under way in trade patterns among NAFTA partners with exports among NAFTA economies growing more slowly than their exports with the rest of the world, reversing the previous 10-year trend. The report finds that lower-cost suppliers, primarily China and India, are displacing North American imports and could weaken North American integration. The report states that furthering continental integration would require "renewed efforts at resolving long-standing trade disputes, new liberalization initiatives, or greater policy harmonization in areas such as border security, labor mobility, or corporate taxation."[59]

If the United States continues to deepen economic integration with Mexico, one area that may need more attention is the issue of the difference in income levels between the two countries. The economic relationship with Mexico is unique because of Mexico's proximity to the United States, but also because of the wide differences in levels of economic development between the two countries. Mexico is the first developing country with which the United States entered into a free trade agreement. In Mexico, NAFTA has had an uneven effect in different parts of the country and it has not been a solution to the problem of poverty and unemployment. Mexico's problem with poverty cannot be attributed directly to NAFTA because it was in existence prior to the agreement. At the time of NAFTA there was hope that Mexico's economy would grow sufficiently to create jobs in urban areas and help alleviate poverty in rural areas. However, the economy did not expand as expected and the problem of poverty continues.

Another issue is whether trade agreements are enough, or are the appropriate policy instrument, to resolve income disparities among trading partners or even within a developing country. The World Bank study on the effects of NAFTA on Mexico concludes that NAFTA has helped to improve economic conditions in Mexico but it has not been enough to narrow the economic disparities with the United States. The authors of the study state, among other things, that Mexico needs to invest more in education, infrastructure, and institutional strengthening to benefit more fully from freer trade.[60] A possible consideration for policymakers is whether to help Mexico improve the quality of education and strengthen its national institutions through foreign aid programs or other mechanisms.

The economic hardship in certain sectors and regions of Mexico has been a major reason behind unauthorized Mexican migration to the United States. Mexican President Felipe

Calderón made his first official visit to the United States as President-elect in early November 2006, after first visiting Canada and several Latin American countries. During his visit, Calderón criticized the recent authorization of fencing along the U.S.-Mexico border and noted that it complicated U.S.- Mexico relations. He asserted that job-creation and increased investment in Mexico would be more effective in reducing illegal migration from Mexico than a border fence. Calderón signaled a shift in Mexican foreign policy when he noted that while immigration is an important issue in the bilateral relationship, it is not the only issue, as trade and economic development are also important.

Under the Fox Administration, Mexico voiced concern about alleged abuses suffered by Mexican workers in the United States and for the loss of life and hardships suffered by Mexican migrants as they use increasingly dangerous methods to cross into the United States. The Fox Administration held the view that the migrants are "undocumented workers" and that because the U.S. market attracts and provides employment for the migrants, it bears some responsibility. During his administration, former Mexican President Vicente Fox pressed proposals for legalizing undocumented Mexican workers in the United States through amnesty or guest worker arrangements as a way of protecting their human rights. In 2004, President Bush proposed an overhaul of the U.S. immigration system to permit the matching of willing foreign workers with willing U.S. employers when no U.S. documented workers could be found to fill the jobs.

The U.S. Senate began consideration of comprehensive immigration reform in May 2007. Mexico had long lobbied for immigration reform in the United States and cautiously watched the debate in 2007 on this measure. Legal immigration reform has stalled in the 110th Congress. A bipartisan compromise proposal for comprehensive immigration reform negotiated with the Bush Administration was introduced in the Senate on May 21, 2007, as S.Amdt. 1150 to S. 1348. A modified version of that compromise (S. 1639) came to the Senate floor the week of June 26, 2007, but a key cloture vote did not pass.[61] It is unclear whether the 110th Congress will again tackle comprehensive immigration reform. It may, however, consider legislation on selected immigration reform issues, such as foreign workers. Additional border security measures may also be considered.

End Notes

[1] See CRS Report RL32724, *Mexico-U.S. Relations: Issues for Congress*, by Mark P. Sullivan and June S. Beittel.

[2] Pew Hispanic Center, *Trends in Unauthorized Immigration: Undocumented Inflow Now Trails Legal Inflow,* October 2, 2008.

[3] CRS Report RL32724, *Mexico-U.S. Relations: Issues for Congress*, p. 7.

[4] Data compiled by CRS using Global Trade Atlas database.

[5] See CRS Report RS21737, *NAFTA at Ten: Lessons from Recent Studies*, by J. F. Hornbeck.

[6] Ibid.

[7] Federal Reserve Bank of Dallas, "The Binational Importance of the Maquiladora Industry," *Southwest Economy,* Issue 6, November/December 1999.

[8] Mexico's export-oriented industries began with the maquiladora program established in the 1960s by the Mexican government, which allowed foreign-owned businesses to set up assembly plants in Mexico to produce for export. Maquiladoras could import intermediate materials duty-free with the condition that 20% of the final product be exported. The percentage of sales allowed to the domestic market increased over time as Mexico liberalized its trade regime. U.S. tariff treatment of maquiladora imports played a significant role in the industry. Under HTS provisions 9802.00.60 and 9802.00.80, the portion of an imported good that was of U.S.-origin entered the United States duty-free. Duties were assessed only on the value added abroad. After

NAFTA, North American rules of origin determine duty-free status. Recent changes in Mexican regulations on export-oriented industries merged the maquiladora industry and Mexican domestic assembly-for-export plants into one program called the maquiladora Manufacturing Industry and Export Services (IMMEX).

[9] Data from Mexico's *Instituto Nacional de Estadística Geografía e Informática* (INEGI), provided by Global Insight, Inc, at the LIX Maquiladora Industry Outlook Meeting on June 8, 2007 in El Paso, Texas.

[10] Ibid.

[11] Vargas, Lucinda, "NAFTA, the U.S. Economy, and Maquiladoras," *El Paso Business Frontier,* 2001.

[12] Federal Reserve Bank of Dallas, *Southwest Economy,* Issue 3, "Spotlight: Maquiladora Data, Mexican Reform Clouds View of Key Industry," May/June 2007.

[13] Based on data from INEGI.

[14] Ibid.

[15] For information on remittances to Latin America see CRS Report RL31659, *Foreign Remittances to Latin America*, by Walter W. Eubanks and Pauline Smale.

[16] EIU ViewsWire, "Mexico Economy: Remittances Home Hit a Record US$16.6 Billion in 2004," February 9, 2005.

[17] *The Dallas Morning News,* "Remittances to Mexico See Biggest Drop in 13 Years," March 7, 2008.

[18] The World Bank, *Remittance Trends 2007,* by Dilip Ratha, Sanket Mohapatra, K.M. Vijayalakshmi, and Zhimei Xu, November 29, 2007.

[19] The Federal Reserve Bank of Dallas report "Workers' Remittances to Mexico," (2004) evaluated the economic impact of worker remittances to Mexico and cites a number of reports by the World Bank and the Mexican government.

[20] Ibid, p. 4.

[21] Joint statement by President Bush, President Calderon, Prime Minister Harper, April 22, 2008.

[22] "U.S., Mexico, Canada Agree to Increase Cooperation," *The Washington Post,* March 24, 2005, p. A4.

[23] "Neighbors Who Are not Always Friends: Bush's Summit with Mexican and Canadian Leaders Will Probably Take Small Steps Toward Bolder Integration," *The Christian Science Monitor,* March 23, 2005, p. 2.

[24] See for example, Corsi, Jerome R., *The Plan to Replace the Dollar with the 'Amero',* May 22, 2006; Corsi, Jerome, *I-69: Yet Another NAFTA Superhighway*, September 12, 2006; or Schlafly, Phyllis, *The NAFTA Superhighway*, August 23, 2006.

[25] EIU, "Mexico Finance: The Peso Crisis, Ten Years On," January 3, 2005.

[26] Banco de Mexico, "Mexico's Monetary Policy Framework Under a Floating Exchange Rate Regime," by Agustín G. Carstens y Alejandro M. Werner, May 1999.

[27] EIU, "Mexico Economy: Mexico Begins to See Benefits of Free-Floating Peso," December 20, 2004.

[28] Joachim Zietz, "Why Did the Peso Collapse? Implications for American Trade," *Global Commerce*, by , Volume 1, No. 1, Summer 1995.

[29] EIU, *Country Report: Mexico,* March 2009.

[30] Ibid.

[31] EIU, *Country Report: Mexico,* March 2009.

[32] The World Bank Group, *Mexico Makes Progress and Faces Challenges in Poverty Reduction Efforts,* June 2004.

[33] The World Bank Group Press Release, "Mexico Makes Progress and Faces Challenges in Poverty Reduction Efforts," July 2004.

[34] Ibid.

[35] Associated Press, "Poverty Level Down, But Still Big Challenge for Mexico," July 28, 2004

[36] Santiago Levy, *Progress Against Poverty,* Brookings Institution, 2006.

[37] Organization of American States, Foreign Trade Information System (SICE), see http://www.sice.oas.org.

[38] *The Asahi Shimbun,* "Mexico: Loving Free Trade Ever Since NAFTA," March 2002. See http://www.facilitycity.com.

[39] *The Asahi Shimbun,* "Japan: Free Trade with Mexico," *The Asahi Shimbun,* March 12, 2004.

[40] The WTO allows member countries to form regional trade agreements, but under strict rules. The position of the WTO is that regional trade agreements can often support the WTO's multilateral trading system by allowing groups of countries to negotiate rules and commitments that go beyond what was possible at the time under the WTO. The WTO has a committee on regional trade agreements that examines regional groups and assesses whether they are consistent with WTO rules. See The World Trade Organization, "Understanding the WTO: Cross-Cutting and New Issues, Regionalism: Friends or Rivals?" http://www.wto.org.

[41] U.S. Commercial Service, *Country Commercial Guide: Mexico,* August 13, 2004, p. 6.

[42] For more information on textile and apparel trade, see CRS Report RL31723, *Textile and Apparel Trade Issues*, by Bernard A. Gelb.

[43] CRS Report 98-783, *NAFTA: Estimates of Job Effects and Industry Trade Trends After 5 1/2 Years*, by Mary Jane Bolle.

[44] For more information, see CRS Report RS21737, *NAFTA at Ten: Lessons from Recent Studies*, by J. F. Hornbeck.

[45] The World Bank, *Lessons from NAFTA for Latin America and the Caribbean,* by Daniel Lederman, William F. Maloney, and Luis Servén, 2005. (Hereinafter *Lessons from NAFTA,* 2005).

[46] Ibid.

[47] Economic convergence can be broadly defined as a narrowing of the disparities in the economic levels and the manufacturing performances of particular countries or their regions. The goal of the theory of economic convergence is to research and analyze the factors influencing the rates of economic growth and real per capita income in countries.

[48] *Lessons from NAFTA*, 2005.

[49] *Economia*, "NAFTA and Convergence in North America: High Expectations, Big Events, Little Time," by William Easterly, Norbert Fiess, and Daniel Lederman, Fall 2003.

[50] Esquivel, Gerardo, and José Antonio Rodríguez-López, "Technology, trade, and wage inequality in Mexico before and after NAFTA," *Journal of Development Economics*, 2003.

[51] *Lessons from NAFTA*, 2005.

[52] See CRS Report RL32724, *Mexico-U.S. Relations: Issues for Congress*, by Mark P. Sullivan and June S. Beittel.

[53] "9th Circuit Considers Injunction to Halt Mexican Truck Pilot Program," *International Trade Daily*, February 13, 2008; Rosalind McLymont, "Long Haul Across the Border," *Shipping Digest*, January 7, 2008; and "Hoffa Blasts Bush Administration's Indifference to NAFTA Harm," *PR Newswire*, March 10, 2008.

[54] Department of Transportation. "Cross-Border Trucking Demonstration Project," March 11, 2008.

[55] *International Trade Reporter,* "Key GOP House Members Urge obama to Develop New Mexico Truck Program," March 26, 2009.

[56] Arshad Mohammed, "WRAPUP 2-U.S. to blame for much of Mexican drug violence," *Reuters News*, March 25, 2009.

[57] "Bush Administration Defends Sugar Deal to Congress," *Inside U.S. Trade*, November 3, 2006; "Grassley, U.S. Industry Welcome Agreement with Mexico on Sugar, HFCS," *International Trade Reporter*, August 3, 2006; and, "U.S., Mexico Reach Agreement on WTO Soft Drink Dispute Compliance Deadline," *International Trade Reporter*, July 13, 2006.

[58] *International Trade Reporter,* "Mexico Initiates WTO Dispute Proceeding Against U.S. 'Dolphin-Safe' Label for Tuna," October 30, 2008.

[59] ITR, "North American Integration Slipping Due to China's Strong Growth, Report Says," Volume 22, Number 8, February 24, 2005.

[60] The World Bank, *Lessons from NAFTA for Latin America and the Caribbean,* by Daniel Lederman, William F. Maloney, and Luis Servén, 2005.

[61] For more details, see CRS Report RL32235, *U.S. Immigration Policy on Permanent Admissions*, by Ruth Ellen Wasem.

In: Mexico: Background and Issues
Editor: Richard C. Bradley
ISBN: 978-1-61728-498-4

Chapter 3

MÉRIDA INITIATIVE FOR MEXICO AND CENTRAL AMERICA: FUNDING AND POLICY ISSUES*

Clare Ribando Seelke

SUMMARY

Increasing violence perpetrated by drug trafficking organizations (DTOs) and other criminal groups is threatening citizen security in Mexico and Central America. Drug-related violence claimed more than 6,500 lives in Mexico in 2009, and several Central American countries have among the highest homicide rates in the world. Mexican DTOs dominate the illicit drug market in the United States and are expanding their operations by forming partnerships with U.S. gangs. As a result, some of the drug-related violence in Mexico has spilled over into the United States.

On October 22, 2007, the United States and Mexico announced the Mérida Initiative, a proposed package of U.S. counterdrug and anticrime assistance for Mexico and Central America that would begin in FY2008 and last through FY2010. Congress appropriated roughly $1.3 billion for Mexico and Central America, as well as Haiti and the Dominican Republic, in the FY2008 Supplemental Appropriations Act (P.L. 110-252), FY2009 Omnibus Appropriations Act (P.L. 111-8), and the FY2009 Supplemental Appropriations Act (P.L. 111-32). Each of these Acts contained human rights conditions on 15% of certain law enforcement and military assistance provided.

Throughout 2009, drug-related violence in Mexico and the potential threat of spillover along the Southwest border focused congressional concern on the pace of implementation of the Mérida Initiative. On December 3, 2009, the Government Accountability Office (GAO) issued a preliminary report for Congress on the status of funding for the Mérida Initiative. By the end of September 2009, GAO found that $830 million of the $1.3 billion in Mérida funds appropriated for Mexico and Central America had been obligated by the State Department,

* This is an edited, reformatted and augmented version of a CRS Report for Congress publication dated January 2010.

but only $26 million of the funds had actually been spent. The pace of implementation has accelerated since that time, particularly in Mexico, but implementation challenges remain.

For FY2010, the Obama Administration requested $450 million in Mérida funding for Mexico and $100 million for Central America. On December 13, 2009, Congress passed the FY2010 Consolidated Appropriations Act (H.R. 3288/P.L. 111-117), which allows for $210.3 million for Mexico and $83 million for Central America under a new Central America Regional Security Initiative (CARSI). These Mexico (Mérida) and Central America (CARSI) funds are subject to the same human rights conditions as those provided in P.L. 111-8. Congress also provided $37 million in P.L. 111-117 for a new Caribbean Basin Security Initiative (CBSI).

During its second session, the 111th Congress is likely to maintain a strong interest in how well U.S. agencies and their foreign counterparts are implementing the Mérida Initiative and the degree to which the nations involved are fulfilling their domestic obligations under Mérida. Congress may also monitor enforcement of Mérida's human rights conditions, particularly with respect to Mexico. Congress is likely to play a role in the design of post-Mérida security cooperation with Mexico, Central America, and the Caribbean Basin during its consideration of the Obama Administration's FY2011 budget request. This chapter provides an overview of the funding provided for the Mérida Initiative, the status of Mérida implementation, and a discussion of some policy issues that Congress may consider as it oversees the Initiative. For related information, see CRS Report RL32724, *Mexico-U.S. Relations: Issues for Congress*, and CRS Report R40582, *Mexico's Drug-Related Violence*.

INTRODUCTION

Heightened drug-related violence in Mexico, including states along the U.S.-Mexico border, and the increasing presence of Mexican drug traffickers and Central American gangs in the United States have focused congressional concern on the pace of implementation of the Mérida Initiative. To date, Congress has appropriated some $1.3 billion to support Mérida programs in Mexico, $248 million for Mérida and a new Central America Regional Security Initiative (CARSI) in Central America, and $37 million for the establishment of a Caribbean Basin Security Initiative.[1] During its second session, the 111th Congress is likely to monitor how Mérida and related funds have been used, progress to date, any planned adjustments in the uses of funds, and post-Mérida plans that are being developed by the Obama Administration.

BACKGROUND

Mexico is a major producer and supplier to the U.S. market of heroin, methamphetamine, and marijuana and the major transit country for cocaine sold in the United States. According to the Department of State's 2009 *International Narcotics Control Strategy Report*, as much as 90% of the cocaine entering the United States now transits through Mexico. A small number of Mexican drug trafficking organizations (DTOs), often mistakenly referred to as "drug cartels,"[2] control the most significant drug distribution operations along the Southwest border. Drug trafficking-related violence in Mexico has spiked dramatically in recent years as DTOs have competed for control of lucrative smuggling routes into the United States.[3]

Since taking office in December 2006, Mexican President Felipe Calderón has made combating the DTOs a centerpiece of his domestic policy agenda. The Calderón government has scored some significant victories against the DTOs, such as the recent killing of Arturo Beltrán Leyva and capture of Teodoro Garcia Simental.[4] However, the government's crackdown, as well as turf wars among rival DTOs, has fueled an escalation in violence throughout the country, including states along the U.S.-Mexico border. In 2008, more than 5,100 people in Mexico were killed in drug-related violence, a 126% increase over 2007.[5] In 2009, conservative estimates indicate that more than 6,500 people, including 35 soldiers and close to 500 police officers, died as a result of drug-related homicides, with the violence largely concentrated in five states.[6] In many areas of those states, such as Ciudad Juarez, Chihuahua, which accounted for roughly 31% of the drug-related homicides recorded in Mexico during 2009, violence has remained at elevated levels even with the presence of large numbers of federal troops and police officials.

Mexican DTOs are increasingly expanding their operations into Central America[7], a volatile region where the governments of some countries – particularly Guatemala, El Salvador, and Honduras – are already dealing with some of the highest violent crime rates in the world.[8] Central American officials have even less training and equipment to deal with DTOs, organized crime, and criminal gangs than their Mexican counterparts. In addition, as with Mexico, Central America continue to have problems with impunity, police corruption, and human rights abuses by security forces that have hindered the performance and reputation of their law enforcement and judicial systems.

The Development of the Mérida Initiative

Prior to 2007, neither Mexico nor any of the countries in Central America had received large amounts of U.S. counternarcotics (CN) assistance.[9] In FY2007, for example, Mexico received $36.7 million in CN assistance and the only Central American countries to receive CN funds were Guatemala ($1.9 million) and Panama ($3.3 million).

In response to the Mexican government's request for increased cooperation and assistance, in October 2007 the United States and Mexico proposed the Mérida Initiative, a package of U.S. counterdrug and anticrime assistance to Mexico and Central America.[10] As proposed, the Mérida Initiative was to provide some $1.4 billion in assistance, largely in the form of equipment and training, from FY2008 through FY2010. According to the State Department, the four primary goals of the Mérida Initiative are to: 1) break the power and impunity of criminal organizations; 2) assist the Mexican and Central American governments in strengthening border, air, and maritime controls; 3) improve the capacity of justice systems in the region; and, 4) curtail gang activity in Mexico and Central America and diminish the demand for drugs in the region. Within these over-arching goals, the State Department developed specific objectives and performance measures that can be used to evaluate the Mérida Initiative (see "Monitoring Progress").[11]

According to its proponents, the Mérida Initiative is more than just a foreign assistance package, it is a new kind of regional security partnership between the United States, Mexico and Central America. Analysts and U.S. officials have repeatedly said that for the Initiative to be successful, all the countries involved will have to accept their "shared responsibility" to tackle domestic problems contributing to drug trafficking and crime in the region, including U.S. drug demand.[12] Since President Calderón took office, Mexico has increased security spending, including a reported $5 billion increase in the 2009 budget, mobilized thousands of soldiers and police to drug trafficking "hot-spots" throughout the country, and enacted judicial and law enforcement reforms.[13] The Obama Administration has, among other measures, posted more agents from the Bureau of Alcohol, Tobacco, Firearms, and Explosives (ATF) and Immigrations and Customs Enforcement (ICE) along the Southwest border to help intercept arms and bulk cash flowing into Mexico.[14] Central American leaders have regularly met to develop ways to better coordinate their security and counterdrug efforts through the Central American Integration System (SICA).

FUNDING THE MÉRIDA INITIATIVE

Mexico

FY2008 Supplemental Appropriations

In June 2008, the 110th Congress appropriated $352 million in FY2008 supplemental assistance and $48 million in FY2009 bridge fund supplemental assistance for Mexico in P.L. 110-252, the FY2008 Supplemental Appropriations Act (see Table 1 for funding for Mexico by year and aid account). In contrast to the Bush Administration, which requested all Mérida funding in the International Narcotics Control and Law Enforcement (INCLE) account, Congress divided the funding for Mexico in P.L. 110-252 between the INCLE, Foreign Military Financing (FMF), and Economic Support Fund (ESF) aid accounts. Congress limited the amount of FMF and INCLE available to provide equipment to the Mexican Army/Air Force and Navy and made 15% of FMF and INCLE contingent on meeting certain human rights conditions.[15] (See Appendix A for the final language of the human rights conditions in P.L. 110-252). Congress also earmarked $73.5 million for judicial reform, institution building, rule of law, and anti-corruption activities.[16] Congress stipulated that none of the funds may be used for budget support or as cash payments.

According to the Department of State,[17] which is leading Mérida Initiative implementation, the first tranche of $400 million for the foreign aid program provided in P.L. 110-252 includes funding for the following:

- helicopters (up to five Bell 412 helicopters) and surveillance aircraft (up to two CASA maritime patrol aircraft) to support interdiction and rapid response of Mexican law enforcement agencies;
- non-intrusive inspection equipment, ion scanners, and canine units for Mexican customs, the new Mexican federal police and the military to interdict trafficked drugs, arms, cash, and persons;
- technologies and secure communications to improve data collection and storage;
- and technical advice and training to strengthen the institutions of justice in order to improve vetting for the Mexican police force, to provide case management software

to track investigations through the legal process, to support offices of citizen complaint and professional responsibility, and to promote the establishment of witness protection programs.

As of late July 2009, Congress was still withholding some $57.0 million in FY2008 supplemental INCLE and FMF funds pending submission of a State Department human rights progress report for Mexico. In early August 2009, press reports indicated that the State Department had decided to delay submission of a favorable human rights report for Mexico to Congress due to the likelihood that it would have been rejected by Senate appropriators.[18] U.S. and Mexican human rights groups had urged the State Department not to issue a favorable report on the Mexican government's human rights record because they maintained that the Mexican military has failed to investigate, prosecute, or punish human rights violations committed by its forces.[19] After receiving additional information from the Mexican military regarding its efforts to prosecute soldiers charged with human rights and other abuses, the State Department issued a somewhat favorable report to Congress on August 13, 2009, thereby meeting the statutory requirements in P.L. 110-252 for the release of the FMF and INCLE funds that had been on hold.[20]

FY2009 Omnibus and Supplemental Appropriations

The Bush Administration requested $450 million in INCLE funding for Mexico under Mérida in its FY2009 budget request, placing more emphasis on assistance to non-military agencies. In March 2009, the 111th Congress passed the Omnibus Appropriations Act, (P.L. 111-8) providing $300 million for Mexico within the INCLE, ESF, and FMF accounts with not less than $75 million for judicial reform, institution building, anti-corruption, and rule of law activities. The measure continues the same human rights conditions originally set forth in P.L. 110-252. In P.L. 111-8, human rights conditions apply to 15% of the total funds provided, not including assistance for judicial reform, institution building, anti-corruption, and rule of law activities.[21] The same human rights progress report submitted to Congress in mid-August 2009 by the State Department met the statutory requirements in P.L. 111-8 for the release of roughly $31.5 million in FMF and INCLE funds that had been on hold.

On April 9, 2009, the Obama Administration submitted a FY2009 supplemental request that included an additional $66 million in INCLE assistance to acquire three Blackhawk helicopters, along with spare parts and support for those helicopters, for Mexico's civilian Secretariat for Public Security (SSP).[22] On June 24, 2009, President Obama signed the FY2009 supplemental appropriations measure passed by Congress (H.R. 2346/P.L. 111-32) that includes $160 million in INCLE assistance and $260 million in FMF for Mexico, $354 million more than the Administration's request. The $160 million in INCLE funds can be used to supply the Mexican federal police with items such as forensics and nonintrusive inspection equipment, computers, training, and fixed and rotary wing aircraft (including the requested Blackhawk helicopters). The $260 million in FMF funding is for expedited aviation assistance to the Mexican Navy. P.L. 111-32 also appropriates significant funds to other U.S. agencies, including the Departments of Justice and Homeland Security, to increase security on the Southwest border. Of the $420 million in FY2009 supplemental assistance to Mexico, 15% of the $160 million in INCLE assistance is subject to the same human rights conditions set forth in the FY2009 omnibus appropriations measure (P.L. 111-8, section 7045(e) of

Division H).[23] However, the FMF funds appropriated in P.L. 111-32 are not subject to human rights conditions.

Table 1. FY2008 – FY2010 Mérida Funding for Mexico by Aid Account ($ in millions)

Account	FY2008 Supp. (P.L. 110-252)	FY2009 Bridge (P.L. 110-252)	FY2009 (P.L. 111-8)	FY2009 Supp. (P.L. 111-32)	FY2010 P.L. 111-117)	Account Totals
ESF	20.0	0.0	15.0	0.0	15.0	50.0
INCLE	215.5	48.0	246.0	160.0	190.0	859.5
FMF	116.5	0.0	39.0	260.0	5.3	420.8
Total	**352.0**	**48.0**	**300.0**	**420.0**	**210.3**	**1,330.3**

Sources: U.S. Department of State, FY2008 Supplemental Appropriations Spending Plan, FY2009 Appropriations Spending Plan, and FY2009 Supplemental Spending Plan. FY2010 Consolidated Appropriations Act (P.L. 111-117).

Notes: ESF=Economic Support Fund; FMF=Foreign Military Financing; INCLE=International Narcotics Control and Law Enforcement.

FY2010 Appropriations

For FY2010, the Obama Administration requested $450 million in INCLE assistance for Mexico for helicopters, fixed-wing aircraft, and surveillance systems for Mexico's SSP; helicopters for the Mexican Navy; and non-intrusive inspection equipment for the SSP, the Mexican military and Customs. The Administration sought support for law enforcement training programs in investigative techniques and ethics, as well as anti-corruption training for internal watchdog units within the Attorney General's Office (PGR) and SSP. The Administration's FY2010 request also included funding for ongoing rule of law reforms.

On December 13, 2009, Congress passed the FY2010 Consolidated Appropriations Act (H.R. 3288/P.L. 111-117), which allows for $210.3 million for Mexico in the INCLE, ESF, and FMF accounts subject to the same human rights conditions as P.L. 111-8. While Congress provided less funding for Mérida-related programs in Mexico and Central America than the Administration's FY2010 request, Congress had appropriated significantly more for Mexico than requested in the FY2009 supplemental spending measure, and considered $254 million of this as forward funding of FY2010. In the Joint Explanatory Statement to P.L. 111-117, the conferees direct the Secretary of State to submit a report to within 90 days of the enactment of the Act addressing how prior Mérida funds have been used, progress to date, any planned adjustments in the uses of funds, and post-Merida plans. Table 1 describes the various funding levels addressed above.

Non-Mérida Assistance for Mexico

In addition to funding provided through the Mérida Initiative, Mexico continues to receive U.S. assistance through other State and Defense Department assistance accounts, some of which is for security and counterdrug programs. For example, in FY2009 Mexico received roughly $0.8 million for military training programs funded through the State Department's International Military Education and Training Account (IMET), up from $0.4 million in FY2008. Apart from the Mérida Initiative, the U.S. Department of Defense (DOD) provided a $13 million counterterrorism training and equipment package to the Mexican military in FY2008.[24] In addition, while DOD only provided some $3.1 million in CN training assistance to Mexico in FY2008, DOD assistance expanded to roughly $28.2 million in FY2009 in order to complement Mérida programs.[25] On December 16, 2009, Congress appropriated an additional $50 million in funding for counternarcotics communication equipment for Mexico in the FY2010 Department of Defense Appropriations Act (H.R. 3326/P.L. 111-118).[26]

Central America

FY2008 Supplemental Appropriations

The FY2008 Supplemental Appropriations Act (P.L. 110-252) included $60 million in Mérida funds for Central America. As with Mexico, Congress divided the funding for Central America between several different accounts (see Table 2). In addition to changing the account structure, Congress shifted the bulk of funding for Central America from public security and law enforcement programs to institution building, rule of law, and development programs. It did so by earmarking $25 million in ESF funds for the creation of an Economic and Social Development Fund for Central America. Of the ESF funds provided, $20 million are being administered by the U.S. Agency for International Development (USAID) for youth violence prevention, community policing, and community development programs in violence-prone areas. The other $5 million in ESF funds are supporting educational and cultural exchange programs administered by the State Department. Congress also earmarked $1 million to support the International Commission against Impunity in Guatemala (CICIG).[27]

As with Mexico, P.L. 110-252 required that 15% of INCLE and FMF assistance be withheld until the Secretary of State reports that the Central American governments are taking steps to create police complaints commissions, reform their judiciaries, and investigate and prosecute military and police forces who have been credibly alleged to have committed human rights violations. (see Appendix A for the final language of the human rights conditions). The State Department submitted human rights progress reports for Belize, Costa Rica, the Dominican Republic, El Salvador, Haiti, Honduras, and Panama on April 30, 2009, and for Guatemala on August 18, 2009. The State Department was unable to report on progress made by Nicaragua, and on August 13, 2009, reprogrammed $252,600 in FY 2008 INCLE funds withheld from Nicaragua to support efforts in Belize, Costa Rica, and Panama.

FY2009 Appropriations

The Bush Administration requested $100 million in FY2009 funds for Central America under the Mérida Initiative. In the FY2009 Omnibus Appropriations Act, P.L. 111-8, Congress provided $105 million in funding for Central America subject to similar human rights conditions as in P.L. 110-252. The explanatory statement to the FY2009 omnibus bill provides $70 million in INCLE for the region. It also stipulates that $15 million of the FMF funds appropriated must support maritime security programs and that $12 million of the ESF appropriated must fund USAID's Economic and Social Fund for Central America. On August 27, 2009, the Secretary of State reported on progress made by Belize, Costa Rica, El Salvador, Guatemala, and Panama, meeting the 15% withholding statutory requirement. Some

$1.73M in FY 2009 INCLE funds remains withheld pending the submission of the 15% report to Congress for Honduras and Nicaragua.

Table 2. FY2008 – FY2010 Mérida Funding for Central America by Aid Account ($ in millions)

Account	FY2008 Supp. (P.L. 110-252)	FY2009 (P.L.111-8)	FY2010 (P.L.111-117)[a]
ESF	25.0	18.0	n/a
INCLE	24.8	70.0	n/a
NADR	6.2	0.0	n/a
FMF	4.0	17.0	n/a
Total	**60.0**	**105.0**	**83.0**

Source: U.S. Department of State, FY2008 Supplemental Appropriations Spending Plan, FY2009 Appropriations Spending Plan, and "Summary and Highlights, International Affairs, Function 150, Fiscal Year 2010."

Notes: ESF=Economic Support Fund; FMF=Foreign Military Financing; INCLE=International Narcotics Control and Law Enforcement; NADR=Non-proliferation, Anti-terrorism and Related Programs.

a. P.L. 111-117 does not provide a funding breakdown for Central America by aid account.

FY2010 Appropriations

For FY2010, the Obama Administration requested $100 million in INCLE assistance for Central America to enhance regional capability to protect citizen security, combat illegal trafficking and build stronger justice sector institutions. According to the request, funding would support U.S. anti-gang efforts, provide equipment and technical assistance for community policing and juvenile justice systems, and implement anti-corruption measures.

On December 13, 2009, Congress passed the FY2010 Consolidated Appropriations Act (H.R. 3288/P.L. 111-117), which allows for "up to" $83 million for Central America to combat drug trafficking and organized crime, and for judicial reform, institution building, anti-corruption, rule of law, and maritime security. The Act places Central America funding into a new Central America Regional Security Initiative (CARSI), which splits Central America from the Merida Initiative. These CARSI funds are subject to the same human rights conditions as those provided in P.L. 111-8. The Joint Explanatory Statement to P.L. 111-117 directs the Secretary of State to submit a report within 90 days of the enactment of the Act detailing the threats to be addressed, goals, and expected results of the programs that have been funded thus far in Central America (as well as Haiti and the Dominican Republic) through Mérida and CARSI.

The Caribbean

Although not included in the original Mérida request, Congress dedicated $2.5 million in INCLE funding for Haiti and $2.5 million for the Dominican Republic, two major drug transit countries in the Caribbean, in P.L. 110-252 and again in P.L. 111-8. In Haiti, Mérida funds are being used to install a secure communications network for the Haitian National Police

(HNP), support the HNP's drug interdiction efforts, and provide training for Haitian judicial officials. In the Dominican Republic, Mérida funds are being used to support police professionalization programs, provide logistical support to interdiction units, and train judicial authorities in implementing the new criminal procedure code. A portion of the Mérida funds for each country is also supporting the U.N. Stabilization Mission in Haiti (MINUSTAH).

For 2010, the Obama Administration did not seek Mérida Initiative funding for Haiti and the Dominican Republic in its budget request, but proposed a new security regime for the Caribbean, the Caribbean Basin Security Initiative (CBSI). The FY2010 Consolidated Appropriations Act (H.R. 3288/P.L. 111-117) provided "not less than" $37 million for CBSI, of which "not less than" $21 million is to be used for social justice and education programs.

Other Mérida Legislation in the 111th Congress

H.R. 2410 (Berman) Foreign Relations Authorization Act, Fiscal Years 2010 and 2011. Introduced May 14, 2009; House Committee on Foreign Affairs held markup and ordered the bill reported. House approved June 22, 2009. Title IX, Subtitle A of the bill, as introduced, consists of actions to enhance the Mérida Initiative, including the designation of a high-level coordinator within the Department of State to implement the program; the addition of Caribbean Community (CARICOM) countries to the Mérida Initiative; the establishment and implementation of a program to assess the effectiveness of assistance provided under the Mérida Initiative; within 180 days and not later than December 1 of each year thereafter, a reporting requirement regarding the programs and activities carried out under the Mérida Initiative. Title IX, Subtitle B of the bill would require the President to establish an inter-agency task force on the prevention of illicit small arms trafficking in the Western Hemisphere; increase penalties for illicit trafficking in small arms and light weapons; and express congressional support for the ratification by the United States of the Inter-American Convention Against the Illicit Manufacturing of and Trafficking in Firearms, Ammunition, Explosives, and Other Related Materials (CIFTA).

H.R. 3238 (Kirkpatrick) Introduced July 16, 2009; referred to Committees on Homeland Security and Foreign Affairs. Committee on Homeland Security held markup and ordered the bill reported November 17, 2009. The bill would require the Secretary of Homeland Security, in consultation with the Secretary of State, to submit a report on the effects of the Mérida Initiative on the border security of the United States.

Status of Implementation

There has been increasing concern in Congress about the slow delivery of Mérida assistance. U.S. officials reportedly attributed early delays in disbursal of FY2008 funds to U.S. government contracting regulations, negotiations with Mexico and other countries about what equipment is actually needed, and the difficulty of delivering an aid package that involves so many agencies and offices.[28] More recent delays in Mérida implementation have also occurred because Congress did not pass an FY2009 appropriations bill until well into the 2009 fiscal year, and as a result of ongoing consultations between the State Department and congressional appropriators on the contents of the spending plans and human rights progress reports required by the Mérida appropriations legislation.

On December 3, 2009, the Government Accountability Office (GAO) issued a preliminary report for Congress on the status of funding for the Mérida Initiative.[29] By the end of September 2009, GAO found that $830 million of the $1.3 billion in Mérida funds appropriated for Mexico and Central America had been obligated by the State Department, but only $26 million of the funds had actually been spent. The report attributed delays in Mérida implementation to "(1) statutory conditions on the funds, (2) challenges in fulfilling administrative procedures [required for obligation and expenditure of the funds][30], and (3) the need to enhance institutional capacity on the part of both recipient countries and the United States to implement the assistance."[31]

In a written response to the GAO report, the State Department acknowledged that implementation delays had occurred, but stated that it had devoted significant time to working with partner governments to prepare for the disbursement and coordination of future Mérida assistance. The State Department also criticized the GAO's use of "expended funds" as its primary performance measure, since this measure did not account for ongoing programs such as the training of 3,000 Mexican federal police investigators at the new Federal Police Academy or equipment that had been ordered.[32] According to data provided by the State Department, as of November 27, 2009, some $359 million in Mérida funding was actively supporting projects in Mexico and Central America.[33]

State Department officials in Mexico City have reported significant progress in Mérida implementation since the GAO reporting period ended. According to an equipment report provided by State Department officials, roughly $77.2 million worth of equipment was delivered to Mexico by the end of December 2009, including 30 ion scanners and five Bell helicopters for the Mexican Army. Another $135.5 million in equipment is scheduled to be delivered by June 2010, including a $50 million CASA surveillance aircraft for the Mexican Navy and three UH-60 helicopters for the SSP. With respect to Mérida-funded training programs, 42% of training projects were reported to have achieved "significant progress" in implementation by mid-November 2009, including those involving police professionalization and continuing education, prison reform, prosecutorial capacity building, and human rights training programs.[34]

Although the pace of implementation has quickened since the GAO reporting period ended in September 2009, some 30% of FY2008 Mérida training programs remained stalled as of mid-November 2009.[35] Those programs include efforts to strengthen vetted units against money laundering and organized crime, help law schools and bar associations train lawyers in the new judicial system, and efforts to improve internal controls and citizen participation programs at the Attorney General's Office (PGR). Similarly, some 43% of FY2008 Mérida-funded equipment projects had yet to show significant progress in implementation by mid-November. Those projects would provide equipment to strengthen and modernize multi-agency organized crime and money laundering units, asset forfeiture units at the PGR, and the Financial Intelligence Unit of the Secretary of Finance (the lead agency implementing programs against money laundering).

Policy Issues

A broad consensus appears to be shared by the Administration, Congress and the policy community on the need for the United States to support neighboring governments in Mexico and Central America that are struggling to address drug-related violence. President Obama reiterated his support for President Calderón's "courageous effort" to take on the DTOs during a press conference held in Mexico after the conclusion of the North American Leaders Summit on August 10, 2009.[36] In 2009, Congress held numerous hearings on the heightened drug-related violence in Mexico, and its potential spillover effects on the United States. During its second session, the 111th Congress is likely to closely monitor the efficacy of assistance provided through the Mérida Initiative and compliance with Mérida's human rights conditions. Congress may also play a significant role in designing post-Mérida security cooperation with Mexico, Central America, and the Caribbean as it considers the Obama Administration's FY2011 budget request.

When Secretary of State Hillary Clinton traveled to Mexico on March 25 – 26, 2009, she commented on the importance of bilateral cooperation under the Initiative. During her trip, she acknowledged that an "insatiable demand for illegal drugs" in the United States "fuels the drug trade."[37] With regard to the United States as a source of the weapons that arm the drug traffickers, Clinton also acknowledged that "our inability to prevent weapons from being smuggled across the border to arm these criminals causes the deaths of police, soldiers and civilians."[38] Congress is likely to continue to examine how well the U.S. government is demonstrating its "shared responsibility" to tackle domestic problems contributing to drug trafficking and crime in the region, including U.S. drug demand. This section of the report raises some questions and policy issues Congress is likely to consider at it oversees implementation of the Mérida Initiative.

Is Mérida the Right Drug Control Approach?[39]

Unless programs like the Mérida Initiative are woven into a more holistic U.S. drug policy focusing on reducing demand as well as supply, many analysts predict that they are unlikely to have a significant impact on drug flows in the region.[40] In February 2009, a non-governmental, independent study group called the Latin American Commission on Drugs and Democracy—cochaired by former presidents from Brazil, Colombia, and Mexico—concluded that the current international drug control model has failed and called for a new policy focused more on "harm reduction" through prevention and treatment than on criminalizing drugs. As a comparison, many studies, including an October 2008 report by the Government Accountability Office (GAO), have concluded that while Plan Colombia, a centerpiece of U.S. international drug control efforts, improved security conditions in Colombia, it did not significantly reduced the amount of drugs flowing into the United States.[41]

These concerns have recently been echoed by Members of Congress. The Western Hemisphere Drug Policy Commission Act of 2009, H.R. 2134 (Engel), passed by the House on December 8, 2009, would establish a commission to evaluate U.S. drug control policies and programs directed at the Western Hemisphere and to provide recommendations on how to improve U.S. international and domestic drug policies.

Early assessments of the likely impact of the Mérida Initiative varied significantly. Mérida supporters described the initiative as a security cooperation partnership against drug traffickers and organized criminal groups, rather than a foreign assistance program. They urged Congress to fully fund Mérida in order to help build the capacity of both military and civilian institutions in partner nations to carry out bilateral and regional counterdrug efforts.[42] Others were more skeptical, maintaining that fighting the drug trade will require more than providing equipment and training for Mexican and Central American military and police forces. They asserted that Mérida needs to include more funding to address the weak civilian judicial and law enforcement institutions, as well as the underlying societal problems, such as poverty and corruption, that have allowed the drug trade to flourish in the region. They also emphasized the importance of addressing U.S. and European drug demand.[43]

Balancing "Hard-side" and "Soft-side" Assistance

During the 110th Congress, debates emerged within Congress about the balance of security vs. institution-building funding in the Bush Administration's FY2008 supplemental request for Mexico. Several Members of Congress opposed the request's apparent emphasis on providing expensive equipment to the Mexican military with its poor human rights record. In response, Administration officials contended that the Calderón government specifically requested security assistance from the United States because Mexican law enforcement and military forces were being outgunned by the drug cartels. They assured Members of Congress that military and police units receiving U.S. equipment and training would be properly vetted.[44]

As noted above, Congress has employed a variety of measures to ensure that various "soft-side" programs receive support from the Mérida Initiative. These have included limiting the FMF and INCLE funds available to provide equipment to the Mexican military, and earmarking $73.5 million in FY2008 supplemental funds and $75 million in FY2009 assistance for institution building, rule of law, and anti-corruption activities in Mexico. Similarly, Congress reduced border security and counterdrug assistance for Central America in the FY2008 supplemental in order to free up $25 million in ESF funds for an Economic and Social Development Fund for the region. Congress provided an additional $12 million for the Economic and Social Development Fund in the FY2009 omnibus measure, but did not set aside specific money to support it in FY2010.

With respect to funding for Mexico, several studies have criticized the Mérida Initiative for focusing too much on technology transfer and not enough on capacity-building and institutional reform. In addition to increasing funding for existing rule of law, human rights, and anti-corruption programs, these studies have identified several other "soft-side" programs and approaches that could be implemented. One study urged U.S. support for the establishment of constabulary forces and community policing programs in order to improve police-community relations. Another suggested financing micro-credit, job training, and alternative livelihoods programs aimed at addressing the poverty that has led some people to collaborate with the DTOs.[45] Still another urged the United States to consider channeling a larger proportion of assistance to state and local entities, particularly initiatives aimed at improving transparency and accountability in government.[46]

Monitoring Progress

U.S. and Mexican security experts have urged Congress to look at a range of indicators when evaluating the Mérida Initiative, rather than merely measuring its effects on drug seizures and flows. Congress asked the State Department to include a list of performance measures for each portion of the Mérida Initiative in its FY2008 supplemental spending plan. For example, some indicators that might indicate that Mérida is helping break the power and impunity of criminal organizations, might include trends in narcotics flows from Mexico to the United States, changes in the amount of illicit materials seized, and the number of high-profile drug traffickers arrested.[47] As previously stated, the Joint Explanatory Statement to the FY2010 Consolidated Appropriations Act directed the State Department to submit a report to congressional appropriators within 90 days on progress that has been made thus far in implementing the Mérida Initiative.

State Department officials have warned, however, that sometimes certain indicators can be misleading. For example, drug seizures in Mexico decreased in 2008 as compared to 2007. Rather than attributing a decline in seizures to some deficiency in Mexican CN efforts, U.S. law enforcement officials believe that traffickers have been forced to seek alternate routes because of better enforcement in Mexico.[48] This trend could continue with Mérida implementation.

U.S. officials also maintain that some of the most important results of Mérida thus far may be impossible to quantify, such as the increase in communication and cooperation that has developed as a result of the Initiative among U.S., Mexican, and Central American law enforcement and security officials.[49] There appears to be a particularly strong sense of co-responsibility and high level of cooperation in implementing the Mérida Initiative among high-ranking U.S. and Mexican officials. This is in sharp contrast to the past, when mutual mistrust hindered bilateral counterdrug efforts. The U.S. and Mexican governments have designed a multi-level working group structure to design and implement bilateral security efforts. By April 2010, U.S. policy-planners from the State Department's Narcotics Affairs Section (NAS), which oversees Mérida implementation, and Mexican officials from 16 partner agencies will be co-located in a new bilateral office, the first of its kind at any U.S. Embassy.

Interagency Coordination

The Mérida Initiative is a wide-ranging foreign assistance package with diverse program components that are being carried out by a wide range of U.S. agencies under the leadership of the State Department. For NAS in Mexico City, which is still in the process of hiring all of its Mérida-related positions, tracking the funding and implementation of all 43 FY2008 Mérida programs in Mexico has proven to be no small feat. (Most FY2009-funded programs have yet to commence). NAS has had to negotiate a large number of complicated inter-agency agreements to delineate funding streams and agency responsibilities for particular programs, some of which are still being finalized.

In addition, as noted in the GAO report, it has taken time for U.S. agencies charged with implementing Mérida programs to deploy "sufficient personnel to effectively manage the sevenfold increase in U.S. law enforcement-related assistance to Mexico"[50] that has occurred as a result of the Mérida Initiative. Some agencies, such as the State Department, are further along in that process than others, which has caused delays in some training programs involving expertise that can only be provided by particular U.S. agencies and offices (including training provided by the Department of Justice's Office of Overseas Prosecutorial Development, Assistance, and Training). Other agencies, like the Federal Bureau of Investigation, have had to shift their staff's focus away from strictly engaging in operations in Mexico towards planning and carrying out training programs for their Mexican counterparts.

Role of the Department of Defense

When the Mérida Initiative was first announced, analysts from across the political spectrum praised the fact that it did not appear to involve an active role for U.S. military forces in Mexico or Central America.[51] Some were pleased that civilian officials from the Central American Integration System (SICA) and the State Department designed the Central American portion of the proposal, rather than military personnel from the Central American Armed Forces Conference (CFAC) and Southcom.[52] Although DOD may not have taken a leadership role in designing Mérida, it is administering assistance provided to Mexico and Central America through the FMF aid account. Apart from the Mérida Initiative, DOD provided a $13 million counterterrorism training and equipment package to the Mexican military in FY2008.[53] In addition, while DOD only provided some $3.1 million in CN training assistance to Mexico in FY2008, DOD assistance expanded to approximately $28.2 million in FY2009 in order to complement Mérida programs.[54]

According to DOD officials in Mexico City, Mérida has "opened doors" for U.S.-Mexican military cooperation, and may result in increased DOD and State Department-funded training and equipment for the Mexican military. In an interview, one top DOD official predicted that the Mexican military will remain actively involved in anti-drug efforts for the foreseeable future. He also maintained that while DOD is unlikely to provide Mexico with the same *amount* of funds it has provided to Colombia, the same *variety* of programs will likely be funded, including training in how to work with police forces, conduct anti-drug operations and investigations, and pursue the leaders of drug trafficking organizations.[55]

U.S. Pledges under the Mérida Initiative

In the U.S. and Mexico joint statement announcing the Mérida Initiative, the United States government pledged to "intensify its efforts to address all aspects of drug trafficking (including demand-related portions) and continue to combat trafficking of weapons and bulk currency to Mexico."[56] Many security experts argue that this pledge may be even more important to the success of regional counterdrug and anticrime efforts than any amount of U.S. foreign aid provided to Mexico or Central America.[57] However, Mérida was proposed and funded as a foreign assistance package without any companion legislation on the domestic side. As such, it may prove difficult for Congress to monitor the degree to which the U.S. government is fulfilling its domestic pledges under the Mérida Initiative.

Weapons Trafficking[58]

U.S. officials estimate that 90% of the firearms recovered from crime scenes in Mexico originated in the United States.[59] Mexican drug cartels and enforcer gangs are reportedly buying semiautomatic versions of AK-47 and AR-15 style assault rifles, and other military-style firearms in the United States. The cartels often obtain their weapons through "straw purchases," whereby people who are legally qualified buy the weapons from licensed gun dealers or at gun shows in border states and sell them to smugglers who take them across the border.

ATF began a Southwest border initiative dubbed Project Gunrunner in FY2004 that aims to disrupt illegal flows of weapons from the United States into Mexico. In FY2006 and FY2007, around 100 ATF special agents and 25 industry operations investigators were dedicated to Project Gunrunner, while by March 2009, the numbers had increased to 148 special agents and 59 industry operations investigators.[60] From FY2004 through June 2009, ATF referred 882 cases for prosecution involving more than 1,838 defendants, including almost 415 cases for firearms trafficking involving more than 1,135 defendants and almost 13,382 guns.[61]

In addition to these efforts in the United States, ATF received $4.5 million in Mérida funds and $4.5 million in asset forfeiture funds from the Department of the Treasury for the deployment of eTrace firearms tracking technology to U.S. Consulates in Mexico to combat arms trafficking.[62] In FY2008, Mexico submitted more than 7,500 recovered guns for tracing, showing that most originated in Texas, Arizona, and California.[63]

The Department of Homeland Security, especially ICE and CBP, are also involved in taking action to stop the southbound flow of weapons to Mexico. Both ICE and CBP have the authority to enforce export provisions of the Arms Exports Control Act. In collaboration with Mexican law enforcement authorities, ICE launched a new bilateral program against weapons smuggling in June 2008 known as Operation *Armas Cruzadas*. Among other activities, the program involves intelligence sharing and joint law enforcement efforts with vetted Mexican units. As DHS reported in March 2009, the operation has resulted in more than 100 criminal arrests, 42 convictions, and the seizure of more than 400 weapons.[64]

According to DHS, the Mexican government began a pilot program in February 2009 to screen incoming vehicles to look for guns, bulk cash, and other contraband, and planned to expand the program across the entire border.[65] In addition, under the Mérida Initiative, the United States will be providing non-intrusive inspection equipment that will assist Mexican officials to prevent arms and cash smuggling from the United States.[66]

Some analysts have suggested that the U.S. government could further expand its efforts against gun trafficking to Mexico. They have advocated for, among other things, improving regulations to combat "straw purchases," better regulating how weapons that are particularly attractive to criminal groups (such as "vest-buster" handguns and anti-armor rifles) are marketed, and enacting an effective assault weapons ban.[67]

Others have called for the U.S. Senate to act on a pending treaty, the Inter-American Convention Against the Illicit Manufacturing of and Trafficking in Firearms, Ammunition, Explosives, and Other Related Materials.[68] According to the Department of State, the convention will help shut down the illicit transnational arms market that fuels the violence associated with drug trafficking, terrorism, and international organized crime. The treaty, which was signed by the United States in 1997, entered into force in July 1998. It was submitted to the Senate for its advice and consent in June 1998.[69]

Drug Demand

U.S. drug demand fuels a multi-billion dollar illicit industry that has enhanced the power of DTOs and other allied gangs and organized criminal groups. In 2007, more than 35 million people in the United States reported using illicit drugs or abusing prescription drugs. Some studies have suggested that addressing drug demand through a combination of treatment programs for heavy users and prevention programs is more successful and cost-effective than supply reduction programs.[70] Nevertheless, the U.S. drug control budget has continued to emphasize supply-side programs, including drug crop eradication in source countries, interdiction, and domestic law enforcement efforts, rather than demand reduction efforts. From FY2002 through the FY2009 budget request, funding for supply-side programs reportedly increased by almost 57%, whereas support for demand reduction efforts increased by less than 3%.[71] Supply reduction efforts now account for nearly two-thirds of the federal drug control budget.

U.S. pledges to intensify domestic demand reduction efforts in order to complement the Mérida Initiative have yet to be reflected in new budgetary priorities. The FY2010 federal drug control request submitted by the Obama Administration included slightly less funding for demand reduction programs (-0.8%) than what was enacted in FY2009.[72] Ongoing debates about the proper balance of funding for supply reduction vs. demand reduction programs are likely to continue in the 111th Congress.[73]

Bulk Cash Smuggling

Interrupting the flow of money from drug sales in the United States to Mexico, estimated to range from $15 billion to $25 billion annually,[74] may be one of the most effective ways to disrupt the activities of the Mexican DTOs. A portion of this money is used to buy weapons in the United States to arm the DTOs and their drug enforcers. Other drug proceeds are used to corrupt law enforcement and public officials enabling the DTOs to continue to operate with impunity. Some analysts believe that the U.S. Treasury is doing a good job of making it difficult to launder money within financial institutions. Therefore, the preferred mode to transfer drug proceeds by the Mexican DTOs is through shipments of bulk cash.[75]

In order to address the problem of bulk cash smuggling, the DEA has carried out bulk cash seizures with the FBI, ICE, and CBP. In 2005, ICE and CBP launched a program known as "Operation Firewall," which increased operations against bulk cash smuggling in the U.S.-Mexico border region. Since 2005, Operation Firewall has resulted in 583 arrests and the seizure of more than $282 million.[76] Many operations have been carried out in coordination with Mexican customs and the Mexican money laundering vetted unit. In 2008, ICE created a Trade Transparency Unit (TTU) in Mexico. Mexican TTU representatives are receiving training and technical support from ICE officials in how to identify cross-border trade anomalies that could be indicative of bulk cash smuggling.

Mexico Policy Issues

As the U.S. Congress oversees implementation of the Mérida Initiative, it is likely to maintain an interest in what the Mexican government is doing to combat the drug cartels and reform its law enforcement and judicial systems. Congress may want to ensure that U.S. and

Mexican counternarcotics programs are complementing, rather than duplicating each other's efforts. Congress may also want to monitor the Mexican government's anti-corruption efforts, as well as its ability to hold police and military forces accountable for human rights abuses.

Domestic Counterdrug Efforts and Strategy

President Calderón has made combating drug trafficking and organized crime a top priority of his administration. He increased Mexico's security budget from roughly $2 billion in 2006 to a reported $9.3 billion for 2009.[77] He has mobilized thousands of soldiers and federal police to arrest drug traffickers, establish check points, burn marijuana and opium plants, and interdict drug shipments. President Calderón has also used extradition as a major tool to combat drug traffickers, extraditing 95 individuals in 2008 and a record 107 individuals in 2009.[78] These efforts, combined with increased collaboration with U.S. law enforcement agencies, have resulted in some significant government victories against the DTOs – including the recent killing of Arturo Beltrán Leyva and capture of Teodoro Garcia Simental.[79]

Despite these victories, the persistent and increasingly brazen violence committed by the drug traffickers, which has occurred partially in response to government pressure, has led to increasing criticism of Calderón's aggressive anti-drug strategy.[80] Academics and human rights groups have added to this criticism by asserting that Calderón's increasing reliance on military forces to perform public security functions has exposed the military to corruption and resulted in a growing number of human rights violations by security forces.[81] Mexican officials are reportedly revising their military-led strategy in Ciudad Juarez, and recently deployed 2,000 federal police to set up checkpoints and patrol the city. The Mexican government may also increase funding for social and economic development programs to address the root causes of violence in Juarez and other border communities.[82] U.S. officials have pledged to reprogram FY2009 Mérida funding to complement Mexican government efforts. To that end, a high-level bilateral assessment team traveled to Tijuana/San Diego in early December and Ciudad Juarez/El Paso in mid January 2010.

Police Reform and Anti-Corruption Efforts

Instances of corruption of law enforcement and government officials have been a significant problem that has made the campaign against drug cartels more difficult. In October 2008, an elite unit within the federal Attorney General's office for Special Investigations of Organized Crime (SIEDO) was implicated in a scandal involving payoffs for sensitive information about antidrug activities, with at least 35 officials fired or arrested.[83] In November 2008, the former head of SIEDO was arrested and accused of accepting bribes from a drug cartel. The former investigative agency within the PGR, the Federal Agency of Investigations (AFI), which was created in 2001, was also widely criticized for corruption by 2005 and largely disbanded in June 2009.[84]

Corruption has also plagued federal, state, and municipal police forces. In a particularly egregious example of DTO infiltration at the municipal level, 10 local police in Michoacán have been arrested and charged with murdering 12 federal anti-drug agents in July 2009.[85]

President Calderón has taken steps to reform the country's federal, state, and municipal police forces and to crack down on corruption within the police and other government institutions. Calderón has reorganized the two federal police agencies under a single commander, established a new police training institute, and created a national database through which police can share information and intelligence.[86] President Calderón initially proposed the creation of one unified Federal Police force under the SSP, but two laws passed in May 2009 creating a Federal Police force under the SSP and a Federal Ministerial Police force under the PGR to replace the discredited AFI, both with some investigative functions. His government has begun to test the competency of state and local police forces and to reward units whose officers meet certain standards with higher budgets. President Calderón has also purged hundreds of corrupt police officers and government officials at all levels of government.

The State Department's 2008 human rights report, issued in March 2009, recognized the Mexican government's efforts to reform and professionalize the police force, although it highlighted that corruption and impunity, particularly at the state and local levels, remain endemic problems. Some security experts have also praised his federal police reform efforts, but expressed concern that "advances in police reform are being undermined by the slow pace of judicial reform."[87] Analysts have suggested that the Calderón government consider implementing other reforms, including, but not limited to, strengthening police professionalization programs, establishing a career track within federal and state police forces, encouraging community-oriented policing, and developing internal and external review mechanisms for police performance.

Implementation of Judicial Reforms

The Mexican judicial system has been widely criticized for being opaque, inefficient, and corrupt. It is plagued by long case backlogs, a high pre-trial detention rate (some 40% of Mexican inmates are simply awaiting trials), and an inability to secure convictions. In June 2008, President Calderón signed a judicial reform decree after securing the approval of Congress and Mexico's states for an amendment to Mexico's Constitution. Under the reform, Mexico has eight years to replace its trial procedures, moving from a closed door process based on written arguments to a public trial system with oral arguments and the presumption of innocence until proven guilty. In addition to oral trials, the judicial system is expected to adopt additional means of alternative dispute resolution, which should help make it more flexible and efficient.

Implementing these judicial reforms has brought with it significant challenges, which include the need to update law school curricula, retrain current legal professionals, build new courtrooms, improve forensic technology, and encourage the use of alternative dispute resolution. Many observers hope that the federal government can learn how to identify and overcome those challenges by looking at the experiences that states such as Chihuahua and Oaxaca have had with support from USAID, in adopting an accusatorial justice system.[88] Others predict that progress "is likely to be very slow as capacity constraints and entrenched interests in the judicial system delay any changes."[89] Still others have echoed the concerns expressed in the previously cited Woodrow Wilson Center briefing paper, which argued that "the Calderón government is devoting more of its political and economic capital to modernizing the police...[than to] strengthening the independence and capacity of the justice system [including the PGR]."[90]

Protection of Human Rights

Both the Mexican police and military have poor human rights records. According to the State Department's most recent human rights report, there were credible reports of police involvement in extrajudicial killings, kidnappings for ransom, and torture. There has been increasing concern that the Mexican military, which has had less human rights training and is less accountable to civilian authorities than the police, is committing more human rights abuses as it is increasingly tasked with carrying out public security functions.[91] According to Mexico's Human Rights Commission (the CNDH), complaints of human rights abuses by the Mexican military increased from 182 in 2006 to 1,230 in 2008.[92] Amnesty International released a new report in December 2009 on alleged cases of human rights abuses committed by Mexican military forces engaged in counterdrug efforts that occurred between October 2008 and August 2009.[93]

In addition to expressing concerns about current human rights abuses being committed, Mexican and international human rights groups have criticized the Mexican government for failing to hold military and police officials accountable for past abuses. On July 13, 2009, Human Rights Watch issued a statement asserting that "Mexican military courts...have not convicted a single member of the military accused of committing a serious human rights violation."[94] The head of the Mexican military's human rights office held a press conference on July 23 , 2009, to dispute those assertions, but reportedly did not provide details on particular cases that had been successfully prosecuted in the military justice system.[95]

Human rights organizations generally lauded the inclusion of human rights conditions (described in Appendix A) in Mérida Initiative appropriations legislation. In the summer of 2009, U.S. and Mexican human rights groups urged the State Department not to issue a favorable report on the Mexican government's human rights record. They maintained that the Mexican military has failed to investigate, prosecute, or punish human rights violations committed by its forces.[96]

On August 13, 2009, the State Department submitted its human rights progress report for Mexico to Congress, thereby meeting the statutory requirements for FY2008 supplemental and FY2009 regular funds that had been on hold to be released. While acknowledging that serious problems remain, the report outlines steps that the Mexican government has made to improve police transparency and accountability, consult with Mexican human rights organizations and civil society on the Mérida Initiative, investigate and prosecute allegations of human rights abuses by security forces, and prohibit the use of torture. The report acknowledges that human rights complaints against the Mexican military have "increased almost six-fold" since the beginning of the Calderon government. It also states that "the opaqueness of the [Mexican] military court system makes it difficult to analyze the nature and type of complaints filed, the status of cases against members of the military alleged to have violated human rights, or the results of the military prosecution."[97] Human rights groups have sharply criticized the State Department's assessment of Mexico's human rights progress.[98]

BEYOND THE MÉRIDA INITIATIVE

U.S.-Mexican Security Cooperation

With the arrival of U.S. Ambassador Carlos Pascual in August 2009 and as part of the FY2011 budget preparation process, U.S. and Mexican officials began to revise the strategic framework underpinning U.S.-Mexican security cooperation. The U.S. and Mexican Ambassadors have since publicly stated that they anticipate future funding requests associated with that cooperation to focus more on institution-building, including law enforcement training, than on equipment.[99] In interviews, NAS officials confirmed that the post-Mérida bilateral security cooperation strategy is likely to focus on four pillars: 1) disrupting the operational capacity of organized crime, 2) institutionalizing Mexico's capacity to sustain the rule of law (police and judicial reform), 3) creating a 21st century border structure, and 4) building strong and resilient communities.

Thus far, the Calderón government has focused much of its efforts on dismantling the power of the DTOs (pillar one), but many security experts believe that the government, with U.S. support, needs to focus more on addressing the country's weak judicial institutions (pillar two). With impunity rates hovering around 98%[100], many experts maintain that it is crucial for Mexico to implement the judicial reforms passed in the summer of 2008 and focus on fighting corruption at all levels of government. In order for Mexico to transition to an accusatorial system with oral trials by 2016, some argue that U.S.-funded judicial training programs, some of which are just getting started, may have to be significantly expanded. Federal police reform is well underway, but serious questions remain as to when and how the federal police will take over the anti-drug functions currently being carried out by the Mexican military. It also remains to be seen how federal reform efforts (and U.S. efforts to support them) will be expanded to include state and municipal police forces. Security experts have also identified improving police-community relations, respect for human rights, and the prevention and punishment of street crime in Mexico as important issues that need to be addressed.

Pillar three focuses on making the U.S.-Mexican border more secure and more efficient, as well as helping Mexico better patrol its southern border with Guatemala and Belize. It involves programs aimed at improving border management, infrastructure, and technology, as well as enhancing country and bilateral efforts to stop northward flows of drugs and southward flows of cash and weapons.

Pillar four of the aforementioned strategy would be a new focus for U.S.-Mexican cooperation, and may include targeted efforts to assist at-risk youth and curb unemployment and other social problems in communities plagued by drug trafficking and violence. The types of programs under consideration are not unlike those that have been recommended by some critics of the Mérida Initiative's initial emphasis on training and equipping Mexican security forces.[101] In many ways, some resemble the types of programs that have been implemented by USAID in gang-infested communities in Central America, as well as violent cities in Colombia and Brazil.

Cooperation with Central America and the Central American Regional Security Initiative (CARSI)

A number of policy issues have emerged involving the Central American portion of the Mérida Initiative, which, as of FY2010, has been split away from the Mérida Initiative into a new Central American Regional Security Initiative (CARSI). According to H.Rept. 111-187, addressing drugs and crime in Central America requires a longer term commitment than the three-year Mérida program. Some analysts specializing in Central American security issues hope that by splitting Central America away from U.S.-Mexican security cooperation programs, the sub-region will receive more focus, funding, and attention from Congress and the Administration. Others disagree, asserting that it is important to have an integrated approach to counterdrug and anti-crime programs in Mexico and Central America, as the Mérida Initiative was initially designed to do. Some policy issues that have emerged during congressional consideration of the Central American portion of the Mérida Initiative include:

- **Funding:** When the Mérida Initiative was announced, Central American leaders and some Members of Congress expressed concerns about the funding disparity between the Mexican and Central American portions of the Initiative.[102] Lingering questions remain about the adequacy of the funds provided, as well as how much of those funds should be spent on regional programs versus bilateral programs in the seven Central American countries.

- **Type of Funds Provided:** In the FY2008 Supplemental Appropriations Act, Congress reduced the funds appropriated for law enforcement programs in Central America in order to increase funding for institution-building, rule of law, and development programs. Members have and will likely continue to debate how funding should be balanced between the various program components, particularly how much funding should support law enforcement programs and drug interdiction efforts versus institution-building and rule of law activities.

- **Pace of Implementation:** As previously stated, the December 2009 GAO report on the status of Mérida funding has raised serious concerns among Members of Congress about the slow pace of implementation. While the pace of implementation in Mexico has quickened, many projects in Central America continue to be stalled.

- **Instability in Particular Countries:** As a result of the June 2009 ouster of President Zelaya, some Mérida assistance for Honduras has been put on hold. The issue of how to deal with instability in particular countries is likely to arise again during Mérida and CARSI implementation.

- **Interagency Coordination:** Debates are likely to continue concerning what U.S. agency is best equipped to carry out Mérida and CARSI programs, including the issue of whether there is a role for the U.S. Southern Command in anticrime efforts, and how U.S. programs should be coordinated with those funded by other donors.

- **Anti-gang Policies:** There is ongoing disagreement over the level and combination of preventive and suppressive policies that should be used in Central America to address the gang problem. Proponents of law enforcement solutions maintain that Central American law enforcement officials lack the capacity and resources to target gang leaders effectively, share data, and conduct thorough investigations that lead to successful prosecutions. Human rights groups tend to emphasize the importance of prevention and rehabilitation programs.

- **U.S. Deportation Procedures:** Congress may also maintain an interest in how U.S. deportation procedures for individuals with criminal records might be improved and whether U.S. assistance should be provided to help receiving governments reintegrate deportees.

The Caribbean Basin Security Initiative[103]

The Obama Administration did not include Haiti and the Dominican Republic in its FY2010 request for Mérida. Instead, the Administration requested $45 million in initial funding for projects that are being developed as part of a new security dialogue with Caribbean Community (CARICOM) member states[104] and the Dominican Republic. When President Obama announced the new security cooperation plan, the Caribbean Basin Security Initiative (CBSI), at the Summit of the Americas in April 2009, he said that it would likely involve increased U.S. assistance to help the region address such challenges as transnational crime, illicit trafficking, and maritime and aviation security.

Initial U.S.-Caribbean meetings were held in Suriname, Barbados, and the Dominican Republic in 2009, and a ministerial meeting is expected to take place in Washington early this year where a political declaration, action plan, and framework for the Caribbean Basin Security Initiative will be adopted. As described in the State Department's FY2010 Congressional Budget Justification for Foreign Operations, the CBSI would have three components: 1) assistance for air and maritime assets and command, control, and communications architecture; 2) assistance for social justice and economic development projects, with programs targeted at youth development and training; and 3) assistance for programs to enhance the rule of law and anti-crime efforts. The CBSI is being developed through a process of dialogue with Caribbean nations, which are expected to establish complementary programs with their own funding.

Rather than appropriating Mérida funds for Haiti and the Dominican Republic, as in FY2008 and FY2009, Congress provided "not less than" $37 million in P.L. 111-117 for the CBSI, of which "not less than" $21 million should be for social justice and education programs.

Appendix A. Conditions on FY2008 Supplemental Assistance for Mérida

Mexico

The FY2008 Supplemental Appropriations Act (P.L. 110-252), which includes the first tranche of funding provided for the Mérida Initiative, has softer human rights conditions than earlier House and Senate versions, in large part because of Mexico's objections that some of the conditions would violate its national sovereignty. The Secretary of State, after consultation with Mexican authorities, is required to submit a report on procedures in place to implement Section 620J of the Foreign Assistance Act (FAA) of 1961. That section of the FAA "prohibits assistance to any unit of the security forces of a foreign country if the Secretary of State has credible evidence that such unit has committed gross violations of human rights." An exception to this prohibition is provided in Section 620J if the Secretary of State determines and reports to Congress that the government of such country is taking effective measures to bring the responsible members of the security forces unit to justice.

In P.L. 110-252, human rights conditions require that 15% of INCLE and FMF assistance be withheld until the Secretary of State reports in writing that Mexico is taking action in four human rights areas:

- improving transparency and accountability of federal police forces;
- establishing a mechanism for regular consultations among relevant Mexican government authorities, Mexican human rights organizations, and other relevant Mexican civil society organizations, to make consultations concerning implementation of the Mérida Initiative in accordance with Mexican and international law;
- ensuring that civilian prosecutors and judicial authorities are investigating and prosecuting, in accordance with Mexican and international law, members of the federal police and military forces who have been credibly alleged to have committed violations of human rights, and the federal police and military forces are fully cooperating with the investigations; and
- enforcing the prohibition, in accordance with Mexican and international law, on the use of testimony obtained through torture or other ill-treatment.

Central America, Haiti and the Dominican Republic

P.L. 110-252 includes similar conditions on assistance provided to Central America, Haiti and the Dominican Republic. As with Mexico, The Secretary of State is required to submit a report on procedures in place to implement Section 620J of the Foreign Assistance Act (FAA) of 1961 in order for Mérida funding to be released.

Other human rights conditions require that 15% of INCLE and FMF assistance be withheld until the Secretary of State reports in writing that the governments of the countries in Central America, Haiti, and the Dominican Republic are taking action in three areas:

- establishing police complaints commissions with authority and independence to receive complaints and carry out effective investigations;
- implementing reforms to improve the capacity and ensure the independence of the judiciary; and
- investigating and prosecuting members of the federal police and military forces who have been credibly alleged to have committed violations of human rights.

End Notes

[1] Congress also appropriated $5 million in P.L. 110-252 and again in P.L. 111-8 for Mérida-related programs in Haiti and the Dominican Republic.

[2] The term drug cartel remains the term used colloquially and in the press, but some experts disagree with this because "cartel" often refers to price-setting groups and it is not clear that Mexican drug trafficking organizations are setting illicit drug prices.

[3] For more information, see CRS Report R40582, *Mexico's Drug-Related Violence* , by June S. Beittel

[4] Elliot Spagat, "Mexico-U.S. Cooperation Cited in 2nd Drug Lord Arrest," *Associated Press*, January 12, 2010.

[5] Figures for 2008 and 2009 are drawn from the Trans-Border Institute (TBI), "Drug Violence in Mexico: Data and Analysis from 2001-2009," January 2010, citing data gathered by *Reforma* newspaper. For a description as to why *Reforma* data are used instead of other sources, see p. 2-3 of the TBI report, available at: http://www.justiceinmexico.org/resources/pdf/drug_violence.pdf.

[6] Ibid. According to the *Reforma* data, the states that accounted for the largest proportions of all drug-related homicides in Mexico in 2009 were Chihuahua (31%), Sinaloa (12%), Guerrero (10%), Durango (10%), and Michoacán (6%). The overall rate and number of drug-related homicides declined significantly in Baja California in 2009 as compared to the previous year, although there was an uptick in violence in that state in November and December.

[7] The Central American countries include Belize, Costa Rica, El Salvador, Guatemala, Honduras, Nicaragua, and Panama.

[8] U.N. Development Program (UNDP), "Informe Sobre Desarrollo Humano Para América Central 2009-2010: Abrir Espacios a la Seguridad Ciudadana y el Desarrollo Humano," October 2009.

[9] For an evaluation of previous U.S. counternarcotics assistance to Mexico, see Government Accountability Office, "U.S. Assistance Has Helped Mexican Counternarcotics Efforts, but Tons of Illicit Drugs Continue to Flow into the United States," August 17, 2007.

[10] The U.S. and Mexican joint statement on the Mérida Initiative highlighted counterdrug and anticrime efforts of both countries, including Mexico's 24% increase in security spending in 2007 under President Felipe Calderón and U.S. efforts to reduce weapons, human, and drug trafficking along the Mexican border. Although the statement did not announce additional funding for U.S. domestic efforts, it cited several examples of such efforts to combat drugs and crime that are already in place. Those examples included the 2007 Southwest Border Counternarcotics Strategy and the 2008 National Drug Control Strategy. See U.S. Department of State and Government of Mexico, "Joint Statement on the Mérida Initiative," October 22, 2007.

[11] U.S. Department of State, ,"FY2008 Supplemental Appropriations Spending Plan, Mexico, Central America, Haiti, and the Dominican Republic," September 9, 2008, pp. 16-39.

[12] Andrew Selee, "U.S.-Mexico Cooperation: A New Opportunity?" *Americas Quarterly*, Summer 2009; U.S. Department of State, Secretary of State Hillary Rodham Clinton, "Remarks with Mexican Foreign Secretary Patricia Espinosa After Their Meeting," Mexico City, Mexico, March 25, 2009.

[13] Figure cited in U.S. Department of State, "Mexico- Merida Initiative Report," August 2009.

[14] In June 2009, the U.S. Office of National Drug Control Policy (ONDCP) published the 2009 National Southwest Border Counternarcotics Strategy, which for the first time included a separate chapter on cooperation with Mexico. For information on other recent U.S. border security efforts, see: U.S. Secretary of Homeland Security, "Remarks to Border Security Conference at the University of Texas at El Paso," El Paso, Texas, August 11, 2009.

[15] The human rights conditions in P.L. 110-252 are less demanding than earlier House and Senate versions, largely because of Mexico's objections that some of the original conditions would have violated its national sovereignty. As enacted, the measure reduced the amount of funding subject to human rights conditions, from 25% to 15% of FMF and INCLE, and removed conditions that would have required the Mexican government to try military officials accused of abuses in civilian courts and to enhance the power of its National Human Rights Commission. The legislation also softened the language concerning other conditions.

[16] In addition to the broad $73.5 million earmark, Congress earmarked $3 million to support the creation a national police registry, $10 million for drug demand reduction programs, and $5 million for police training programs.

[17] U.S. Embassy, Mexico, "U.S.-Mexico At a Glance: The Mérida Initiative," September 2008; U.S. Department of State, "FY2008 Supplemental Appropriations Spending Plan, Mexico, Central America, Haiti, and the Dominican Republic," September 9, 2008.

[18] William Booth and Steve Fainaru, "Leahy Blocks Positive Report on Mexico's Rights Record," *Washington Post*, August 5, 2009.

[19] Letter from Amnesty International and Other Human Rights Groups to Secretary of State Hillary Clinton, "Human Rights Concerns to Inform the U.S. Department of State's Merida Initiative Reporting on Mexico, July 24, 2009.

[20] William Booth, "Mexico May Get More Anti-Drug Aid," *Washington Post Foreign Service*, August 18, 2009.

[21] P.L. 111-8 also has a provision requiring that prior to the procurement or lease of aircraft, that the Director of the Defense Security Cooperation Agency, in consultation with the Secretary of State, shall submit to the Committees on Appropriations an analysis of alternatives for the acquisition of all aircraft.

[22] Another $16 million in reprogrammed Mérida Initiative funds previously appropriated in P.L. 110-252 would be used to pay for maintenance of the helicopters.

[23] These INCLE funds will be on hold until the human rights progress report for FY2010 is submitted by the State Department. Email from State Department official, January 11, 2010.

[24] In the FY2006-FY2008 annual Department of Defense (DOD) authorization bills, Congress provided DOD with authority to train and equip foreign military forces to perform counterterrorism operations. This "Section 1206" authority, as it is known, enables DOD to use defense funds to conduct or support train and equip programs such as those usually provided under State Department security assistance authorities and budgets. U.S. Department of Defense, "Section 1206 Programs Fact Sheet." July 29, 2009.

[25] Section 1022 of the National Defense Authorization Act for Fiscal Year 2008 (P.L. 110-181) extends Section 1033(b) of the National Defense Authorization Act for Fiscal Year 1998 to make available train and equip authorities to Mexico. Estimates of DOD CN support to Mexico for FY2008 and FY2009 are from U.S. Department of Defense, "Fact Sheet: Current DOD CN Support to Mexico," July 2009.

[26] Funding for this equipment is listed as "Digital Communications Equipment" on p.352 of the Joint Explanatory Statement for the FY2010 Defense Appropriations Act (H.R. 3326/P.L.-111-118).

[27] In December 2006, the United Nations and the Guatemalan government signed an agreement to establish the International Commission against Impunity in Guatemala (CICIG) to investigate illegal security groups and clandestine organizations, some of which have been tied, directly or indirectly, to the Guatemalan state. In August 2007, the Guatemalan Congress ratified the UN-Guatemala agreement allowing the creation of the CICIG. The CICIG was inaugurated on January 11, 2008.

[28] William Booth and Steve Fainaru, "U.S. Aid Delays in Drug War Criticized," *Washington Post*, April 5, 2009. A cursory review of Mérida program documents indicates that at least ten U.S. agencies and offices are involved in implementing aspects of the Initiative. Those agencies and offices include, but are not limited to: the State Department; USAID; Department of Defense; ICE, Customs and Border Protection, and Coast Guard within the Department of Homeland Security; Federal Bureau of Investigation, U.S. Marshals Service, DEA, the Office of Overseas Prosecutorial Development, Assistance, and Training, and the International Criminal Investigative Training Assistance Program within the Department of Justice; the Treasury Department; and the Bureau of Alcohol, Tobacco, Firearms, and Explosives.

[29] The GAO is scheduled to issue a more detailed follow-up report on Mérida implementation in the summer of 2010.

[30] Prior to the disbursal of INCLE funding for Mérida, for example, the State Department had to negotiate and sign Letters of Agreement with the countries that were to receive those funds. On December 3, 2008, the United States and Mexico signed a Letter of Agreement, allowing $197 million in Mérida funds to be disbursed.

[30] By the end of June 2009, all the Central American countries, Haiti, and the Dominican Republic had signed Letters of Agreement with the United States.[30]

[31] U.S. Government Accountability Office (GAO), "Status of Funds for the Mérida Initiative," December 3, 2009, GAO 10-253R, available at: http://www.gao.gov/products/GAO-10-253R.

[32] Ibid, p. 26-7.

[33] Roughly $12.3 million of that funding was supporting programs in Central America. Data provided in an email from State Department official, January 13, 2010.

[34] Government of Mexico, Technical Secretariat of the National Security Council, Implementation Tracking System of Merida Initiative Projects, November 20, 2009.

[35] Ibid.

[36] The White House, Office of the Press Secretary, "Press Conference by President Obama, President Calderón of Mexico, and Prime Minister Harper of Canada," Guadalajara, Mexico, August 10, 2009.

[37] Mary Beth Sheridan, "On Mexico Trip, Clinton Criticizes U.S. Drug Policy," *Washington Post*, March 26, 2009; and Mark Lander, "Clinton Says Demand for Illegal Drugs in the U.S. 'Fuels the Drug Trade' in Mexico," *New York Times*, March 26, 2009.

[38] Ibid.

[39] For more information on U.S. international drug control policy, see CRS Report RL34543, *International Drug Control Policy*, by Liana Sun Wyler.

[40] See, for example, International Crisis Group, "Latin American Drugs II: Improving Policy and Reducing Harm," March 14, 2008.

[41] Government Accountability Office, "Plan Colombia: Drug Reduction Goals Were Not Fully Met, But Security Has Improved; U.S. Agencies Need More Detailed Plans for Reducing Assistance," October 2008, GAO-09-7.

[42] American Enterprise Institute, "Five Perspectives on the Mérida Initiative: What it is and why it Must Succeed," March 4, 2008; Heritage Foundation, "Executive Summary: Mexico, Drug Cartels, and the Merida Initiative: A Fight We Cannot Afford to Lose," by Ray Walser, July 23, 2008.

[43] Washington Office on Latin America (WOLA), "The Mérida Initiative and Citizen Security in Mexico and Central America," March 19, 2008; Council on Foreign Relations, "Task Force Report: U.S.-Latin America Relations: A New Direction for a New Reality," May 2008.

[44] Senate Foreign Relations Committee, "Hearing on Mexico and Central America Counternarcotics Aid," November 15, 2007.

[45] Hal Brands, "Mexico's Narco-Insurgency and U.S. Counterdrug Policy," Strategic Studies Institute, May 2009.

[46] See, for example, Schaefer et al., "Security in Mexico: Implications for U.S. Policy Options," RAND Corporation, 2009.

[47] For a complete list of those indicators, see U.S. Department of State, ,"FY2008 Supplemental Appropriations Spending Plan, Mexico, Central America, Haiti, and the Dominican Republic," September 9, 2008, pp. 16-39.

[48] U.S. Department of State, *2009 International Narcotics Control Strategy Report*, February 27, 2009.

[49] Interview with State Department officials, July 13, 2009.

[50] GAO, December 2009, p. 14.

[51] Heritage Foundation, July 2008; WOLA, March 2008.

[52] U.S. Department of State, Office of Language Services Translating Division, "Not All That is Gold Glitters and Not All That Glitters is Gold," by Joel Fyke and Maureen Meyer, published in Foreign Affairs en Español, vol. 8, no. 1.

[53] In the FY2006-FY2008 annual Department of Defense (DOD) authorization bills, Congress provided DOD with authority to train and equip foreign military forces to perform counterterrorism operations. This "Section 1206" authority, as it is known, enables DOD to use defense funds to conduct or support train and equip programs such as those usually provided under State Department security assistance authorities and budgets. U.S. Department of Defense, "Section 1206 Programs Fact Sheet." July 29, 2009.

[54] Section 1022 of the National Defense Authorization Act for Fiscal Year 2008 (P.L. 110-181) extends Section 1033(b) of the National Defense Authorization Act for Fiscal Year 1998 to make available train and equip authorities to Mexico. Estimates of DOD CN support to Mexico for FY2008 and FY2009 are from U.S. Department of Defense, "Fact Sheet: Current DOD CN Support to Mexico," July 2009.

[55] Interview with DOD official from the Office of Defense Coordination at the U.S. Embassy in Mexico City, December 8, 2009.

[56] U.S. Department of State and Government of Mexico, "Joint Statement on the Mérida Initiative," October 22, 2007.

[57] Brookings Institution, November 2008.

[58] For more information, see CRS Report R40733, *Gun Trafficking and the Southwest Border*, by Vivian S. Chu and William J. Krouse

[59] U.S. Embassy, Mexico City, Mexico, "U.S.-Mexico, "U.S.-Mexico at a Glance: Combating Illicit Firearms," February 2009.

[60] Department of Justice (DOJ), Statement of William Hoover, Assistant Director for Field Operations, ATF, and Anthony P. Placido, Assistant Administrator for Intelligence Division, DEA, before Senate Committee on the Judiciary, Subcommittee on Crime and Drugs, March 17, 2009.

[61] DOJ, Statement of Anthony P. Placido, Assistant Administrator for Intelligence Division, DEA, and Bill McMahon, Deputy Assistant Director, ATF, before the House Homeland Security Committee, Subcommittee on Border, Maritime, and Global Counterterrorism, July 16, 2009.

[62] Ibid.

[63] U.S. Department of Justice, "Department of Justice Announces Resources for Fight against Mexican Drug Cartels," Fact Sheet, March 24, 2009.

[64] U.S. Department of Homeland Security, "Statement of Mark Koumans, Deputy Assistant Secretary, Office of International Affairs," before House Committee on Appropriations, Subcommittee on Homeland Security, March 10, 2009.

[65] Ibid.

[66] U.S. Department of State, "Statement of David T. Johnson, Assistant Secretary of State, Bureau of International Narcotics and Law Enforcement Affairs," before the House Committee on Foreign Affairs, Subcommittee on the Western Hemisphere, March 18, 2009.

[67] Tom Diaz, Violence Policy Center, "Disrupting Arms Trafficking to Mexico," October 17, 2008.

[68] Peter DeShazo and Johnna Mendelson Forman, "A treaty that can help stem drug violence in Mexico," *Washington Times*, February 24, 2009.
[69] U.S. Department of State, The Inter-American Convention Against the Illicit Manufacturing of and Trafficking in Firearms, Ammunition, Explosives, and Other Related Materials," Fact Sheet, March 25, 2009.
[70] P. Rydell and S. Everingham, "Controlling Cocaine Supply Versus Demand Programs," RAND: Santa Monica, C.A., 1994; David Boyum and Peter Reuter, An Analytic Assessment of U.S. Drug Policy, Washington, D.C.: American Enterprise Institute, 2005.
[71] "FY02-FY09 Budget Emphasizes Least Effective Ingredients of Drug Policy," Carnevale Associates, February 2008.
[72] U.S. Office of National Drug Control Policy, *National Drug Control Strategy: FY2010 Budget Summary*, May 7, 2009, p. 13.
[73] For more information on U.S. domestic drug policy, see CRS Report RL32352, *War on Drugs: Reauthorization and Oversight of the Office of National Drug Control Policy*, by Mark Eddy.
[74] Woodrow Wilson International Center for Scholars Mexico Institute, *The United States and Mexico: Towards a Strategic Partnership*, January 2009.
[75] Testimony of Andrew Selee, Director of the Mexico Institute, Woodrow Wilson Center before the House Subcommittee on National Security and Foreign Affairs of the Committee on Oversight and Government Reform, March 12, 2009.
[76] U.S. Department of Homeland Security, Statement of John T. Morton, Assistant Secretary, ICE, before the House Appropriations Subcommittee on Homeland Security, November 19, 2009.
[77] Steve Fainaru and William Booth, "As Mexico Battles Cartels, The Army Becomes the Law," *Washington Post*, April 2, 2009.
[78] Email from Mexican Embassy in Washington D.C., January 12, 2010.
[79] Elliot Spagat, "Mexico-U.S. Cooperation Cited in 2nd Drug Lord Arrest," *Associated Press*, January 12, 2010.
[80] José de Cordoba and Joel Millman, "Mexico Ramps up Drug War With a Surge on Rio Grande," *Wall Street Journal*, December 22, 2009; Jorge C. Castañeda, "What's Spanish for Quagmire?" *Foreign Policy*, January/February 2010.
[81] Jorge Rocha Quintero, "Public Security and Human Rights," in *Police and Public Security in Mexico*, edited by Robert A. Donnelly and David A. Shirk. San Diego, CA: University Readers, 2009.
[82] This review has since been reported in the media. See: William Booth and Steve Fainaru, "Mexico Questions its Drug Strategy; Violence in Juarez Prompts Officials to Admit Military Failure," *Washington Post*, December 27, 2009.
[83] Tracy Wilkinson, "Mexico Under Siege: Elite Police Tainted by Drug Gang," *Los Angeles Times*, October 28, 2008.
[84] Donnelly and Shirk, p. 228.
[85] Ken Ellingwood, "Mexico Tackles Legacy of Corrupt Police Force," *Chicago Tribune*, November 18, 2009.
[86] Eric L. Olson, "Police Reform and Modernization in Mexico, 2009" Woodrow Wilson Center, September 2009.
[87] Ibid, p. 7.
[88] David Shirk and Lourna M. Márquez-Carrasquillo, "Border Brief: State Level Judicial Reform Initiatives in Mexico," February 21, 2008.
[89] "Mexico Risk: Legal and Regulatory Risk," *Economist Intelligence Unit-Risk Briefing*, January 8, 2010.
[90] Olson, p. 7.
[91] See testimony by Joy Olson, Washington Office on Latin America, and Lisa Haugaard, Latin America Working Group, before the House Committee on Appropriations, Subcommittee on State, Foreign Operations, and Related Programs, hearing on the Mérida Initiative, March 10, 2009.
[92] Statistics are available in annual reports of Mexico's Human Rights Commission, available at http://www.cndh.org.mx.
[93] Amnesty International, "Mexico: New Reports of Human Rights Violations by Military," December 2009.
[94] Human Rights Watch, "Mexico: U.S. Should Withhold Military Aid: Rights Conditions in Merida Initiative Remain Unmet," July 13, 1009, available at: http://www.hrw.org/en/news/2009/07/13/mexico-us-should-withhold-military-aid.
[95] Booth and Fainaru, August 5, 2009.
[96] Letter from Amnesty International and Other Human Rights Groups to Secretary of State Hillary Clinton, "Human Rights Concerns to Inform the U.S. Department of State's Merida Initiative Reporting on Mexico, July 24, 2009.
[97] U.S. Department of State, "Mexico- Merida Initiative Report," August 2009.
[98] Fundar et al., "Obama Administration's Alleged Release of Mérida Funds: A Violation of U.S. Law That Will Encourage Serious Human Rights Violations in Mexico," August 2009.
[99] Remarks by U.S. Ambassador to Mexico Carlos Pascual and Mexican Ambassador to U.S. Arturo Sarukhan, *US Fed News*, September 28, 2009.
[100] This is figure is widely cited. See, for example, a recent report by the Center of Research for Development (CIDAC), "Índice de Incidencia Delictiva y Violencia 2009," August 2009, p. 9.

[101] Some have suggested financing micro-credit, job training, and alternative livelihoods programs aimed at addressing the poverty that has led some people to collaborate with the DTOs. See, for example, Hal Brands, "Mexico's Narco-Insurgency and U.S. Counterdrug Policy," Strategic Studies Institute, May 2009.

[102] Manuel Roig-Franzia, "Central Americans See Peril in Bush's Anti-Drug Priorities," *Washington Post*, November 29. 2007.

[101] Some have suggested financing micro-credit, job training, and alternative livelihoods programs aimed at addressing the poverty that has led some people to collaborate with the DTOs. See, for example, Hal Brands, "Mexico's Narco-Insurgency and U.S. Counterdrug Policy," Strategic Studies Institute, May 2009.

[102] Manuel Roig-Franzia, "Central Americans See Peril in Bush's Anti-Drug Priorities," *Washington Post*, November 29. 2007.

[103] This section was drafted by Mark P. Sullivan, Specialist in Latin American Affairs.

[104] Currently 14 independent Caribbean Basin countries are CARICOM members: Antigua and Barbuda, the Bahamas, Barbados, Belize, Dominica, Grenada, Guyana, Haiti, Jamaica, St. Kitts and Nevis, St. Lucia, St. Vincent and the Grenadines, Suriname, and Trinidad and Tobago.

In: Mexico: Background and Issues
Editor: Richard C. Bradley

ISBN: 978-1-61728-498-4

Chapter 4

MEXICO'S DRUG-RELATED VIOLENCE*

June S. Beittel

SUMMARY

Drug-related violence in Mexico has spiked in recent years as drug trafficking organizations (DTOs) have competed for control of smuggling routes into the United States. Drug trafficking issues are prominent in Mexico because the country has for at least four decades been among the most important producers and suppliers of heroin, marijuana and (later) methamphetamine to the U.S. market. Today it is the leading source of all three drugs and is now the leading transit country for cocaine coming from South America to the United States. Although previous Mexican governments had accommodated some drug trafficking in the country, when President Felipe Calderón came into office in December 2006 he made battling the Mexican drug trafficking organizations a top priority. He has raised spending on security and sent thousands of troops and federal police to combat the DTOs in states along the U.S.-Mexico border and throughout the country. In response to the government's crackdown, the DTOs have responded with escalating violence.

In recent years, drug trafficking violence in Mexico has claimed thousands of lives and reached a level of intensity and ferocity that has exceeded previous periods of drug-related violence. The government's intensified campaign against the DTOs resulted in changes in the structure of these criminal organizations. The seven major DTOs in Mexico have reconfigured. The fracturing of some of the most powerful drug trafficking syndicates and the reemergence of once powerful DTOs have led to bloody conflict within and among the DTOs. Today a small number of DTOs control the lucrative drug trafficking corridors through which drugs flow north from Mexico into the United States and high-powered firearms and cash flow south fueling the narcotics trade.

President Calderón has demonstrated what has been characterized as an unprecedented willingness to cooperate with the United States on counterdrug measures. In October 2007, both countries announced the Mérida Initiative to combat drug trafficking, gangs and

* This is an edited, reformatted and augmented version of a CRS Report for Congress publication dated May 2009.

organized crime in Mexico and Central America. To date, the U.S. Congress has appropriated a total of $700 million for Mexico under the Mérida Initiative. The program, which combines counternarcotics equipment and training with rule of law and justice reform efforts, is still in its initial stages of implementation.

The scope of the drug violence and its location—much of it in northern Mexico near the U.S.-Mexico border—has been the subject of intense interest in Congress. The 111th Congress has held more than a dozen hearings dealing with the increased violence in Mexico as well as U.S. foreign assistance and border security efforts. This chapter examines the causes for the escalation of the violence in Mexico. It provides a brief overview of Mexico's counterdrug efforts, a description of the major DTOs, the causes and trends in the violence, the Calderón government's efforts to crackdown on the DTOs, and the objectives and implementation of the Mérida Initiative as a response to the violence in Mexico. For related information about Mexico and the Mérida Initiative, see CRS Report RL32724, *Mexico-U.S. Relations: Issues for Congress*, and CRS Report R40135, *Mérida Initiative for Mexico and Central America: Funding and Policy Issues*. For more information on international drug policy, see CRS Report RL34543, *International Drug Control Policy*

DRUG TRAFFICKING IN MEXICO

Today Mexico is a major producer and supplier to the U.S. market of heroin, methamphetamine, and marijuana and the major transit country for cocaine sold in the United States. According to the Department of State's 2009 *International Narcotics Control Strategy Report*, as much as 90% of the cocaine entering the United States now transits through Mexico. A small number of Mexican DTOs control the most significant drug distribution operations along the Southwest border. The criminal activities of these Mexican DTOs reach well beyond the towns and cities of the border, extending along drug trafficking routes into cities across the United States. The Mexican DTOs have exhibited many characteristics of organized crime such as being organized in distinct cells and controlling subordinate cells that operate throughout the United States.[1]

In the U.S. Justice Department's *National Drug Threat Assessment 2009* (published in December 2008), Mexican drug trafficking organizations were identified as the greatest drug trafficking threat to the United States worldwide. Today's situation arose with the closing of the Caribbean route through which drugs, and particularly cocaine from Colombia, was channeled to the United States in an earlier era. With increased U.S. efforts to interdict narcotic smugglers in the Caribbean and Florida in the late 1980s and 1990s, the Colombian drug cartels began subcontracting with Mexican DTOs to smuggle cocaine into the United States across the Southwest border. By the late 1990s, Mexican DTOs had pushed aside the Colombians and gained greater control and market share of cocaine trafficking into the United States. Mexican DTOs now dominate the wholesale illicit market in the United States.[2]

The Mexican DTOs, often referred to as "drug cartels,"[3] have become increasingly violent. The *National Drug Threat Assessment* states that Mexico's DTOs now "control most of the U.S. drug market," with distribution capabilities in 230 U.S. cities. Mexican President Felipe Calderón began his assault on organized crime shortly after he took office in December

2006 and made combating the DTOs a centerpiece of his policy. The Calderón government has devoted billions of dollars[4] to the offensive against Mexico's entrenched drug trafficking organizations, and deployed 45,000 soldiers and thousands of federal police in nearly a dozen of Mexico's states in the fight.[5]

More than 5,600 people died in drug trafficking violence in Mexico in 2008, more than double the prior year. This escalation in the level of violence was matched by a growing ferocity.

Beginning in early 2008, there was an increase in assassinations of high-level law enforcement officials, gruesome murders including beheadings, violent kidnappings, use of a growing and varied arsenal of high-powered weapons, and one incidence of indiscriminate killing of civilians.[6] The battle for control of the multi-billion dollar drug trade has been—and continues to be—brutal. While the U.S. and Mexican media began to shift their attention away from the sensational crimes allegedly committed by the Mexican DTOs in late spring, the high numbers of killings have continued, exceeding an estimated 2,000 thus far in 2009.

Background on Mexico's Anti-drug Efforts

For many years, the export of illegal narcotics to the United States, which shares a nearly 2,000-mile border with Mexico, was tolerated by the Mexican government. The Mexican government pursued an overall policy of accommodation, according to numerous accounts.[7] Under this system, arrests and eradication took place, but due to the effects of widespread corruption, the system was "characterized by a working relationship between Mexican authorities and drug lords" through the 1990s.[8]

In the 1980s and 1990s, U.S.-Mexico counternarcotics efforts were often marked by mistrust. Beginning in 1986, when the U.S. President was required to certify whether drug producing and drug transit countries were cooperating fully with the United States, Mexico usually was criticized for its efforts leading to increased Mexican government criticism of the U.S assessment. Reforms to the U.S. drug certification process enacted in September 2002 (P.L. 107-228) essentially eliminated the annual drug certification requirement, and instead required the President to designate and withhold assistance from countries that had "failed demonstrably" to make substantial counternarcotics efforts.[9] In the aftermath of these reforms, U.S. bilateral cooperation with Mexico on counternarcotics efforts improved considerably during the administration of Vicente Fox (2000-2006), and combating DTOs has become a priority of the current Calderón administration.

The election of President Fox in 2000 ended 71 years of one-party rule in Mexico by the Institutional Revolutionary Party (PRI), shifting Mexico toward a more democratic political system. Fox, of the conservative National Action Party (PAN) believed that a more democratic regime could lower internal security spending, a policy he pursued during his term in office.[10] Some critics argue the Fox administration's lack of steady focus on the drug problem led to "lost years" in the battle against the DTOs. Others point to more effective antidrug policies that began under Fox to build the institutional capacity for an effective counterdrug strategy. Under President Fox, the federal police force was purged and reorganized and a more aggressive approach was taken in fighting the DTOs including more arrests, increased seizures of drug shipments and the extradition of major drug kingpins to the

United States. These counternarcotics successes, however, led to a wave of violence as arrests of DTO leaders resulted in bloody turf battles over territory, resources and manpower.[11]

When President Felipe Calderón, (also of the center-right PAN party), won office in December 2006 with a very narrow victory, he made combating the drug cartels a top priority.[12] He called the increased drug violence a threat to the Mexican state and sent thousands of soldiers and federal police to combat cartels in drug trafficking "hot spots." Soldiers and federal law enforcement officials have been tasked with arresting traffickers, establishing check points, burning marijuana and opium fields, and interdicting drug shipments along the Mexican coasts. Many have lauded President Calderón's determination to make battling the DTOs and the pervasive corruption they engender as a hallmark of his new administration.

In 2008, the government's crackdown, and rivalries and turf wars among Mexico's DTOs, fueled an escalation in violence throughout the country, including in northern Mexico near the U.S.-Mexico border. In an effort to control the most lucrative drug smuggling routes in Mexico, rival DTOs have been launching attacks on each other, as well as on Mexican military and police. The violence, as described in more detail below, has continued in 2009 and is posing a serious challenge for Mexico's security forces. Since coming into office in December 2006, President Calderón has deployed some 45,000 troops and 5,000 federal police along the U.S.-Mexico border and throughout the country's interior.[13] Over that time, approximately 10,000 people have been killed in the violence.[14] (For a detailed map of the drug killings since 2007 and other data about the drug war in Mexico, see graphic in the *Washington Post* at http://www.washingtonpost.com/wp-dyn/content/graphic/2009/04/01/GR2009040103531.html).

Major DTOs in Mexico[15]

The major DTOs in Mexico are all polydrug operations (handling methamphetamine, marijuana, cocaine and heroin). Figure 1 shows the approximate areas of influence of the major Mexican DTOs as of May 2009.[16] The recent heightened violence suggests there has been a realignment of control of national markets and transport routes. The seven major cartels that once controlled Mexico have reconfigured. The major criminal organizations that now are reported to dominate the market are described below:

Sinaloa Federation and Cartel—By 2008, a federation dominated by the Sinaloa cartel (which included the Beltrán Leyva Organization and the Carillo Fuentes or Juárez cartel) broke apart. The federation reportedly had controlled a majority of the cocaine passing through Mexico to the United States.[17] The Sinaloa cartel itself remains strong and effective in smuggling cocaine from South America to the United States, but it has lost control of territory in Mexico to its competitors as the result of the inter-cartel battles during 2008. It is headed by Joaquin "El Chapo" Guzman, probably the most wanted drug smuggler in Mexico.[18]

Gulf Cartel—A year ago, the Gulf cartel was considered the most powerful DTO in Mexico, but it has been a steady target of the government campaign and now it is "an open question...whether the cartel is intact."[19] The cartel's headquarters is the northeastern Mexican state of Tamaulipas. The suspected leader of the cartel, Osiel Cardenas Guillen, was arrested in 2003. However, he was not extradited to the United States until 2007. The Gulf cartel no longer controls Los Zetas, formerly their paramilitary enforcement arm. The relationship today between the Gulf cartel and Los Zetas remains unclear though it is likely they still cooperate.[20]

Beltrán Leyva Organization—Until last year, this syndicate was a part of the Sinaloa federation. As part of the Sinaloa federation, it controlled access to the U.S. border in Sonora state. It has become independent of the Sinaloa federation and has grown to be one of the most powerful drug trafficking organizations in Mexico, still controlling large areas of the country. It is believed to be responsible for the May 2008, assassination of acting federal police director Edgar Millán Gomez in Mexico City, and has gone after other high-ranking government officials. This organization has quickly secured narcotics transport routes in the states of Sinaloa, Durango, Sonora, Jalisco, Michoacan, Guerrero and Morelos. Their attempt to take territory from their former Sinaloa partners reportedly unleashed a wave of violence.

Arrellano Felix Organization/Tijuana Cartel—This syndicate, once one of the two most powerful DTOs,[21] was weakened significantly in 2008 by both U.S. and Mexican law enforcement efforts to capture their highest ranking leadership. The arrest of Eduardo "El Doctor" Arrellano Felix, in October 2008, the last of the Arrellano brothers to be captured or killed, was symbolic of its demise. This cartel split into two groups whose conflict for dominance led to extensive violence in the Tijuana area.

Vicente Carillo Fuentes Organization/Juárez Cartel—This organization is based in Ciudad Juárez in Chihuahua state, across the border from El Paso, Texas. It operates in much of northern Chihuahua state and part of Nuevo Leon and Sonora states. Over the past year there has been an ongoing violent battle between Sinaloa (their former partner) and this cartel for control of Juárez.[22] The Juárez cartel has a longstanding alliance with the Beltrán Leyva Organization. Some analysts fear that this once very powerful cartel will again grow in power after splitting from Sinaloa.

Los Zetas—This group of former military counternarcotics commandos,[23] known for its violence and effective use of tactics and weaponry, has grown in power even though it lost Daniel Perez Rojas. He was arrested in Guatemala this past year and was allegedly the leader of the group's activities in Central America. Los Zetas, since their split with the Gulf cartel, have contracted themselves to a variety of drug trafficking organizations throughout the country, notably the Beltrán Leyva Organization. The Zetas who formed as fearsome enforcers for the Gulf cartel have gained power under suspected Zeta leader Heriberto Lazcano. In 2009, U.S. authorities have come to believe this organization may be operating as an independent DTO.[24]

Los Zetas quickly established a reputation as one of the most violent enforcer gangs with military-level expertise in intelligence, weaponry and operational tactics. Some argue that the escalation in violence in 2007 and 2008 can be traced in part to them.[25] They have also brazenly engaged directly with the Mexican military in firefights. A previous period of intense Zeta-led violence was "the cross-border killing spree engaged in by Gulf cartel Zeta operatives in the Laredo-Nuevo Laredo area during 2004-2005" according to DEA Special Agent Joseph M. Arabit.[26] This precedent for the current "epidemic" of DTO killings in the border region demonstrates the inherent violence of drug gangs.[27] The enforcer gangs employed by the cartels have gained power as they fill voids in cartel leadership following arrests by the Mexican government. Los Zetas have reportedly recruited former Guatemalan special forces, Kaibiles, to join them and have contracted with members of violent Central American gangs, such as *Mara Salvatrucha* (MS-13), to act as distributors.

Other Groups and Emergent Cartels

Other enforcer gangs have modeled themselves on the Zetas, but are generally considered less sophisticated assassins.[28] The Sinaloa cartel formed heavily-armed enforcer gangs, the Negroes and the Pelones, who have battled with the Zetas over contested turf. La Familia Michoacana, once a criminal group affiliated with the Sinaloa cartel and now described by the DEA as an "emergent cartel," is active in the struggle for control of drugs arriving from Colombia in the seaports of Michoacán, Guerrero, Oaxaca and Chiapas states. La Familia was among three DTOs designated as significant foreign narcotics traffickers under the Foreign Narcotics Kingpin Designation Act, on April 15, 2009 by President Barack Obama in advance of his trip to Mexico to meet with President Calderón.[29] Four days after this designation, which imposes U.S. financial sanctions on group members, the Mexican government arrested an entire party of suspected La Familia members at a christening hosted by Rafael Cedeña Hernández, allegedly the number two in the gang.[30]

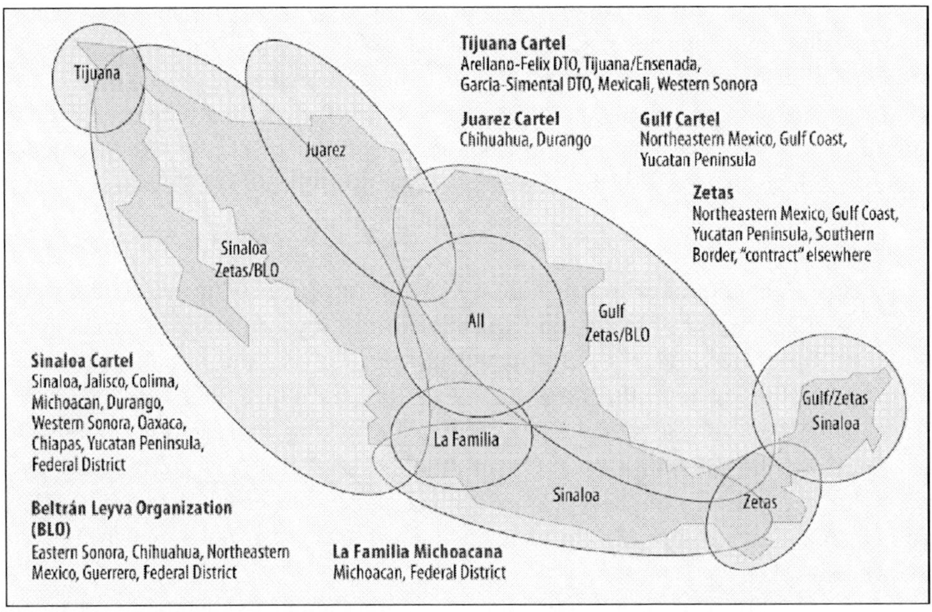

Source: U.S. Drug Enforcement Administration, May 2009, adapted by CRS Graphics.

Figure 1. Mexican DTOs Area of Influence

Source: ESRI Community Data, adapted by CRS Graphics.

Figure 2. Map of Mexico

DTOs and their violent enforcers have moved into other profitable criminal activities to supplement their income including kidnapping, human trafficking, extortion and a network of other illegal businesses. The surge in violence due to inter- and intra-cartel conflict over lucrative drug smuggling routes or "plazas" has been matched by an increase in kidnapping for ransom (sometimes ending with the death of the victim) and a brisk business in other criminal enterprises. Some argue that this diversification into alternative criminal activities may be a sign that U.S. and Mexican drug enforcement measures are suppressing drug trafficking profits.[31]

The Mexican State v. The DTOs

The growth and dramatic character of the violence, the targeting of civil and law enforcement officials, and the direct battle with police and military units, have led some observers to question the strength of the Mexican government, even characterizing it as potentially a "failing" state. A report released in December 2008 by the U.S. Joint Forces Command argued that Mexico potentially could face rapid and sudden collapse in the future because the government, its politicians, police, and judicial infrastructure are under sustained assault by criminal gangs and drug cartels.[32] In late March 2009, however, U.S. Director of National Intelligence Dennis Blair asserted to reporters that "Mexico is in no danger of becoming a failed state."[33] Moreover, during Secretary of State Hillary Clinton's trip to Mexico in March 2009, the Secretary said that the Mexican government was making "great progress" against the drug cartels, and asserted that she does not believe "that there are any ungovernable territories in Mexico."[34]

Mexican officials have strongly contested the claim that Mexico is a failed or failing state. Indeed, Mexican officials claim the heightened violence may be a sign that the cartels are losing ground and turning on each other as their markets shrink.[35] Former Director of the U.S. Office of National Drug Control Policy (2001-2009), John P. Walters, agrees with this assessment.[36] The Mexican government acknowledges that the country does face a significant challenge from well-financed criminal gangs through violence and corruption, but asserts that the description of Mexico as a failed or failing state "grossly distorts the facts on the ground." According to the government, "by all significant measure, Mexico has a functioning state," that provides education, health, security and other government services to millions of people.[37]

Some observers have noted that the DTOs are not seeking to defeat the state, but rather subvert it. The competition to control drug trafficking routes frequently puts the DTOs in battles with state security forces. Effective control of trafficking routes depends upon corrupt government officials and law enforcement.[38] Each year the Mexican drug trafficking organizations repatriate huge sums of money from drug sales in the United States to Mexico, estimated to range from $15 billion to $25 billion annually.[39] Some of this money is used to buy weapons in the United States to arm the DTOs and their enforcers, while other proceeds are used to corrupt law enforcement and public officials to enable the DTOs to operate with impunity.

Pervasive Corruption and the Drug Trade

The large sums of cash generated by drug sales and smuggled back to Mexico is used to corrupt Mexican law enforcement and public officials to either ignore cartel activities or to actively support and protect them. Corruption of local, state and federal police has resulted in Calderón's reliance on the military to combat DTOs, and remains a major challenge for U.S.-Mexican law enforcement cooperation. Corruption of government officials has also been a significant problem that has made the campaign against DTOs more difficult. In late October 2008, an elite unit within the federal Attorney General's office known as SIEDO was implicated in a scandal involving payoffs for sensitive information about antidrug activities, with at least 35 officials and agents fired or arrested.[40] In November 2008, the former head of SIEDO, Noe Ramirez Mandujano, was arrested and accused of accepting bribes from a drug cartel. In October and November of 2008, two former heads of Interpol in Mexico were arrested for alleged ties to the Sinaloa cartel.[41] In early December 2008, President Calderón stated that some 11,500 public employees had been sanctioned for corruption in the two years since he took office. In late May 2009, the federal government made its largest-ever arrest of politicians and senior officials in an anti-drug operation in the President's home state of Michoacan. Ten mayors and 18 other government and police officials, including state prosecutors and the heads of state and municipal police, were detained for alleged ties to the drug gangs.[42]

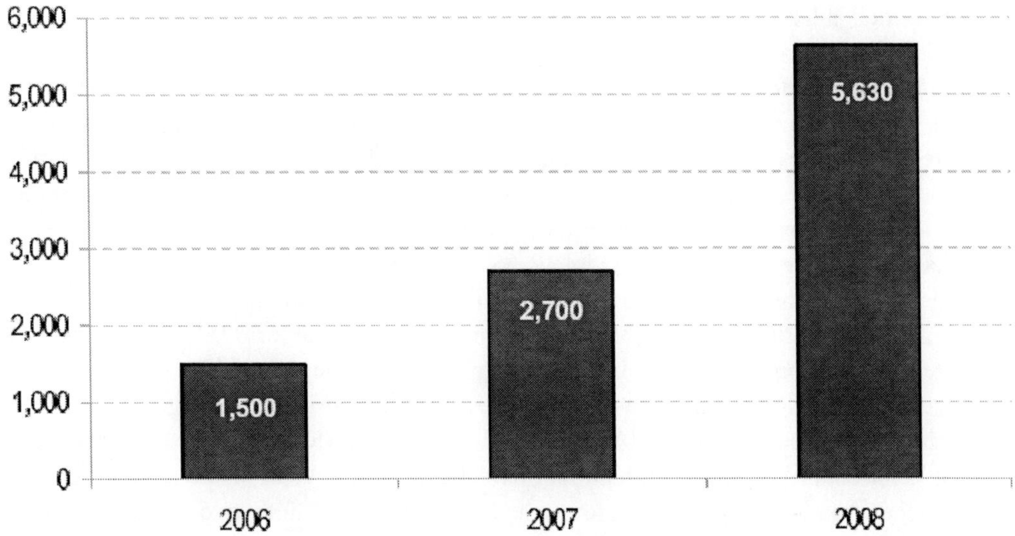

Source: Mexico City's daily newspaper, El Universal. Adapted by CRS Graphics.

Figure 3. Cartel-Related Killings 2006-2008

ESCALATION OF VIOLENCE IN 2008 AND 2009

While there has been a variance in available statistics on drug-related killings in Mexico, the overall trend has been a dramatic increase since 2007. Newspapers and other media organizations track drug trafficking crime by keeping daily tallies which are considered to be representative of the overall situation.[43] At times, the Mexican government and Mexican officials have used different numbers, but the trend has still been in the same upward direction. For example, in April 2009 the Mexican Attorney General said at a bilateral security forum in Cuernavaca that 5,600 people had been killed in DTO violence in 2008[44] in contrast to a graphic published on the Mexican Embassy website which indicates there were more than 6,800 drug-related killings last year.[45]

Using as a base the Mexican Attorney General's statistics of more than 5,600 killed in drug trafficking violence in 2008, this represented a 110% increase over 2007.[46]Among those murdered were 522 Mexican military and law enforcement officials according to recent testimony of the U.S. Department of State.[47] In the first two months of 2009, the violence grew with almost 1,000 drug-related killings in Mexico or 146% more than in the comparable period in 2008.[48] According to the same publication, the 1000th murder in 2008 did not take place until April 22 (compared to February in 2009), suggesting the pace of killings have continued to rise rapidly.[49] (See **Figure 3**, for the tally of drug killings 2006-2008).

Causes for the Spiraling Violence

The violence in Mexico has included the assassination of high level government officials as well as gruesome murders (often carried out with garish one-upmanship) and kidnappings.

Mexican officials have argued that the extraordinary violence has resulted from government successes in disrupting drug transit routes, and that the violence has been concentrated in a few border cities. Others have noted less positive trends. The willingness of DTO gunmen to take on the army directly rather than avoid confrontation has been a pattern in recent encounters.[50] Some estimate that those employed by the major DTOs in Mexico may number up to 100,000 or more, approaching parity with the Mexican armed forces.[51] Moreover, areas of conflict appear to be spreading into new territory including to the southern border with Guatemala suggesting the heightened violence may not end soon.[52]

The DEA reports that inter-cartel conflict (between and among members of different DTOs) and intra-cartel conflict (between members of the same DTO) have long been associated with Mexico's criminal drug enterprises. The new variable is the Calderón government's crackdown which in DEA's assessment has driven "in large measure...the current surge in violence."[53] The violence and brutality of the Mexican DTOs has escalated as they battle for control of multi-billion dollar narcotics markets. With the break up of both the Sinaloa federation into competing groups and the Gulf DTO into two factions (and the suspected transformation of Los Zetas from largely an enforcer group into a competing cartel), the opportunities for violence have mushroomed. Conclusions about the current alliances, objectives and the internal structure of the cartels are difficult to draw because the situation is highly fluid, and, of course, quite secretive.[54]

Several analysts have characterized 2008 as a year of flux and turmoil as the drug cartels battled for market dominance and responded violently to their government's unprecedented campaign against them. In evaluating the progress of the government crackdown, one think tank's annual assessment of Mexico's drug war concludes: "The increased turbulence in inter-cartel relations has produced unprecedented levels in violence that shows no sign of abating."[55] The realignment of Mexico's drug syndicates in 2008 and their violent turf battles appear to be the result of a splintering of the so-called Sinaloa federation of DTOs, the split in the Gulf cartel and the reemergence of DTOs once thought to be obsolete which are battling for control of national markets and transport routes.[56] What was once a bi-polar competition between the powerful Gulf cartel and the Sinaloa federation has been transformed by the government's anti-crime initiatives into significant inter-cartel and intra-cartel violence.

Violence is a tool of the drug trafficking business and the objectives of the violence seem to vary. Much of the violence has been a result of conflict between the cartels for control of territory, to punish betrayals and inflict revenge against the government's successes. Violence is also used to intimidate government officials, the police and the general public. The cartels prefer to intimidate and subvert a government rather than to bring it down according to one analysis because an intimidated government can deflect effective law enforcement initiatives and it allows the drug cartels to operate largely undisturbed.[57] The cartels may also be using violence against the government to reestablish patterns of protection by corrupt officials that prevailed in much of Mexico for many years.[58]

Kidnapping for money has also increased significantly in Mexico. In 2008, 1,028 persons were kidnapped, 31% of them concentrated in the Federal District and the state of Mexico. Reportedly at least 69 of those abducted were murdered.[59] The actual number of kidnappings is reportedly far higher, according to the State Department's human rights report on Mexico. In August 2008, the killing of a kidnap victim, Fernando Martí, the 14-year-old son of a wealthy businessman, resonated throughout Mexico. It prompted demonstrations calling for the government to take action against the escalation in violence. Kidnapping victims have not only included the rich, but also working class Mexicans whose families have been asked to pay as little as $500 in ransom.[60] In late October 2008, the five-year-old son of a poor family, was kidnapped from a Mexico City market and then killed by injecting acid into his heart.[61] In December 2008, an American anti-kidnapping negotiator, Felix Batista, was abducted in Saltillo, the capital of the border state of Coahuila. His fate remains unknown.

Mexican officials have urged the United States to cut off the flow of high-powered guns to the Mexican DTOs which they believe have also increased the violence. The Mexican government estimates that 2,000 firearms are smuggled across the Southwest border daily.[62] For many observers, this north-to-south "iron river," as it has been called, has arguably increased since 2004, when the federal ban on assault weapons in the United States expired. On April 16-17, 2009, when President Obama traveled to Mexico to meet with President Calderón to discuss cooperation in the fight against the escalating drug violence and other bilateral issues he acknowledged that "more than 90% of the guns recovered in Mexico come from the United States."[63] Drug cartel enforcers are purchasing semiautomatic versions of AK-47 and AR-15 style assault rifles and other military-style weapons including .50 caliber snipers rifles in the United States. With these weapons, some estimate the cartel gunmen may be able to match the firepower of units of the military or law enforcement in small engagements. In addition, a small percentage of the weapons which have been seized by Mexican authorities from drug crimes are military-grade weapons such as portable shoulder-fired anti-tank rocket launchers and grenade launchers (although the source of these weapons is far less clear).[64] President Calderón urged President Obama to clamp down on the flow of arms southward during their meetings.

Location of the Violence and Mexico's Drug War Strategies

Cartel-related killings are highly concentrated in a few states. In 2008, more than 60% of the killings took place in Baja California, Sinaloa and Chihuahua and within those states killings were reportedly concentrated in three cities: Tijuana, Culiacán and Ciudad Juárez. In 2008, by far the greatest numbers of drug-related homicides took place in Chihuahua state where highly contested Ciudad Juárez is located just across the border from El Paso, Texas.[65] (See Figure 2, Map of Mexico). Ciudad Juárez is a strategic location for both drugs and weapons trafficking and it has emerged as a key battleground. The dominant Sinaloa cartel has competed for control of the city with the local Juárez (or Carillo Fuentes) DTO.[66] The violence in Juárez has continued in 2009. In February, the police chief resigned after cartel gunmen left written warnings on the bodies of a slain police officer and prison guard that they would kill one officer every 48 hours until he left his post.[67] Three days after his resignation, a convoy of police vehicles escorting state governor José Reyes Baeza in Chihuahua city, was fired upon, allegedly by cartel gunmen.[68]

President Calderón has demonstrated an unmatched willingness to collaborate with the United States on joint counterdrug measures. He has mobilized tens of thousands of military troops to confront the DTOs in drug trafficking "hotspots." For example, in February 2009 he sent a surge of 5,000 troops to hyperviolent Juárez , supplementing 2,500 troops and federal police already in place there. The Mexican military took over all the local law enforcement functions and the running of the prisons in the border city. With more troops added in March that brought the overall federal force to 10,800, (approximately 8,000 military) the murder rate in Ciudad Juárez finally began to fall.[69]

President Calderón's crackdown significantly disrupted the cartels' operations in 2008, and this has continued in 2009. In March 2009, in an effort to increase pressure on the drug cartels, the Mexican authorities offered rewards for information leading to the capture of 24 of the top drug traffickers, with each reward set at $2 million.[70] Since the government's crackdown, large caches of weapons and drugs have been seized, key members of the cartels arrested, and a record number have been extradited to the United States.

While such action has been popular, the Calderón Administration may be "racing against the clock" to maintain public support. Frustration may grow if the drug war in Mexico fails to produce more measurable results and the public is unlikely to tolerate a bloody war with the DTOs indefinitely. In mid-term elections in July 2009, the PRI is expected to win more seats in the national legislature and in local and state elections than Calderón's PAN party. According to a poll by the Mexican newspaper *Reforma* on March 1, 2009, 40% of Mexicans disapprove of how Calderón has handled drug trafficking and his broader security program.[71]

The militarization of law enforcement in Mexico has also been criticized by Mexican civil society and human rights organizations.[72] The Calderón government has argued that the military will be needed in its domestic security role until at least 2013 because state and local police have been too compromised by corruption, and only the military can compete with the heavy weaponry of the DTOs. In a report released in April 2009, Human Rights Watch alleges serious human rights violations by the military.[73] The report describes 17 cases involving more than 70 victims in what it describes as "egregious crimes" such as enforced disappearances, killings, torture, rapes, and arbitrary detention. Several of the cases are from 2007 and 2008. Also, according to Mexico's National Human Rights Commission (CNDH), human rights violations by Mexican security forces have surged. In 2008, CNDH reported more than 1,200 complaints of human rights abuses by members of the military.[74] Other concerns about the military involvement in civilian law enforcement include the possibility that the longer these forces serve in this capacity there is an increasing chance they too will be subject to corruption by the DTOs. About 10% of the approximately 10,000 killed in Mexico's drug violence since Calderón came into office are from the Mexican federal police and military.

Notwithstanding the ongoing violence, Mexico continues to have one of the lower homicide rates in the region. At 11 murders per 100,000 according to the Mexican government, it is lower than those in Colombia, Guatemala, El Salvador and Brazil.[75]

THE U.S. POLICY RESPONSE

Violence in Mexico, much of it centered in states close to the Southwest border, has generated widespread concern about spillover into the United States. Secretary of Homeland Security Janet Napolitano noted in March 2009 congressional testimony that the United States has a significant security stake in helping Mexico in its efforts against the drug cartels and organized crime, with three major roles to play: providing assistance to Mexico to defeat the cartels and suppress the flare-up of violence in Mexico; taking action on the U.S. side of the border to cripple smuggling enterprises; and guarding against and preparing for the possible spillover of violence into the United States. Secretary Napolitano noted that there already has been a limited increase in drug-related violence in the United States (such as a rise in kidnappings and weapons violations in cities close to the border such as Phoenix), but maintained that the increase is not the same kind or nearly the same scale as in Mexico.[76]

Through a range of federal agencies including the Department of Homeland Security, the Department of Justice, and the Department of State, the United States has taken numerous measures to increase border security and cooperate with Mexico to combat the drug cartels. Initiatives have been started or strengthened to deny the DTOs illicit arms, to reduce money laundering and bulk cash smuggling (the preferred mode of transferring drug proceeds by the Mexican DTOs), [77] to reduce the trafficking of drug precursor chemicals and to suppress human smuggling.[78] Direct assistance to Mexico to support its efforts against the DTOs is provided under the Mérida Initiative with implementation led by the Department of State.

The U.S. Congress has also expressed concern over the situation in Mexico and potential "spillover" effects in the United States. Thus far in 2009, the 111th Congress has held 14 hearings on Mexico's drug trafficking violence and border security and U.S. foreign assistance. (See Appendix for a listing of the hearings).

The Mérida Initiative[79]

The United States and Mexico issued a joint statement on October 22, 2007, announcing a multi-year plan for $1.4 billion in U.S. assistance to combat drug trafficking and other criminal organizations in Mexico and Central America. The Mérida Initiative, named for the location of a March 2007 meeting between Presidents Bush and Calderón, expands bilateral and regional cooperation to combat organized crime, DTOs, and criminal gangs. To carry out the Mérida _ Initiative, the Bush Administration requested $500 million for Mexico in a FY2008 supplemental appropriations request and another $450 million for Mexico in the FY2009 regular foreign aid request, for a total request of $950 million. To date Congress has appropriated a total of $700 million for Mexico under the Mérida Initiative: with $352 million in FY2008 supplemental assistance and $48 million in FY2009 bridge funds, both funded by P.L. 110-252, and $300 million in regular FY2009 assistance funded in the Omnibus Appropriations Act, 2009 (P.L. 111-8), signed into law in March 2009.

The objective of the Mérida Initiative, according to the October 2007 joint statement, is to maximize the effectiveness of our efforts to fight criminal organizations—so as to disrupt drug-trafficking (including precursor chemicals), weapons trafficking, illicit financial activities, and currency smuggling, and human trafficking.[80] The joint statement highlighted efforts of both countries, including Mexico's 24% increase in security spending in 2007, and U.S. efforts to reduce weapons, human, and drug trafficking along the Mexican border. Although the statement did not announce additional funding for U.S. domestic efforts, it cited several efforts to combat drugs and crime that are already in place. Those included the 2007 Southwest Border Counternarcotics Strategy, the 2008 National Drug Control Strategy, and the 2007 U.S. Strategy for Combating Criminal Gangs from Central America and Mexico.

The Bush Administration had requested that all proposed funding for the Mérida Initiative be designated for the International Narcotics Control and Law Enforcement (INCLE) account, administered by the Department of State's Bureau of International

Narcotics and Law Enforcement Affairs (INL), but Congress ultimately appropriated the assistance within the INCLE, Foreign Military Financing (FMF), and Economic Support Fund (ESF) accounts (see **Table 1**). Congress also stipulated that none of the funds may be used for budget support or as cash payments to Mexico.

The law has human rights conditions softer than earlier House and Senate versions, in large part because of Mexico's objections that some of the conditions would violate its national sovereignty. As enacted, the Secretary of State, after consultation with Mexican authorities, is required to submit a report on procedures in place to implement Section 620J of the Foreign Assistance Act (FAA) of 1961. That section of the FAA "prohibits assistance to any unit of the security forces of a foreign country if the Secretary of State has credible evidence that such unit has committed gross violations of human rights." An exception to this prohibition in Section 620J is if the Secretary of State determines and reports to Congress that the government of such country is taking effective measures to bring the responsible members of the security forces unit to justice. The report is a condition to release 15% of the INCLE and FMF assistance under Mérida.

In March 2009 legislative action on P.L. 111-8, Congress provided $300 million for Mexico under the Mérida Initiative within the INCLE, ESF, and FMF accounts, with not less than $75 million for judicial reform, institution building, anti-corruption, and rule of law activities. The measure has human rights conditions similar to those in P.L. 110-252. It requires that prior to the procurement or lease of aircraft, that the Director of the Defense Security Cooperation Agency, in consultation with the Secretary of State, shall submit to the Committees on Appropriations an Analysis of Alternatives for the acquisition of all aircraft for the Mérida Initiative.

On April 9, 2009, the Obama Administration submitted a FY2009 supplemental request that includes an additional $66 million in INCLE assistance for Mexico under the Mérida Initiative. According to the request, the assistance would be used to acquire three Blackhawk helicopters for Mexico's civilian Public Security Secretariat to provide them urgently needed air transport capacity, and to provide spare parts and support. On May 14, 2009, the House approved its version of the FY2009 supplemental appropriations measure, H.R. 2346, that would increase funding levels to $160 million in INCLE funding (an increase of $94 million) and an additional $310 million in FMF funding for a total of $470 million for Mexico. (In addition, the supplemental request and House-approved version of the bill also included $350 million in Department of Defense Operation and Maintenance for counternarcotics and other activities, including assistance to other Federal agencies, on the U.S. border with Mexico.) On May 21, 2009, the Senate approved its version of the FY2009 supplemental that included $66 million in INCLE assistance for Mexico, the same amount as the Administration's request. (The Senate bill shifts $350 million requested for the Department of Defense for Southwest border security to domestic agencies, and adds $250 million for related activities.)[81]

For FY2010, the Obama Administration requested $450 million in the INCLE account for Mexico under the Mérida Initiative. It is unclear if Congress would fund the full amount requested for FY2010 if it ends up appropriating the $470 million for Mexico in the House-approved version of the FY2009 supplemental appropriations bill.

Table 1. FY2008 to FY2010 Mérida Funding for Mexico by Aid Account ($ in millions)

Account	FY2008 Suppl. Funds (P.L. 110-252)	FY2009 Bridge Funds (P.L. 110-252)	FY2009 Omnibus (P.L. 111-8)	FY2009 House-approved Supplemental (H.R. 2346)	FY 2009 Senate-approved Supplemental (H.R. 2346)	FY2010 Request
ESF	20.0	0.0	15.0	0.0	0.0	0.0
INCLE	215.5	48.0	246.0	160.0	66.0	450.0
FMF	116.5	0.0	39.0	310.0	0.0	0.0
Total	352.0	48.0	300.0	470.0	66.0	450.0

Source: U.S. Department of State, FY2008 Supplemental Appropriations Spending Plan; P.L. 111-8, Omnibus Appropriations Act 2009 (Division H and Joint Explanatory Statement, H.R. 1105); H. Rpt. 111-105; and U.S. Department of State, "Summary and Highlights, International Affairs, Function 150, Fiscal Year 2010."

Implementation of Mérida

The growth and dramatic character of the violence in Mexico and the potential threat for spillover north of the border has focused concern on the pace of the implementation of Mérida aid in both countries. Increasing criticism from Mexican officials has been reported as well as from Members of the U.S. Congress about the slowness of delivery of promised assistance to Mexico under the Mérida Initiative. When Secretary of State Hillary Clinton traveled to Mexico on March 25 – 26, 2009, she commented on the importance of bilateral cooperation under the Initiative and she expressed concern about the slow pace of implementation.[82] In her testimony before the House Foreign Affairs Committee on April 22, 2009, she repeated that concern.[83]

According to the Department of State,[84] which is leading Mérida Initiative implementation, the first pot of $400 million for the foreign aid program provided in P.L. 110-252 includes funding for the following:

- helicopters (up to five Bell 412 helicopters) and surveillance aircraft (up to two CASA maritime patrol aircraft) to support interdiction and rapid response of Mexican law enforcement agencies;
- non-intrusive inspection equipment, ion scanners, and canine units for Mexican customs, the new Mexican federal police and the military to interdict trafficked drugs, arms, cash, and persons;
- technologies and secure communications to improve data collection and storage;
- and technical advice and training to strengthen the institutions of justice, to improve vetting for the Mexican police force, to provide case management software to track investigations through the legal process, to support offices of citizen complaint and professional responsibility, and to promote the establishment of witness protection programs.

On December 3, 2008, the United States and Mexico signed a Letter of Agreement, allowing $197 million of the first pot of Mérida funds to be disbursed.[85] Later in December, the governments of Mexico and the United States met to coordinate implementation of the

Mérida Initiative through a cabinet-level High Level group reflecting the urgency on both sides of the border to address the growing violence in Mexico. According to the State Department, a working-level meeting was held February 3, 2009, in Mexico City "with the aim of accelerating the implementation of the 48 projects through nine working groups for Mexico under the Initiative." This meeting was followed by another on March 2, 2009.[86]

Only the initial phases of implementation have begun. Although some programs are scheduled to become operational starting in the spring through the end of 2009, others that fund military equipment have a longer procurement process. This is especially true for assistance in the Foreign Military Financing (FMF) account that provides for equipment such as Bell helicopters and CASA surveillance aircraft that may take from one to two years for delivery to Mexico. According to press reports, just $7 million of the initial $400 million pot of assistance has been spent, while U.S. officials have attributed delays to cumbersome U.S. government contracting regulations, negotiations with Mexico about what equipment is actually needed, and the difficulty of delivering an aid package that involves so many agencies and has some four dozen programs.[87]

The 111th Congress has expressed interest in cooperating with the Mexican government as it battles the DTOs and tries to bring the mayhem and violence down to a level that can be managed as a public security rather than a military concern. The heightened violence in Mexico, much of it in cities and states that border the United States, has been the focus of 14 congressional hearings to date.[88] On April 16, 2009, President Obama made his first trip to Mexico to discuss common security issues and cooperation and other issues in the bilateral relationship. In advance of the trip, the President added three Mexican DTOs (Sinaloa cartel, Los Zetas and La Familia Michoacana) to the list of drug kingpins subjecting them to financial sanctions under the U.S. Foreign Narcotics Kingpin Designation Act (P.L. 106-120). The President also urged the Senate to provide its advice and consent to the pending CIFTA treaty.[89] Congressional hearings indicate that further initiatives are likely, including a significant increase of Mérida funding in the FY2009 supplemental appropriations bill and in the President's FY2010 budget request. Motivated by concern about Mexican spillover violence and the corrosive impact of Mexican drug trafficking on the stability of Mexico's democracy and economy, further appropriations in the foreign operations and domestic context may be forthcoming.

APPENDIX. HEARINGS ON INCREASED DRUG VIOLENCE IN THE 111TH CONGRESS

This compilation of selected hearings, prepared by Julissa Gomez-Granger, Information Research Specialist with the Knowledge Services Group of CRS, focuses on increasing violence in Mexico as well as U.S. foreign assistance and border security programs.

House

U.S. Congress. House. Committee on the Judiciary. Subcommittee on Crime, Terrorism, and Homeland Security. *Escalating Violence in Mexico and the Southwest Border as a Result of the Illicit Drug Trade*. Hearing held May 5, 2009.

Witnesses: Stuart G. Nash, Associate Deputy Attorney General, and Director Organized Crime Drug Enforcement Task Forces (OCDETF), U.S. Department of Justice; Salvador Nieto, Deputy Assistant Commissioner, Office of Intelligence and Operations Coordination, U.S. Customs and Border Protection, DHS; Janice Ayala, Deputy Assistant Director, Office of Investigations, U.S. Immigration and Customs Enforcement, DHS; Anthony Placido, Assistant Administrator for Intelligence, U.S. Drug Enforcement Administration, U.S. Department of Justice; William J. Hoover, Acting Deputy Director, Bureau of Alcohol, Tobacco, Firearms and Explosives, U.S. Department of Justice

Available at: http://judiciary.house.gov/hearings/hear_090506.html

U.S. Congress. House. Committee on Homeland Security. Subcommittee on Emergency Communications, Preparedness and Response. *Examining Preparedness and Coordination Efforts of First Responders Along the Southwest Border*. Hearing held March 31, 2009.

Witnesses: Richard Barth, Acting Assistant Secretary, Office of Policy, DHS; Janice Ayala, Deputy Assistant Director, Office of Investigations, U.S. Immigration and Customs Enforcement, DHS; Maj. Gen. Peter Aylward, Director, Joint Staff, National Guard Bureau; Sigifredo Gonzalez Jr., Sheriff, Zapata County, Texas; Larry Dever, Sheriff, Cochise County, Arizona

Available at: http://www.cq.com/display.do?dockey=/ cqonline/prod/data/ docs/html/ transcripts/ congression al/111/congressionaltranscripts111-000003091913.html@ committees & metapub =CQ-CONGTRANSCRIPTS&searchIndex=0&seqNum=23#speakers

U.S. Congress. House. Committee on Appropriations. Subcommittee on Commerce, Justice, Science and Related Agencies. *Drug Enforcement Administration*. Hearing held March 26, 2009.

Witness: Michelle M. Leonhart, Acting Administrator, Drug Enforcement Administration

Available at: http://appropriations.house.gov/Subcommittees/sub_cjs.shtml

U.S. Congress. House. Committee on Appropriations. Subcommittee on Commerce, Justice, Science and Related Agencies. *Federal Law Enforcement Response to US-Mexico Border Violence*. Hearing held March 24, 2009.

Witnesses: Bill Newell, Special Agent in Charge, ATF Phoenix Division; Joseph Arabit, Special Agent in Charge, Drug Enforcement Administration, El Paso, TX; Phil Gordon, Mayor, City of Phoenix ; David Shirk, Assistant Professor and Director of the Trans-Border Institute

Available at: ht tp://appropriations.house.gov/Subcommittees/sub_cjs.shtml

U.S. Congress. House. Committee on Foreign Affairs. Subcommittee on the Western Hemisphere. *Guns, Drugs and Violence: The Merida Initiative and the Challenge in Mexico.* Hearing held March 18, 2009.

Witnesses: David Johnson, Assistant Secretary of State, Bureau of International Narcotics and Law Enforcement Affairs, U.S. Department of State; Roberta S. Jacobson, Deputy Assistant Secretary of State, Bureau of Western Hemisphere Affairs, U.S. Department of State; M. Kristen Rand, Legislative Director, Violence Policy Center; Andrew Selee, Ph.D., Director, Mexico Institute, Woodrow Wilson International Center for Scholars; Michael A. Braun, Managing Partner, Spectre Group International, LLC

Available at: http://foreignaffairs.house.gov/hearing_notice.asp?id=1055

U.S. Congress. House. Committee on Oversight and Government Reform. Subcommittee on National Security and Foreign Affairs. *Money, Guns, and Drugs: Are U.S. Inputs Fueling Violence on the U.S.-Mexico Border?* Hearing held March 12, 2009.

Witnesses: Andrew Selee, Director, Woodrow Wilson Center Mexico Institute; Michael Braun, Former DEA Assistant Administrator; Tom Diaz, Senior Policy Analyst, Violence Policy Center; Jonathan Paton, Arizona State Senate

http://www.cq.com/display.do?dockey=/cqonline/prod/data/docs/html/transcripts/congres sion al/111/congressionaltranscripts111-000003074885.html@committees&metapub=CQ-CONGTRANSCRIPTS&searchIndex=2&seqNum=109#speakers

U.S Congress. House. Committee on Homeland Security. Subcommittee on Maritime and Global Counterterrorism. Border Violence: *An Examination of DHS Strategies and Resources*. Hearing held March 12, 2009.

Witnesses: Roger T. Rufe, Jr., Director, Office of Operations Coordination, DHS; Alonzo, Pena, Attache, U.S. Embassy, Mexico City, DHS; John, Leech, Acting Director, Office of Counternarcotics Enforcement, DHS; Salvador, Nieto, Deputy Assistant Commissioner, Intelligence and Operations Coordination, Customs and Border Protection; Kumar, Kibble, Deputy Director, Office of Investigations, Immigration and Customs Enforcement

Available at: http://www.cq.com/display.do? dockey=/cqonline/ prod/data/docs/html/ transcripts/ congression al/111/congressionaltranscripts111-000003074816. html@committees & metapub=CQ-CONGTRANSCRIP TS &searchIndex=2 &seqNum= 110#speakers

U.S. Congress. House. Committee on Appropriations. Subcommittee on Homeland Security. *Department of Homeland Security Response to Violence on the Border with Mexico.* Hearing held March 10, 2009.

Witnesses: Mark Koumans, Deputy Assistant Secretary of Homeland Security for International Affairs; Jayson Ahern, Acting Commissioner, Customs and Border Protection, DHS; Marcy Forman, Director, Office on Investigations, Immigration and Customs Enforcement, DHS; David Aguilar, Chief, U.S. Border Patrol

Available at: http://appropriations.house.gov/Subcommittees/sub_dhs.shtml

U.S. Congress. House. Committee on Appropriations. Subcommittee on Homeland Security. *Secure Border Initiative and Control of the Land Border*. Hearing held March 10, 2009.

Witnesses: Jayson Ahern, Acting Commissioner, Customs and Border Protection, DHS; David Aguilar, Chief, U.S. Border Patrol; Mark Borkowski, Executive Director, Secure Border Initiative

Available at: http://appropriations.house.gov/Subcommittees/sub_dhs.shtml

U.S. Congress. House. Committee on Appropriations. Subcommittee on State, Foreign Operations, and Related Programs. *Merida Initiative*. Hearing held March 10, 2009.

Witnesses: Thomas Shannon, Assistant Secretary of State for Western Hemisphere Affairs; David Johnson, Assistant Secretary of State for International Narcotics Control and Law Enforcement; Rodger Garner, Mission Director for Mexico, Agency for International Development; Lisa Haugaard, Executive Director, Latin American Working Group; Joy Olson, Director, Washington Office on Latin America; Ana Paula Hernandez, General Director, Colectivo por una Politica Integral hacia las Drogas

Available at: http://www.cq.com/display.do? dockey=/cqonline/prod/ data/docs/html/ transcripts/ congression al/111/congressionaltranscripts111-000003073406. html@committees &metapub=CQ-CONGTRANSCRIPTS&searchIndex=2&seqNum=131 or at: http://appropriations.house.gov/Subcommittees/sub_sfo.shtml

Senate

U.S. Congress. Senate. Committee on Foreign Relations. *U.S.-Mexico Border Violence*. Field hearing held March 30, 2009. El Paso, Texas.

Witnesses: Jamie Esparza, District Attorney, El Paso, TX; William McMahon, Deputy Assistant Director, US Bureau of Alcohol, Tobacco, Firearms and Explosives, Washington, DC; Joseph Arabit, Special Agent in charge, Drug Enforcement Administration, El Paso, TX; Ricardo Garcia Carriles, Former Police Chief of Ciudad Juarez, El Paso, TX ; The Honorable Harriet C. Babbitt, Former Ambassador to Organization of American States, Washington, DC; Howard Campbell, Professor, University of Texas at El Paso

Available at: http://foreig.senate.gov/hearings/2009/hrg090330a.html

U.S. Congress. Senate. Committee on Homeland Security and Governmental Affairs. *Southern Border Violence*. Hearing held March 25, 2009.

Witnesses: Janet Napolitano, Secretary of Homeland Security; James B. Steinberg, Deputy Secretary of State; David W. Ogden, Deputy Attorney General, Department of Justice

Available at: http://www.cq.com/ display.do?dockey=/ cqonline/prod/data/docs/ html/ transcripts/ congression al/111/congressionaltranscripts111-000003084334.html @committees &metapub=CQ-CONGTRANSCRIPTS&searchIndex=7&seqNum=7#speakers

U.S. Congress. Senate. Committee on Homeland Security and Governmental Affairs. *Southern Border Violence: State and Local Perspectives*. Field hearing held April 20, 2009. Phoenix, Arizona.

Witnesses: Janice K. Brewer, Governor, State of Arizona; Terry Goddard, Attorney General, State of Arizona; Phil Gordon, Mayor, City of Phoenix, Arizona; Octavio Garcia-Von Borstel, Mayor, City of Nogales, Arizona; Ned Norris, Jr., Chairman, Tohono O'odham Nation; Jack F. Harris, Public Safety Manager, City of Phoenix, Arizona; Clarence W. Dupnik, Sheriff, County of Pima, Arizona; Larry Dever, Sheriff, County of Cochise, Arizona

Available at: http://hsgac.senate.gov/ public/index.cfm? Fuseaction=Hearings. Detail&HearingID=f259bf1c-934d-41af-8ff3-72140882b3c3

U.S. Congress. Senate. Senate Judiciary Committee. Subcommittee on Crime and Drugs; with the Senate Caucus on International Narcotics Control. *Law Enforcement Responses to Mexican Drug Cartels*. Joint hearing held March 17, 2009.

Witnesses: Terry Goddard, Attorney General, State of Arizona, Phoenix, AZ; William Hoover, Assistant Director for Field Operations, Bureau of Alcohol, Tobacco, Firearms and Explosives; Anthony P. Placido, Assistant Administrator and Chief of Intelligence, Drug Enforcement Administration; Kumar Kibble, Deputy Director, Office of Investigations, Immigration and Customs Enforcement, DHS; Denise Eugenia Dresser Guerra, Professor, Department of Political Science, Instituto Tecnologico Autonomo de Mexico, Mexico City, Mexico; Jorge Luis Aguirre, Journalist, El Paso, Texas

Available at: http://judiciary

or at: http://www.cq.com/display. do?dockey =/cqonline/prod/ data/docs/html/ transcripts/congressional/111/congressionaltranscripts111-000003078495.html@ committees & metapub =CQ-CONGTRANSCRIPTS&searchIndex=9&seqNum=2#speakers

End Notes

[1] CRS Report RL34215, *Mexico's Drug Cartels*, by Colleen W. Cook.

[2] For more information on the history of the drug cartels in Mexico, see CRS Report RL34215, *Mexico's Drug Cartels*, by Colleen W. Cook.

[3] The term drug cartel remains the term used colloquially and in the press, but some experts disagree with this because "cartel" often refers to price-setting groups and it is not clear that Mexican drug cartels are setting illicit drug prices.

[4] It is unclear precisely how much the Calderón government spends on security. Estimates of $9 - $11 billion have been reported. See "On the trail of the traffickers," *The Economist*, March 7, 2009. The $11 billion figure (a cumulative figure since the beginning of the Calderón administration) was provided in remarks of Manuel Suárez-Mier, Legal Attaché, Embassy of Mexico at "Transnational Criminal Organizations in the Americas: Responding to the Growing Threat," A Colloquium at The George Washington University on January 29, 2009. Another article cites the Mexican government as its source for 2009 spending levels: "This year, the Mexican government will spend $9.3 billion on national security, a 99 percent increase since Calderón took office." See, Steve Fainaru and William Booth, "As Mexico Battles Cartels, The Army Becomes the Law," *Washington Post*, April 2, 2009.

[5] "Mexico: More Bloodshed," Economist Intelligence Unit - Business Latin America, January 12, 2009; Steve Fainaru and William Booth, "As Mexico Battles Cartels, The Army Becomes the Law," *Washington Post*, April 2, 2009.

[6] A grenade attack in Morelia, Michoacan, on Mexico's Independence Day in September 2008, which took place in a crowded public square and resulted in eight deaths and more than 100 injured, was allegedly the work of the Mexican DTOs. See Stratfor, *Mexican Drug Cartels: Government Progress and Growing Violence*, December 11, 2008. Other acts that seem to be an effort to establish a signature of violence such as placing victims'

severed heads or tortured bodies in public places or leaving threatening signs on or near victims' bodies have proliferated since early 2008.

[7] Francisco E. González, "Mexico's Drug Wars Get Brutal," *Current History*, February 2009; Steven B. Duke, "Drugs: To Legalize or Not," *Wall Street Journal*, April 25, 2009; George W. Grayson, *Mexico's Struggle with 'Drugs' and 'Thugs'*, Foreign Policy Association, Headline Series No. 331, New York, NY, Winter 2009.

[8] Francisco E. González, "Mexico's Drug Wars Get Brutal," *Current History*, February 2009.

[9] See CRS Report 98-174, *Mexican Drug Certification Issues: U.S. Congressional Action, 1986-2002*, by K. Larry Storrs.

[10] Jane's Information Group, "Security-Mexico," February 20, 2009.

[11] Francisco González writes: "...the capture of some cartel leaders was tantamount to kicking hornets' nests without having the means to spray the rattled insects."

[12] "Fighting Back—Mexico Declares War on Drug Cartels," *Jane's Intelligence Review*, April 1, 2007.

[13] Vanda Felbab-Brown, *The Violent Drug Market in Mexico and Lessons from Colombia*, The Brookings Institution, Policy Paper, No. 12, Washington, DC, March 2009.

[14] Steve Fainaru and William Booth, "As Mexico Battles Cartels, The Army Becomes the Law," *Washington Post*, April 2, 2009. Note reliable statistics on cartel killings remain illusive, with newspapers and other media organizations in Mexico compiling statistics generally considered to be reflective of the overall situation.

[15] This overview of Mexico's major drug cartels draws extensively from Stratfor, *Mexican Drug Cartels: Government Progress and Growing Violence*, December 11, 2008 and Jane's Information Group, "Security-Mexico," February 20, 2009. For background on the cartels, see CRS Report RL34215, *Mexico's Drug Cartels*, by Colleen W. Cook; "Mexico-U.S.: The Drug Wars- Dissecting the threat perceived in Washington," *Latin News: Security & Strategic Review*, January 2009.

[16] The regions of control shown in **Figure 1** are more fluid than indicated because of the continually changing alliances in this multi-sided conflict.

[17] Jane's Information Group, "Security-Mexico," February 20, 2009.

[18] "Mexico drug violence rises on border despite army," *Reuters News*, May 11, 2009.

[19] Stratfor, Mexican Drug Cartels: Government Progress and Growing Violence. December 11, 2008.

[20] Ibid.

[21] Jane's Information Group, "Security-Mexico," February 20, 2009. The article notes: "In the late 1990s and early 2000s, the two dominant organizations were the Juárez cartel, based in the Texas border city of Ciudad Juárez, and its principal rival the Tijuana cartel, based in the California border city of Tijuana."

[22] The violence in Juárez this past year has been extreme with more than 1,600 homicides in 2008. In December, four policemen in Juárez were killed in a half hour period and one of them decapitated. See coverage in: Tom Miller, "Twilight Zone," *Washington Post*, February 8, 2009.

[23] Most reports indicate that Los Zetas were created by a group of 30 lieutenants and sub-lieutenants who deserted from the Mexican military's Special Air Mobile Force Group (Grupos Aeromóviles de Fuerzas Especiales, GAFES) to the Gulf Cartel in the late 1990s. See CRS Report RL34215, *Mexico's Drug Cartels*, by Colleen W. Cook.

[24] Steve Fainaru and William Booth, "As Mexico Battles the Cartels, The Army Becomes the Law; Retired Soldiers Tapped to Run Police Forces," *Washington Post*, April 2, 2009. See also Samuel Logan, "Los Zetas: Evolution of a Criminal Organization," March 12, 2009, available at http://www.ocnus.net /artman2/publish/Dark_Side_4/ Los_Zetas_Evolution_of_a_Criminal_Organization.shtml.

[25] Jane's Information Group, "Security-Mexico," February 20, 2009.

[26] Testimony of Joseph M. Arabit, Special Agent in Charge, El Paso Division, Drug Enforcement Administration, before the House Appropriations Committee Subcommittee on Commerce, Justice, Science and Related Agencies, March 24, 2009.

[27] Ibid.

[28] CRS Report RL34215, *Mexico's Drug Cartels*, by Colleen W. Cook.

[29] The White House, "FACT SHEET: U.S.-Mexico Discuss New Approach to Bilateral Relationship," April 16, 2009.

[30] "Gang Warns Church," *Latin American Weekly Report*, April 23, 2009.

[31] Jane's Information Group, "Security-Mexico," February 20, 2009. Stratfor, Mexican Drug Cartels: Government Progress and Growing Violence. December 11, 2008.

[32] United States Joint Forces Command, "The Joint Operating Environment 2008: Challenges and Implications for the Future Joint Force," December 2008.

[33] Ken Ellingwood, "Clinton: U.S. Shares Blame for Mexico Ills," *Los Angeles Times*, March 26, 2009; and "Mexico Will Not Become 'Failed State': U.S. Spy Chief," Agence France Presse, March 26, 2009.

[34] U.S. Department of State, Secretary of State Hillary Rodham Clinton, "Remarks with Mexican Foreign Secretary Patricia Espinosa After Their Meeting," Mexico City, Mexico, March 25, 2009.

[35] "On the trail of the traffickers," *The Economist*, March 7, 2009.

[36] John P. Walters, "Drugs: To Legalize of Not," *Wall Street Journal*, April 25, 2009.

[37] Embassy of Mexico, Washington, DC. "Mexico and the Fight Against Drug Trafficking and Organized Crime: Setting the Record Straight," March 2009.

[38] Jane's Information Group, "Security-Mexico," February 20, 2009.

[39] Woodrow Wilson International Center for Scholars Mexico Institute, *The United States and Mexico: Towards a Strategic Partnership*, January 2009.

[40] Tracy Wilkinson, "Mexico Under Siege: Elite Police Tainted by Drug Gang," *Los Angeles Times*, October 28, 2008.

[41] "Ex-heads of Interpol Mexico to face trial for cartel ties," EFE News Service, January 19, 2009.

[42] Marc Lacey, "Mexican Sweep Nets Officials," *New York Times*, May 27, 2009; William Booth, "Police Detain 10 Mexican Mayors Who Are Suspected in Drug Activity," May 27, 2009.

[43] Jane's Information Group, "Security-Mexico," February 20, 2009.

[44] "Calderón scores some successes," *Latin American Regional Report: Mexico & NAFTA*, April 2009.

[45] Embassy of Mexico, Washington, DC. "Mexico and the Fight Against Drug-Trafficking and Organized Crime: Setting the Record Straight," March 2009, available at http://portal.sre.gob.mx/eua/pdf/SettingTheRecordStraightFinal.pdf.

[46] "Mexico-U.S.: The Drugs War—Dissecting the threat perceived in Washington," *Latin American Security & Strategic Review*, January 2009.

[47] Testimony of David T. Johnson, Assistant Secretary, U.S. Department of State, Bureau of International Narcotics and Law Enforcement Affairs, before the Subcommittee on State, Foreign Operations, Related Programs of House Committee on Appropriations, March 10, 2009.

[48] "Cartels add political dimension to 'drugs war'," Latin American Security & Strategic Review, February 2009.

[49] According to the *Latin American Weekly Report*: "Already this year, over 2,000 people have been killed by gang members. This is twice as many as were killed in the same period of 2008. This year, the date at which the 1000th person was killed by gangsters was 20 February. In 2008 the 1,000 death mark was only passed on 22 April." See "Mexican army 'on streets until 2013,;" *Latin American Weekly Report*, April 23, 2009.

[50] "Cartels add political dimension to 'drugs war'," *Latin American Security & Strategic Review,* February 2009. In early May 2009, Joaquin Guzman, the billionaire who reportedly heads the Sinaloa cartel threatened a more aggressive approach toward competitors and U.S. law enforcement, instructing his associates to use deadly force to get deliveries through and protect drug trafficking operations. See Josh Meyer, "Sinaloa cartel may resort to deadly force in U.S.," *Los Angeles Times*, May 6, 2009.

[51] Sara A. Carter, "100,000 foot soldiers in cartels; Numbers rival Mexican army," *Washington Times*, March 3, 2009; Steve Fainaru and William Booth, "As Mexico Battles Cartels, The Army Becomes the Law," *Washington Post*, April 2, 2009.

[52] CRS interview with DEA official on May 6, 2009.

[53] Testimony of Joseph M. Arabit, Special Agent in Charge, El Paso Division, Drug Enforcement Administration, before the House Appropriations Committee Subcommittee on Commerce, Justice, Science and Related Agencies, March 24, 2009.

[54] Jane's Information Group, "Security-Mexico," February 20, 2009.

[55] Stratfor, Mexican Drug Cartels: Government Progress and Growing Violence, December 11, 2008.

[56] Ibid.

[57] Ray Walser, *Mexico, Drug Cartels, and the Mérida Initiative: A Fight We Cannot Afford to Lose*, Heritage Foundation, Executive Summary: Backgrounder No. 2163, Washington, DC, July 22, 2008.

[58] Francisco E. González, "Mexico's Drug Wars Get Brutal," *Current History*, February 2009.

[59] Benito Jiménez y Verónica Sánchez, "Aumentan secuestros," *Reforma* (Mexico), April 5, 2009.

[60] Ken Ellingwood, "In Mexico, A Bounty on Every Head," *Los Angeles Times*, September 1, 2008.

[61] "Killing of 5-Year-Old Kidnapped from Market Shocks Mexico," *New York Times*, November 4, 2008.

[62] Alfredo Corchado, "Mexico's Violence to Intensify Officials from Both Sides of Border May Be Targets, Experts Predict," *Dallas Morning News*, January 4, 2009.

[63] "President Obama and Mexican President Felipe Calderón Hold News Conference," *CQ Newsmaker Transcripts*, April 16, 2009. The 90% figure is disputed because it only covers guns that are recovered and turned over to the U.S. government for tracing. An undetermined fraction of the weapons recovered from crimes by the Mexican government are not turned over to the United States for tracing.

[64] E. Eduardo Castillo and Michelle Roberts, "AP IMPACT: Mexico's weapons cache stymies tracing," *Washington Post*, May 7, 2009.

[65] The violence in Juárez this past year was substantial with more than 1,600 homicides in 2008. In December, four policemen in Juárez were killed in a half hour period and one of them decapitated. See coverage in: Tom Miller, "Twilight Zone," *Washington Post*, February 8, 2009.

[66] Jane's Information Group, "Security-Mexico," February 20, 2009. The article notes that the city is a key entry point for cocaine coming from South America, synthetic drugs from a variety of sources and marijuana cultivated in Sinaloa, Durango, and Chihuahua, as well as a key entry point for firearms flowing the other direction from the United States into Mexico.

[67] David Luhnow and José de Córdoba, "The Perilous State of Mexico," *Wall Street Journal*, February 21, 2009.

[68] "Cartels add political dimension to 'drugs war'," *Latin American Security & Strategic Review,* February 2009.

[69] "'Flooding' strategy tried out in Juárez," *Latin American Security & Strategic Review*, March 2009.

[70] Jose de Cordoba, "Drug Cartels Rise on U.S. Agenda -- As Clinton Plans Visit This Week, Mexico Offers Rewards for Capture of Traffickers," *Wall Street Journal*, March 24, 2009.

[71] Pamela Starr, "PAN Mid-term Election Loss Could Cripple Calderón," *Focal Point*, online newsletter of the Canadian Foundation for the Americas, April 2009. Available at: http://www.focal.ca/publications/focalpoint/fp0409/?lang=e&article=article2.

[72] Miguel Agustin Pro Juárez Human Rights Center, *Human Rights Under Siege: Public Security and Criminal Justice in Mexico*, September 2008.

[73] Human Rights Watch, *Uniform Impunity: Mexico's Misuse of Military Justice to Prosecute Abuses in Counternarcotics and Public Security Operations*, April 2009. Available at: http://www.hrw.org/sites/default/files/reports/mexico0409web.pdf.

[74] Comisión Nacional de Derechos Humanos, (Mexico), "Informe de Actividades del 1 de enero al 31 de diciembre de 2008," Mexico, 2009, p. 36.

[75] Marc Lacey, "Killings in Drug War in Mexico Double in '08," *New York Times*, December 9, 2008. The article cites figures from Mexican Attorney General Eduardo Medina-Mora.

[76] Senate Committee on Homeland Security and Governmental Affairs, Testimony of Secretary of Homeland Security Janet Napolitano, hearing on "Southern Border Violence: Homeland Security Threats, Vulnerabilities, and Responsibilities," March 25, 2009.

[77] Testimony of Andrew Selee, Director of the Mexico Institute, Woodrow Wilson Center before the House Subcommittee on National Security and Foreign Affairs of the Committee on Oversight and Government Reform, March 12, 2009.

[78] The scope of this multi-dimensional response is described in more detail in CRS Report RL32724, *Mexico-U.S. Relations: Issues for Congress*.

[79] For more information, see CRS Report R40135, *Mérida Initiative for Mexico and Central America: Funding and Policy Issues*, by Clare Ribando Seelke and June S. Beittel.

[80] U.S. Department of State and Government of Mexico, "Joint Statement on the Merida Initiative," October 22, 2007.

[81] For more information on the supplemental, see CRS Report R40531, *FY2009 Spring Supplemental Appropriations for Overseas Contingency Operations*, coordinated by Stephen Daggett and Susan B. Epstein.

[82] Secretary of State Hillary Rodham Clinton, "Remarks with Mexican Foreign Secretary Patricia Espinosa After Their Meeting," Mexico City, Mexico, March 25, 2009, available at: http://www.state.gov/secretary/rm/2009a/03/120905.htm. Secretary Clinton stated: "With respect to the helicopters, I am well aware that our long process of approval was cumbersome and challenging for the Mexican Government. We're going to see what we can do to cut that time…We think they are a necessary and important tool in the fight against the drug cartels and criminals. It's also suggested to us we ought to look at this more generally, that it takes too long from a decision to delivery, and we'll see what we can do to shorten that."

[83] Testimony of Secretary of State Clinton before the House Foreign Affairs Committee, April 22, 2009. She stated at the hearing: "On the Mérida Initiative, we've got to get the money flowing. Honestly, I don't understand why it's so hard, and we're really digging deep to figure that out."

[84] U.S. Embassy, Mexico, "U.S.-Mexico At a Glance: The Mérida Initiative," September 2008; U.S. Department of State, "FY2008 Supplemental Appropriations Spending Plan, Mexico, Central America, Haiti, and the Dominican Republic," September 4, 2008.

[85] The $197 million is from the International Narcotics Control and Law Enforcement (INCLE) foreign aid funding account, and will fund equipment, training, and technology programs. In addition, more than $136 million under the Mérida Initiative from the Foreign Military Financing (FMF) and Economic Support Funds (ESF) accounts will be used to support antidrug and anticrime programs. See Embassy of the United States in Mexico, Press Release, "Mérida Initiative Monies Released; Letter of Agreement signed," December 3, 2008.

[86] Testimony of David T. Johnson, Assistant Secretary, U.S. Department of State, Bureau of International Narcotics and Law Enforcement Affairs, before the Subcommittee on State, Foreign Operations, Related Programs of House Committee on Appropriations, March 10, 2009.

[87] William Booth and Steve Fainaru, "U.S. Aid Delays in Drug War Criticized," *Washington Post*, April 5, 2009.

[88] See Appendix for a listing of these hearings in the 111th Congress.

[89] In light of intensified U.S. efforts to curb the flow of weapons to Mexico, the Obama Administration has joined some policy advocates in calling for the U.S. Senate to act on a pending treaty, the Inter-American Convention Against the Illicit Manufacturing of and Trafficking in Firearms, Ammunition, Explosives, and other Related Material, known by its Spanish acronym CIFTA. See, The White House, "FACT SHEET: US-Mexico Discuss New Approach to Bilateral Relationship," April 16, 2009. Available at: http://www.whitehouse.gov /the_press_office/Fact-Sheet-US-Mexico-Discuss-New-Approach-to-Bilateral-Relationship.

In: Mexico: Background and Issues
Editor: Richard C. Bradley

ISBN: 978-1-61728-498-4

Chapter 5

MEXICO'S FREE TRADE AGREEMENTS*

M. Angeles Villarreal

SUMMARY

Mexico has had a growing commitment to trade integration through the formation of free trade agreements (FTAs) since the 1990s and its trade policy is among the most open in the world. Mexico's pursuit of FTAs with other countries not only provides economic benefits, but could also potentially reduce its economic dependence on the United States. The United States is, by far, Mexico's most significant trading partner. About 80% of Mexico's exports go to the United States and 49% of Mexico's imports come from the United States. Mexico's second largest trading partner is China, accounting for approximately 6% of Mexico's exports and imports. In an effort to increase trade with other countries, Mexico has a total of 11 trade agreements involving 41 countries. These include agreements with most countries in the Western Hemisphere including the United States and Canada, Chile, Costa Rica, Nicaragua, Guatemala, El Salvador, and Honduras. In addition, Mexico has negotiated FTAs outside of the Western Hemisphere and entered into agreements with Israel and the European Union in July 2000. Mexico also has an FTA with Japan. The large number of trade agreements, however, has not yet been successful in decreasing Mexico's dependence on trade with the United States.

Economic motivations are generally the major driving force for the formation of free trade agreements among countries, but there are other reasons countries enter into FTAs, including political and security factors. One of Mexico's primary motivations for the unilateral trade liberalization efforts of the late 1980s and early 1990s was to improve economic conditions in the country, which policymakers hoped would lead to greater investor confidence and attract more foreign investment. Trade agreements were also expected to improve investor confidence, attract foreign investment, and create jobs. Mexico may have other reasons for entering into FTAs, such as expanding market access and decreasing its

* This is an edited, reformatted and augmented version of a CRS Report for Congress publication dated August 2009.

reliance on the United States as an export market. The slow progress in multilateral negotiations may also contribute to the increasing interest throughout the world in regional trade blocs. Some countries may see smaller trade arrangements as "building blocks" for multilateral agreements.

Since Mexico began trade liberalization in the early 1990s, its trade with the world has risen rapidly, with exports increasing more rapidly than imports. Mexico's trade balance with all countries went from a deficit of $13.5 billion in 1993 to surpluses of $7.1 billion in 1995 and $6.5 billion in 1996. Since 1998, Mexico's trade balance has remained in deficit, reaching $17.5 billion in 2008. The trade balance with the United States went from a deficit of $2.4 billion in 1993 to a surplus of $82.0 billion in 2008. Exports to the United States increased 447% between 1993 and 2008, from $42.9 billion to $292.6 billion. Mexico's imports from the United States increased 237% during the same time period, from $45.3 billion to $152.6 billion.

In the 110th Congress, issues of concern related to the trade and economic relationship with Mexico involved mostly economic conditions in Mexico, issues related to the North American Free Trade Agreement (NAFTA), the effect of NAFTA on Mexico, and Mexican migrant workers in the United States. The 111th Congress will likely maintain an active interest concerning Mexico on these issues. This chapter provides an overview of Mexico's free trade agreements, its motivations for trade liberalization and entering into free trade agreements, and some of the issues Mexico faces in addressing its economic challenges.

INTRODUCTION

The number of regional trade agreements (RTAs) throughout the world has grown steadily since the early 1990s. One of the reasons for the increasing interest in bilateral or regional trade agreements is the impasse of the Doha Development Agenda (DDA). Many members of the World Trade Organization (WTO) are focusing on regional or bilateral free trade agreements as a key component of their foreign and commercial policy.[1] This interest is evident among industrialized and developing countries, and throughout various world regions, including numerous countries in the Americas, Europe, and Asia. Mexico is a member of the WTO, which permits members to enter into regional trade integration arrangements under certain conditions that are defined within specific WTO rules.[2]

Since the early 1990s, Mexico has had a growing commitment to trade liberalizations and its trade policy is among the most open in the world. Mexico has been actively pursuing free trade agreements with other countries to help promote economic growth, but also to reduce its economic dependence on the United States. The United States is, by far, Mexico's most significant trading partner. Over 80% of Mexico's exports are destined for the United States. In an effort to increase trade with other countries, Mexico has entered into eleven free trade agreements with 41 countries.[3] Mexico has used trade liberalization as one of a number of policy tools to improve economic growth. The government has other programs to promote economic development and to address the issue of poverty.

In the 110th Congress, issues of concern related to the trade and economic relationship with Mexico involved mostly economic conditions in Mexico, issues related to the North American Free Trade Agreement (NAFTA), the effect of NAFTA on Mexico, and Mexican migrant workers in the United States. The 111th Congress will likely maintain an active interest concerning Mexico on these issues. This chapter provides an overview of Mexico's free trade agreements, its motivations for trade liberalization and entering into free trade agreements, and some of the issues Mexico faces in addressing its economic challenges.

MOTIVATIONS FOR TRADE INTEGRATION

Economic motivations are generally the major driving force for the formation of free trade agreements (FTAs) among countries, but there are other reasons countries enter into FTAs, including political and security factors. One of Mexico's primary motivations for the unilateral trade liberalization efforts of the late 1980s and early 1990s was to improve economic conditions in the country, which policymakers hoped would lead to greater investor confidence and attract more foreign investment. This motivation was a major factor in negotiating NAFTA with the United States and Canada. The permanent lowering of trade and investment barriers and predictable trade rules provided by FTAs can improve investor confidence in a country, which helps attract foreign direct investment (FDI). Multinational firms invest in countries to gain access to markets, but they also do it to lower production costs.

Mexico has other motivations for continuing trade liberalization with other countries, such as expanding market access for its exports and decreasing its reliance on the United States as an export market. By entering into trade agreements with other countries, Mexico also may be seeking to achieve economies of scale in certain sectors of the economy and expand its export market. Free trade agreements provide partners with broader market access for their goods and services. Countries can benefit from trade agreements because producers are able to lower their unit costs by producing larger volumes for regional markets in addition to their own domestic markets.[4] When more units of a good or a service can be produced on a larger scale, companies are able to decrease cost of production.

The slow progress in multilateral negotiations in the World Trade Organization (WTO) may also be a factor in Mexico's motivations to enter into FTAs. Some countries see smaller trade arrangements as "building blocks" for multilateral agreements. Other motivations are political. It is possible that Mexico may be seeking to demonstrate good governance by locking in political and economic reforms through trading partnerships. Trade agreements could forge geopolitical alliances and strengthen diplomatic ties. Some analysts believe that the choice of RTA partners is increasingly based on political and security concerns and not so much on economic rationale.[5]

MEXICAN TRADE LIBERALIZATION

From the 1930s through part of the 1980s, Mexico maintained a strong protectionist trade policy in an effort to be independent of any foreign power and as a means to promote domestic-led industrialization. Mexico established a policy of import substitution in the 1930s, consisting of a broad, general protection of the entire industrial sector. Mexico placed tight restrictions on foreign investment and controlled the exchange rate to encourage domestic industrial growth. Mexico also nationalized the oil industry during this time. These protectionist economic policies remained in effect until the country began to experience a series of economic challenges caused by a number of factors.

The 1980s in Mexico were marked by inflation and a declining standard of living. The 1982 debt crisis in which the Mexican government was unable to meet its foreign debt obligations caused an economic collapse in the mid-1980s. Much of the government's efforts in these addressing challenges were placed on privatizing state industries and moving toward trade liberalization. In the late 1980s and early into the 1990s, the Mexican government implemented a series of measures to restructure the economy that included unilateral trade liberalization, replacing import substitution policies with others aimed at attracting foreign investment, lowering trade barriers and making the country competitive in non-oil exports. Mexico had few options but to open its economy through trade liberalization after the debt crisis. In 1986, Mexico acceded to the General Agreement on Tariffs and Trade (GATT), assuring further trade liberalization measures that led to closer ties with the United States.

In 1990, President Carlos Salinas de Gortari approached then-U.S. President George H.W. Bush with the idea of forming an FTA. In 1992, Mexico's first agreement for free trade in goods, the Mexico-Chile FTA, came into force. The NAFTA, an FTA that includes Canada, as well as the United States and Mexico, entered into force two years later in 1994. It contained much broader provisions that included trade in services, government procurement, dispute settlement procedures, and intellectual property rights protection. In 1999, the original text of the Mexico-Chile FTA was later complemented with broader provisions, similar to those under NAFTA. Mexico's main motivation in pursuing FTAs with the United States and other countries was to stabilize the Mexican economy, which had experienced many difficulties throughout most of the 1980s with a significant deepening of poverty, by attracting foreign direct investment. The expectation in Mexico was that FTAs would increase export diversification and help create jobs, increase wage rates, and reduce poverty. At the time NAFTA went into effect, some studies predicted that the agreement to have an overall positive impact on the U.S. and Mexican economies though there would be some adjustment costs.[6]

MEXICO'S TRADE AGREEMENTS

Mexico's pursuit of free trade agreements with other countries is a way to bring benefits to the economy, but also to reduce its economic dependence on the United States. The United States is, by far, Mexico's most significant trading partner. About 82% of Mexico's exports go to the United States and 50% of Mexico's imports come from the United States. Mexico's second largest trading partner is China, accounting for approximately 6% of Mexico's exports and imports.[7] In an effort to increase trade with other countries, Mexico has a total of 11 trade agreements involving 41 countries (see Table 1). These include agreements with many countries in the Western Hemisphere including the United States and Canada, Chile, Bolivia, Costa Rica, Nicaragua, Uruguay, Guatemala, El Salvador, and Honduras.

Mexico has also negotiated free trade agreements outside of the Western Hemisphere and, in July 2000, entered into agreements with Israel and the European Union. Mexico became the first Latin American country to have preferred access to these two markets.

Mexico has completed a trade agreement with the European Free Trade Association of Iceland, Liechtenstein, Norway, and Switzerland. The Mexican government expanded its outreach to Asia in 2000 by entering into negotiations with Singapore, Korea, and Japan. In 2004, Japan and Mexico signed the Economic Partnership Agreement, the first comprehensive trade agreement that Japan signed with any country.[8] However, the large number of trade agreements has not yet been successful in decreasing Mexico's dependence on trade with the United States.

Table 1. Mexico's Free Trade Agreements

Agreement	Agreement Type	Coverage	Date of Signature	Entry into Force	WTO Legal Cover
North American Free Trade Agreement	FTA and EIA[a]	Goods and Services	December 17, 1992	January 1, 1994	GATT Art. XXIV and GATS V
Costa Rica – Mexico	FTA and EIA	Goods and Services	April 5, 1994	January 1, 1995	GATT Art. XXIV and GATS V
Nicaragua – Mexico	FTA and EIA	Goods and Services	December 18, 1997	July 1, 1998	GATT Art. XXIV and GATS V
Chile – Mexico	FTA and EIA	Goods and Services	April 17, 1998	August 1, 1999	GATTS Art. XXIV and GATS V
European Union[b] – Mexico	FTA and EIA	Goods and Services	December 8, 1997	July 1, 2000 (goods)	GATT Art. XXIV and GATS V
				October 1, 2000 (services)	
Israel – Mexico	FTA	Goods	April 10, 2000	July 1, 2000	GATT Art. XXIV
El Salvador – Mexico	FTA and EIA	Goods and Services	June 29, 2000	March 15, 2001	GATT Art. XXIV and GATSV
Guatemala – Mexico	FTA and EIA	Goods and Services	June 29, 2000	March 15, 2001	GATT Art. XXIV and GATS V
Honduras – Mexico	FTA and EIA	Goods and Services	June 29, 2000	June 1, 2001	GATT Art. XXIV and GATS V
EFTA[c] – Mexico	FTA and EIA	Goods and Services	November 27, 2000	July 1, 2001	GATT Art. XXIV and GATS V
Japan – Mexico	FTA and EIA	Goods and Services	September 17, 2004	April 1, 2005	GATT Art. XXIV and GATS V

Source: World Trade Organization, Regional Trade Agreement Database, see http://www.wto.org/.

Notes: The WTO definition of a free-trade area is a group of two or more customs territories in which the duties and other restrictive regulations of commerce (except, where necessary, those permitted under Articles XI, XII, XIII, XIV, XV, and XX of the GATT) are eliminated on substantially all the trade between the constituent territories in products originating in such territories.

a. Economic Integration Agreement (EIA) as defined by the World Trade Organization.

b. Includes Austria, Belgium, Bulgaria, Cyprus, Czech Republic, Denmark, Estonia, Finland, France, Germany, Greece, Hungary, Ireland, Italy, Latvia, Lithuania, Luxembourg, Malta, Netherlands, Poland, Portugal, Romania, Slovak Republic, Slovenia, Spain, Sweden, and United Kingdom.

c. Includes Iceland, Liechtenstein, Norway, and Switzerland.

NAFTA

In 1990, Mexico approached the United States with the idea of forming a free trade agreement. Mexico's main motivation in pursuing an FTA with the United States was to help stabilize the Mexican economy and attract foreign direct investment.[9] The Mexican economy had experienced many difficulties throughout most of the 1980s with a significant deepening of poverty. NAFTA is a free trade agreement that eliminated trade and investment barriers among Canada, Mexico, and the United States. Mexico's intention in entering NAFTA was to increase export diversification by attracting FDI, which would help create jobs, increase wage rates, and reduce poverty.

Upon implementation, almost 70% of U.S. imports from Mexico and 50% of U.S. exports to Mexico received duty-free treatment. The remainder of duties were eliminated over a period of 15 years after the agreement was in effect. The agreement also contains provisions for market access to U.S. firms in most service sectors; protection of U.S. foreign direct investment in Mexico; and intellectual property rights protection for U.S. companies. NAFTA is the first U.S. agreement that addressed environmental and labor concerns by including related provision in separate side agreements to NAFTA. At the time the agreement went into effect, a number of economic studies predicted that the trade agreement would have a positive overall effect on the Mexican economy, narrowing the U.S.-Mexico gap in prices of goods and services and the differential in real wages.

Mexico-Costa Rica

The Mexico-Costa Rica FTA was signed on April 5, 1994, in Mexico City and entered into force on January 1, 1995. It was the first in a series of FTAs negotiated by Mexico loosely based on the NAFTA model of trade agreements. This agreement had been preceded by a partial scope agreement signed by the two countries on July 22, 1982 in which Mexico accorded preferential access to some Costa Rican products. The FTA with Costa Rica phased out tariffs in four stages over a fifteen-year time period. Upon implementation of the agreement, approximately 70% of Mexican goods entered Costa Rica and 80% of Costa Rican goods entered Mexico duty free. By January 1, 2004, almost 97% of trade between the two countries was duty free and by 2009, virtually all tariffs had been eliminated.[10]

In addition to the provisions on national treatment and market access for goods, the agreement contains provisions on agriculture, sanitary and phytosanitary measures, rules of origin, customs procedures, safeguards, standards, cross-border trade in services, investment, government procurement, intellectual property rights protection (IPR), and dispute resolution. Items that are not included in the agreement include energy and basic petrochemicals, telecommunications, financial services, and competition policy. The IPR chapter does not cover patents, industrial designs, and layout designs of integrated circuits.[11]

Mexico-Nicaragua

The FTA with Nicaragua was Mexico's second treaty with a country in Central America, also loosely based on the NAFTA model. It was signed on December 18, 1997, and entered into force on July 1, 1998. Upon implementation, 76% of tariffs on Nicaraguan exports to Mexico and 45% of tariffs on Mexican exports to Nicaragua were eliminated. The remaining tariffs are being phased out in four stages over a fifteen-year period. The agreement is similar to NAFTA and includes provisions on national treatment and market access for goods and services; rules of origin; agriculture; sanitary and phytosanitary measures; telecommunications; financial services; government procurement; investment; IPT; dispute resolution; customs procedures; safeguards; unfair trade practices; standards; and other provisions. It does not include a chapter on competition policy, energy, environment, labor, or transportation.[12] The IPR provisions do not cover patents, industrial designs, and layout designs of integrated circuits.[13]

Mexico-Chile

The Mexico-Chile FTA, completed in 1998, was enacted in Chile on July 7, 1999, and in Mexico on August 1, 1999. Mexico and Chile signed the expanded FTA at the 1998 Summit of the Americas in Santiago, Chile on April 17, 1998. The FTA was expected to deepen the growing trade relationship between the two countries and improve bilateral investment opportunities in both countries. The 1998 agreement replaced an earlier FTA that was reached between the two countries in 1991. It removed tariffs on almost all merchandise trade between the two countries.

The Mexico-Chile FTA includes provisions on national treatment and market access for goods and services; rules of origin; customs procedures; safeguards; standards; agriculture; sanitary and phytosanitary measures; investment; air transportation; telecommunications; temporary entry for business persons; IPR; dispute resolution; and other provisions. It does not include a chapter on energy, environment, or labor.[14] A separate agreement, which was signed simultaneously, includes provisions to avoid double taxation for companies doing business in both countries. The FTA provisions are similar to those under NAFTA, but with no labor and environmental provisions in separate side agreements. Other areas that were not included in the 1998 FTA were financial services, patents, or government procurement.[15]

Mexico-European Union

Negotiations for a free trade agreement between Mexico and the European Union (EU) began in October 1996. The agreement, formally called the Economic Partnership Political Co-ordination and Co-operation Agreement (also known as the Global Agreement), was signed in March 2000 and came into force on July 1, 2000. It was the first transatlantic FTA for the EU. The motivations for the agreement were to expand market access for exports from the EU to Mexico and attract more FDI from the EU to Mexico.[16] On May 17, 2008, Mexico and the European Union agreed on a "strategic association" to further advance trade liberalization and to address climate change issues.[17]

The agreement includes provisions on national treatment and market access for goods and services; government procurement; IPR; investment; financial services; standards; telecommunications and information services; agriculture; dispute settlement; and other provisions. The agreement also includes chapters in which the parties agree to increase cooperation in a number of areas, including mining, energy, transportation, tourism, statistics, science and technology, environment, and other areas.[18] On industrial goods, the EU agreed to eliminate tariffs on 82% of imports by value coming from Mexico on the date of entry into the agreement and to phase out remaining tariffs by January 1, 2003. Mexico agreed to eliminate tariffs on 47% of imports by value from the EU upon implementation of the agreement and to phase out the remaining tariffs by January 1, 2007. In agricultural products and fisheries, signatories agreed to phase out tariffs on 62% of trade within ten years.[19] Tariff negotiations were deferred on certain sensitive products, including meat, dairy products, cereals, and bananas. Most non-tariff barriers, such as quotas and import/export licenses, were removed upon implementation of the agreement. Mexico agreed to phase out import restrictions of new automobiles from the EU by 2007. In government procurement, Mexico agreed to follow provisions similar to those under NAFTA to allow the EU to enter the Mexican market while the EU agreed to follow WTO rules.[20] In services trade, the agreement goes beyond the WTO General Agreement on Trade in Services (GATS). It immediately provided European service operators "NAFTA-equivalent" access to Mexico in a number of areas, including financial services, energy, telecommunications, and tourism.[21]

Mexico-Israel

After two years of negotiations, Mexico and Israel signed a free trade agreement on April 10, 2000 and implemented it on July 1, 2000. The agreement immediately eliminated tariffs on most products traded between Mexico and Israel at the time of the agreement with full tariff elimination scheduled by 2005. Policymakers expected the agreement to provide Mexico with more export access to the Israeli market, increased FDI from Israel to Mexico, and result in increased technology transfer from Israel to Mexico.

The agreement includes provisions on national treatment and market access for goods, rules of origin, customs procedures, emergency actions, competition policy, government procurement, dispute resolution, dispute resolution, and WTO rights and obligations.[22] The agreement covers 98.6% of agricultural goods and 100% of industrial goods. Mexico received immediate duty-free access on 50% of its exports and tariff reductions on 12% of its exports to Israel. Tariff-rate quotas were applied on 25% of Mexican exports to Israel. Most remaining tariff barriers on Mexican exports had a five-year phase out schedule. Israel received immediate duty-free access on about 72% of its exports to Mexico. Another 22.8% of tariffs on Israel exports to Mexico were withdrawn in 2003 and another 4.4% were withdrawn in 2005.[23]

Mexico-El Salvador, Guatemala, and Honduras

Mexico and El Salvador, Guatemala, and Honduras (Northern Triangle) signed a free trade agreement on June 29, 2000. The agreement is often referred to as the Mexico-Northern Triangle FTA, but the WTO has it listed as three separate agreements between Mexico and El Salvador, Guatemala, and Honduras. The agreements with El Salvador and Guatemala entered into force on March 15, 2001, while the agreement with Honduras entered into force on June 1, 2001. Negotiations for the FTA with all three countries began in 1992, stalled for four years, and resumed at the second Tuxtla Summit in 1996. Negotiations ended on May 10, 2000. This agreement was the final of Mexico's NAFTA-type agreements with all Central American countries. Prior to the conclusion of the Mexico-Northern Triangle FTA, Mexico had held separate partial scope agreements with each of the three countries, granting some products preferential access to the Mexican market.

The agreement includes provisions on national treatment and market access for goods and services, the agreement has similar provisions to other Mexican FTAs on agriculture; sanitary and phytosanitary measures; rules of origin; financial services; telecommunications services; temporary entry of business persons; investment; IPR; standards; dispute resolution; safeguards; and unfair trade practices.[24] Upon entry into force of the FTA, approximately 57% of Mexico's exports to the three countries received duty-free treatment. Tariffs on an additional 15% of goods were phased out over a period of three to five years. Mexico eliminated tariffs on 65% of imports from the Northern Triangle countries upon implementation and phased out tariffs on 24% of imports over a three to five year period. Thirty percent of Mexico's agricultural exports received duty-free treatment upon the entry into force of the agreement, another 12% were liberalized over a five-year period, and 41% were liberalized over a period of five to eleven years.[25]

Mexico-European Free Trade Association

Mexico and the European Free Trade Association (EFTA), composed of Iceland, Lichtenstein, Norway, and Switzerland, signed a free trade agreement on November 27, 2000. The agreement entered into force on July 1, 2001. This was the first FTA that the EFTA had concluded with an overseas partner country. Since the agreement entered into force, Mexico and the EFTA have met at least four times to explore possibilities of further trade integration, including agricultural and services trade. In September 2008, the two parties agreed to adopt an amendment on transportation to the agreement to help facilitate trade. They also discussed possibilities of further amendments, such as banning export duties and extending the coverage of trade in processed agricultural products.[26]

The agreement includes provisions on national treatment and market access for goods; agriculture; rules of origin; safeguards; and other provisions.[27] During the first six years, the FTA reduced the average Mexican tariff on EFTA industrial goods from 8% to zero. Mexican industrial exports to the EFTA have been free of duty since the entry into force of the FTA.[28]

Mexico-Japan

Mexico and Japan signed a free trade agreement, formally called an Economic Partnership Agreement (EPA) in September 2004. The EPA was Japan's second free trade agreement, but its most comprehensive bilateral agreement at that time. It was Japan's first agreement to include agricultural products, a factor that resulted in initial opposition in Japan. In addition to the removal of tariff barriers, it includes regulations in other areas, including labor mobility and investment.[29] One of the goals of the Mexico-Japan EPA was to restore the competitiveness of Japanese companies in the Mexican market. Mexico already had free trade with the United States and Canada under NAFTA and with the European Union through an FTA that went into force in July 2000. These two agreements had placed Japanese companies at a disadvantage due to differences in tariff rates and exclusion of Japanese companies from public-works projects in Mexico. Mexico entered the agreement to increase Japanese investment in Mexico, and, thus, create jobs, expand Mexican exports to Japan, expand technology transfer from Japan, and strengthen Mexican industrial competitiveness.[30]

The agreement includes provisions on national treatment and market access for goods; sanitary and phytosanitary measures; standards; rules of origin; customs procedures; safeguards; IPR; dispute settlement; financial services; and government procurement. The agreement also includes chapters in which the two countries agreed to increase cooperation in a number of areas, including vocational education and training, agriculture, tourism, and the environment.[31] The two countries agreed to eliminate tariffs on almost all industrial products within ten years. Tariffs were eliminated immediately in the following areas: electronics, household electric appliances, capital goods, and automobiles. By the year 2015, tariffs will be eliminated on 90% of goods that accounted for 96% in total trade value between the two countries. Prior to the EPA, only 16% of Japanese exports to Mexico entered duty free into the Mexican market, while 70% of Mexican exports to Japan entered duty free. In agriculture, Mexican officials initially called for trade concessions in beef, oranges, pineapples, and leather products, but later agreed to an expansion of Japanese import quotas over a five-year period for pork, beef, chicken, oranges, and orange juice.

These are scheduled to be revised in 2010, the fifth year of the agreement. The value of Mexico's agricultural products exempt from import tariffs was reportedly expected to be less than 50% of its total agricultural exports to Japan.[32] The agreement also allowed for a duty-free quota for motor vehicles and steel upon implementation, with a phase-out scheduled over time. Japan's auto and steel companies were expected to benefit the most from these provisions.[33]

Partial Scope Agreements

Mexico also has a number of partial scope agreements, which are integration agreements with more limited free trade coverage than a free trade agreement. Mexico is a party to the Agreement on the Global System of Trade Preferences Among Developing Countries (GSTP). The GSTP was established in 1988 as a framework for the exchange of trade preferences among developing countries to promote trade among developing countries. The agreement provides tariff preferences on merchandise trade among member countries. It is a treaty to which only Group of 77 member countries may enter.[34] The text of the agreement was adopted after a round of negotiations that was concluded in Belgrade in 1988. The agreement, which entered into force on April 19, 1989, was envisaged as being a dynamic instrument which would be expanded in successive stages in additional rounds of negotiations and reviewed periodically.[35] A second round of negotiations was proposed in the early 1990s to expand trade preferences, but negotiations faltered as members failed to ratify the agreement. In June 2004, GSTP participants launched a third round of negotiations. Forty-four countries have acceded to the agreement.[36]

Mexico is a signatory to the Latin American Integration Association (ALADI), which was established by the Treaty of Montevideo in August 1980 and entered into force on March 18, 1981. ALADI replaced the Latin American Free Trade Association established in1960 with the goal of developing a common market in Latin America. ALADI members include Argentina, Bolivia, Brazil, Chile, Colombia, Cuba, Ecuador, Mexico, Paraguay, Peru, Uruguay, and Venezuela. Signatory countries have sought economic cooperation amongst each other but have made little progress toward forming a common market. They maintain a flexible goal of encouraging free trade without a timetable for instituting a common market. Members approved a regional tariff preference arrangement in 1984 and expanded it in 1987 and 1990.[37]

Mexico is also a member of the Protocol Relating to Trade Negotiations among Developing Countries (PTN). The PTN is a preferential arrangement involving Bangladesh, Brazil, Chile, Egypt, Israel, Mexico, Pakistan, Paraguay, Peru, Philippines, Republic of Korea, Serbia, Tunisia, Turkey, and Uruguay. It was signed in December 1971 and became effective on February 11, 1973.

Table 2. Mexico's Partial Scope Agreements

Agreement	Coverage	Date of Signature	Entry into Force	WTO Legal Cover
Global System of Trade Preferences Among Developing Countries (GSTP)[a]	Goods	April 13, 1988	April 19, 1989	Enabling Clause
Latin American Integration Association (ALADI)[b]	Goods	August 12, 1980	March 18, 1981	Enabling Clause
Protocol on Trade Negotiations (PTN)[c]	Goods	December 8, 1971	February 11, 1973	Enabling Clause

Source: World Trade Organization, Regional Trade Agreement Database, see http://www.wto.org/.

[a] Includes Algeria, Argentina, Bangladesh, Benin, Venezuela, Bolivia, Brazil, Cameroon, Chile, Colombia, Cuba, Ecuador, Egypt, Former Yugoslav Republic of Macedonia, Ghana, Guinea, Guyana, India, Indonesia, Islamic Republic of Iran, Iraq, Republic of Korea, Democratic People's Republic of Korea, Libyan Arab Jamahirlya, Malaysia, Mexico, Morocco, Mozambique, Myanmar, Nicaragua, Nigeria, Pakistan, Peru, Philippines, Singapore, Sri Lanka, Sudan, Tanzania, Thailand, Trinidad and Tobago, Tunisia, Vietnam, and Zimbabwe.

[b] Includes Argentina, Venezuela, Bolivia, Brazil, Chile, Colombia, Cuba, Ecuador, Mexico, Paraguay, Peru, and Uruguay.

[c] Includes Bangladesh, Brazil, Chile, Egypt, Israel, Republic of Korea, Mexico, Pakistan, Paraguay, Peru, Philippines, Serbia, Tunisia, Turkey, Uruguay.

MEXICO'S MERCHANDISE TRADE

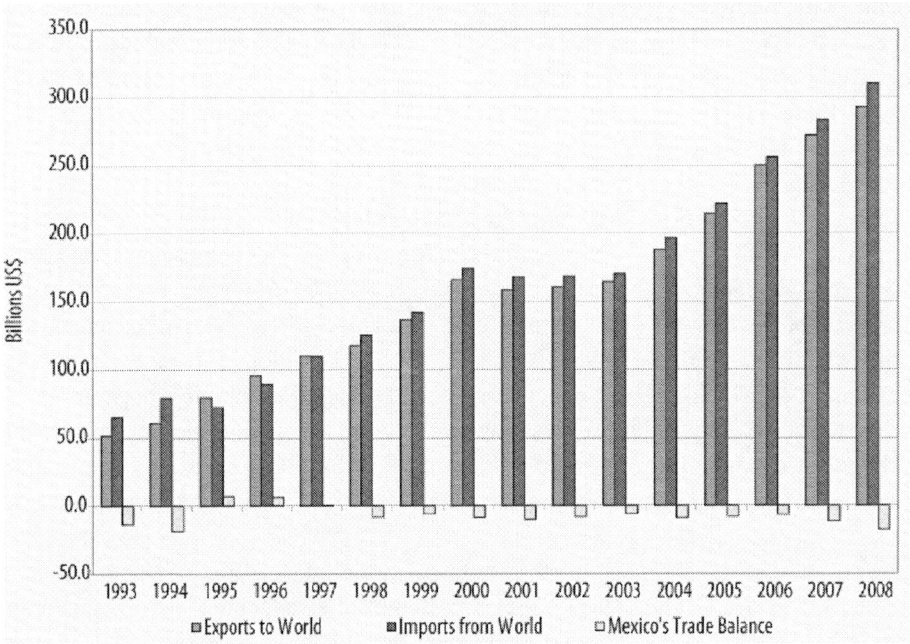

Source: Compiled by CRS using data from Mexico's Ministry of Economy.

Figure 1. Mexico's Merchandise Trade with All Countries

Table 3. Composition of Trade: 2008

Mexico's Exports		Mexico's Imports	
Product (HTS 8-digit level)	**Value (Billions US$)**	**Product (HTS 8-digit level)**	**Value (Billions US$)**
Crude Petroleum Oil	43.6	Gasoline	14.6
Color TV Apparatus	18.1	Liquid Crystal Devices NESOI[a]	4.7
Mexico's Exports		**Mexico's Imports**	
Product (HTS 8-digit level)	**Value (Billions US$)**	**Product (HTS 8-digit level)**	**Value (Billions US$)**
Automobiles	16.1	Automobiles (between 1500 and 3000 cm$^{3)}$	4.3
Mobile Telephones	8.6	Processors and Controllers NESOI[a]	4.1
Wire Harnesses for Automobiles	4.3	Automobiles (larger than 3,000 cm$^{3)}$	3.3
Total	292.6	Total	310.1

Source: Mexico's *Subsecretaría de Negociaciones Comerciales Internacionales*. Compiled by CRS.
[a] NESOI is defined as not elsewhere specified or indicated.

Since the early 1990s, Mexico’s trade with the world has risen rapidly, with exports increasing more rapidly than imports. Mexico’s exports to all countries increased 465% between 1993 and 2008, from $51.8 billion to $292.6 billion (see Figure 1). Mexico’s imports from all countries increased 374% during the same time period from $65.4 billion to $310.1 billion. Mexico’s trade balance went from a deficit of $13.5 billion in 1993 to surpluses of $7.1 billion in 1995 and $6.5 billion in 1996. Since 1998, Mexico’s trade balance has remained in deficit, reaching $17.5 billion in 2008.

Trade with the United States

Mexico’s trade with the United States has increased rapidly since the early 1990s, with exports increasing more rapidly than imports. Mexico’s exports to the United States increased 447% between 1993 and 2008, from $42.9 billion to $234.6 billion (see Figure 2). Mexico’s imports from the United States increased by 237% during the same time period, from $45.3 billion to $152.6 billion. Mexico’s trade balance with the United States went from a deficit of $2.4 billion in 1993 to a surplus of $82.0 billion in 2008.

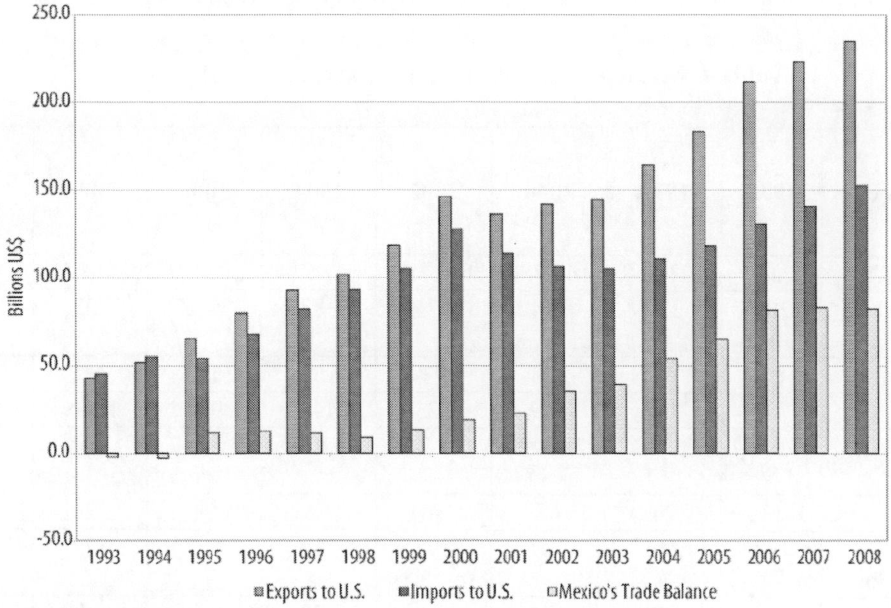

Source: Compiled by CRS using data from Mexico’s Ministry of Economy.

Figure 2. Mexico’s Merchandise Trade with the United States

Trade Trends since Liberalization

One of Mexico’s primary motivations in seeking free trade agreements with other countries after NAFTA took effect was to decrease its dependence on the United States as a trading partner. However, the share of Mexico’s exports going to the United States has remained consistently high since NAFTA and the rest of Mexico's FTAs took effect. Over 80% of Mexico's exports are destined for the United States and approximately half of Mexico's imports come from the United States. In 1995, the year after NAFTA took effect, 82.0% of Mexico's exports went to the United States. The U.S. market share of exports rose to 87.0% in 1999 and remained at about the same level until 2005 when it declined to 84.7%. In 2008, the U.S. share decreased to 80.1%. Between 1996 and 2008, Mexico's total exports doubled from $96.0 billion to $292.7 billion (see Table 3). Exports to countries that have FTAs with Mexico increased considerably during this time period, with exports to Israel experiencing the highest percentage increase (1,592%). NAFTA partners (Canada and the United States) ranked first among Mexico's export markets in 2008, followed by the European Union, Japan, and Chile.

Mexico's total imports increased 247% between 1996 and 2008. Imports from NAFTA trading partners increased by 134% during this time period (see Table 4). Imports from its other FTA trading partners increased more rapidly during these years, with imports from Honduras and Chile experiencing the highest rates of growth (increases of 5,000% and 1,416%, respectively). In 2008, NAFTA countries ranked first as sources of imports ($162.1 billion), followed by the European Union ($39.2 billion), and Japan ($16.3 billion). Mexico's imports from countries with which it has not entered into FTAs increased by over 1000% between 1996 and 2008, from $7.3 billion to $86.0 billion, as shown in **Table 4**.

Table 4. Mexico's Exports by FTA Partners (Millions US$)

Partners	1996	1998	2000	2002	2004	2006	2008	% Change 1996-2008
NAFTA	82,017	103,668	149,784	144,889	167,814	216,976	241,687	195%
Costa Rica	209	290	354	373	387	522	922	341%
Nicaragua	61	65	123	93	151	522	371	508%
Chile	781	736	549	323	443	905	1,589	104%
European Union	3,555	3,988	5,799	5,626	6,818	10,967	17,080	381%
Israel	13	24	67	56	62	91	220	1,592%
El Salvador	177	246	307	292	317	497	772	336%
Guatemala	375	623	574	548	673	935	1,388	270%
Honduras	107	146	149	156	182	285	459	329%
EFTA	200	132	131	172	119	154	643	222%
Japan	1,251	552	1,115	1,194	1,191	1,594	2,068	65%
Rest of World	7,258	7,123	7,169	7,324	9,842	16,477	25,467	251%
Total	96,004	117,593	166,121	161,046	187,999	249,925	292,666	205%

Source: Mexico's Ministry of Economy with data from *Banco de México*. Compiled by CRS.

Table 5. Mexico's Imports from FTA Partners (Millions US$)

FTA Partners	1996	1998	2000	2002	2004	2006	2008	% Change 1996-2008
NAFTA	69,280	95,549	131,551	111,037	116,154	137,687	162,066	134%
Costa Rica	58	87	180	416	852	789	777	1,240%
Nicaragua	12	14	27	27	52	78	119	892%
Chile	171	552	894	1,010	1,464	2,470	2,593	1,416%
European Union	7,800	11,846	15,057	16,950	21,657	28,938	39,160	402%
Israel	79	137	297	250	402	429	524	563%
El Salvador	19	25	20	36	50	59	71	274%
Guatemala	77	81	91	117	230	356	501	551%
Honduras	5	12	13	25	66	123	255	5,000%
EFTA	484	648	851	872	1,074	1,386	1,693	250%
Japan	4,132	4,537	6,466	9,349	10,583	15,295	16,326	295%
Rest of World	7,352	11,885	19,011	28,590	44,226	68,442	86,047	1,070%
Total	89,469	125,373	174,458	168,679	186,810	256,052	310,132	247%

Source: Mexico's Ministry of Economy with data from *Banco de México*. Compiled by CRS.

Eighty-three percent of Mexico's exports are destined for NAFTA trading partners, with the United States accounting for 80% of these exports. The percentage of exports going to the United States and Canada increased from 85% in 1996 to 90% in 2002, and then decreased in the following years, as shown in Table 5. Exports to the European Union accounted for 6% of Mexico's total exports in 2008. The share of Mexico's imports from NAFTA trading partners decreased from 77% in 1996 to 52% in 2008 (see Table 5). The share of Mexico's imports from the European Union increased from 9% in 1996 to 13% in 2008, while the share from non-FTA countries increased from 8% to 28%. Imports from Japan accounted for 5% of Mexico's imports in 2008, while imports from Chile and other FTA partners accounted for 3%. Although Mexico does not have an FTA with China, Mexico's imports from China increased considerably during this period. Imports from China increased from $760 million in 1996 to $34.8 billion in 2008, an increase of over 4000%.

Table 6. Market Share of Exports and Imports by FTA Partner

	1996	1998	2000	2002	2004	2006	2008
Market Share of Mexico's Exports[a]							
NAFTA	85%	88%	90%	90%	89%	87%	83%
EU	4%	3%	3%	3%	4%	4%	6%
Japan	1%	0%	1%	1%	1%	1%	1%
Chile	1%	1%	0%	0%	0%	0%	1%
Other FTA Partners	1%	1%	1%	1%	1%	1%	1%

Table 6. (Continued)

	1996	1998	2000	2002	2004	2006	2008
Rest of World	8%	6%	4%	5%	5%	7%	9%
Market Share of Mexico's Imports[a]							
NAFTA	77%	76%	75%	66%	62%	54%	52%
EU	9%	9%	9%	10%	12%	11%	13%
Japan	5%	4%	4%	6%	6%	6%	5%
Chile	0%	0%	1%	1%	1%	1%	1%
Other FTA Partners	1%	1%	0%	2%	2%	2%	2%
Rest of World	8%	9%	11%	17%	24%	27%	28%

Source: Compiled by CRS using data from Mexico's Ministry of Economy. a. Totals may not add due to rounding.

Economic Policy Challenges for Mexico

One of Mexico's primary motivations in seeking FTAs with other countries has been to decrease its reliance on the United States as an export market. Though Mexico's total exports have increased substantially since it began trade liberalization, the United States continues to be the dominant export market for Mexican goods. Over 80% of Mexico's exports were destined for the U.S. market in 2007. The reliance of Mexico on the United States as an export market makes the country more susceptible to economic conditions in the United States. The adverse effects of the financial crisis on the U.S. economy have negatively affected economic growth in Mexico. After years of economic stability, Mexico's real gross domestic product (GDP) is forecast to contract 5.8% or more in 2009 and unemployment is expected to rise considerably. In addition, the slowdown in the U.S. economy has resulted in lower demand for Mexican goods in the United States which has an adverse effect on industrial production in Mexico.[38]

Mexico is facing increasing challenges in addressing issues related to productivity and the competitiveness of its exports. Some economists believe that countries in Latin America need to become more competitive in the global economy in order to promote economic growth and reduce poverty. They argue that if Latin American countries are going to prosper, they must improve labor skills and technology to be more competitive in the global economy.[39] Over the past several years, Mexico has been facing increasing competition from China and other Asian economies in the manufacturing sector. In 2003, China replaced Mexico as the second-highest source of U.S. imports. This has presented challenges to Mexico's manufacturing sector and some economists argue that Mexico has fallen behind in its comparative advantage in exporting in industries with intermediate wages and technological sophistication.[40] They argue that Mexico must invest more in education and telecommunications infrastructure to increase productivity and remain competitive.

The emergence of China in the global marketplace has drawn comparisons between the industrial policies of China and Mexico. Some analysts believe that Mexico should make more progress in scientific research to attract and create high-tech industries, such as China has done. They argue that China's policy to help attract foreign direct investment, which initially consisted of special zones with preferential fiscal and customs policies and later modified to establish scientific and technical research facilities, should serve as an example to Mexico's industrial policy. They believe that Mexico's approach has been a combination of fiscal and customs policies to enhance its comparative advantage of sharing a 2000-mile border with the United States, but that Mexico did little to promote scientific and technical research. They add that Mexican programs have not fostered or encouraged research and development activities to facilitate the creation of technological enterprises.[41]

A primary motivation for entering into free trade agreements is to improve economic conditions and create jobs. In the case of Mexico, an additional key motivation has been to address the issue of poverty by creating jobs for the poor. Mexico has made an effort to make trade agreements a tool for promoting economic development and combating poverty, but it is only part of the overall effort of the Mexican government to address these issues. Mexico has implemented a compensatory policy to address poverty through its *Oportunidades* program (formerly known as Progresa). This program provides cash transfers to families in poverty who demonstrate that they regularly attend medical appointments and can certify that children are attending school.[42] The program has been successful in bringing more economic stability to the country and reducing poverty but it has not helped the country's productivity and may not be a long-term solution. Some argue that such programs result in a dependence for cash transfers and do not help poor workers obtain formal sector jobs with prospects for increasing productivity.[43]

IMPLICATIONS FOR U.S. INTERESTS

Mexico's numerous free trade agreements and its trade liberalization policy are of interest to U.S. policymakers because of the implications for U.S.-Mexico trade and the overall relationship of the two countries. There is an interdependent relationship between the two countries, as highlighted by the recent slowdown in the U.S. economy and the adverse effects on the Mexican economy. Economic conditions in Mexico are important to the United States because of the proximity of Mexico to the United States, the close trade and investment interactions, and other social and political issues. Another implication for the United States is the effect of Mexico's FTAs on U.S. exports to Mexico. The liberalization of Mexico's trade and investment barriers to other countries has resulted in increasing competition for U.S. goods and services in the Mexican market. However, trade flows are also affected by other factors such as exchange rates, economic growth, and investor confidence, and it is difficult to isolate these effects.

A number of studies suggest that while Mexico's trade liberalization policy, mainly NAFTA, may have brought economic and social benefits to the Mexican economy as a whole, the benefits have not been evenly distributed throughout the country. Wages and employment tend to be higher in states experiencing higher levels of FDI and trade. In terms of regional effects, initial conditions in Mexico determined which Mexican states experienced stronger economic growth as a result of trade liberalization. States with higher levels of telecommunications and transportation infrastructure gained more benefits than poorer states with lower levels of education, infrastructure, and institutional capacity. This affects the United States because Mexican workers who have lost their job due to trade liberalization may migrate to other areas in Mexico or to the United States to seek jobs.[44]

To address issues affecting trade, U.S. policymakers may consider closer cooperation with Mexico to develop complementary policies to ensure that all segments of the two countries benefit from economic integration. The United States and Mexico, along with Canada, have increased cooperation on economic and security issues through the Security and Prosperity Partnership of North America, but there may be additional options that could be considered by both countries.[45] One issue on which a number of economists and other analysts have agreed upon is that Mexico needs to invest more in education, infrastructure, and institutional strengthening to benefit more fully from freer trade. A possible option to address this issue is to create a bilateral or trilateral fund for development that focuses on building infrastructure, improving education and human capital, and creating more opportunities for research and development. U.S. and Mexican policymakers have informally talked about expanding the mandate of the North American Development Bank (NADBank).[46] A number of Members of the U.S. Congress and elected officials from Mexico have discussed the possibility of expanding the mission of the NADBank to go beyond environmental and border issues and consider creating an infrastructure fund that would be managed by NADBank to provide investment in infrastructure, communications, or education.

End Notes

[1] See CRS Report RL32060, *World Trade Organization Negotiations: The Doha Development Agenda, by Ian F. Fergusson, World Trade Organization Negotiations: The Doha Development Agenda*, by Ian F. Fergusson.

[2] For more information on the specific sets of rules governing regional trade agreements among WTO members, see *Regional Trade Agreements: Rules* on the WTO website, see http://www.wto.org.

[3] World Trade Organization (WTO), Regional Trade Agreement Database, see http://www.wto.org/

[4] For more information on the costs and benefits of regional trade agreements, see Cohen, Stephen D., Robert A. Blecker, and Peter D. Whitney, *Fundamentals of U.S. Foreign Policy*, Westview Press, 2003, pp. 49-79.

[5] Crawford, Jo-Ann and Roberto V. Fiorentino, *The Changing Landscape of Regional Trade Agreements*, World Trade Organization Discussion Paper No. 8, 2005, p. 16.

[6] United States International Trade Commission (USITC), *The Likely Impact on the United States of a Free Trade Agreement with Mexico*, USITC Publication 2353, February 1991.

[7] Data compiled by CRS using Global Trade Atlas database.

[8] The Asahi Shimbun, "Japan: Free Trade with Mexico," March 12, 2004.

[9] Hufbauer, Gary Clyde, and Jeffrey J. Schott, *NAFTA Revisited,* Institute for International Economics, October 2005, p. 3.

[10] Salazar-Xirinachs, José Manuel and Maryse Robert, editors, *Toward Free Trade in the Americas*, April 2001, p. 98.

[11] Decreto de promulgación del Tratado de Libre Comercio entre los Estados Unidos Mexicanos y la República de Costa Rica. See WTO Regional Trade Agreement Database, see http://www.wto.org.

[12] *Tratado de Libre Comercio Chile*. See WTO Regional Trade Agreement Database, see http://www.wto.org.

[13] Salazar-Xirinachs, José Manuel and Maryse Robert, editors, *Toward Free Trade in the Americas*, April 2001, p. 99.

[14] Decreto Promulgatorio del Tratado de Libre Comercio entre el Gobierno de los Estados Unidos Mexicanos y el Gobierno de la República de Nicaragua. See WTO Regional Trade Agreement Database, http://www.wto.org.

[15] Bureau of National Affairs (BNA), *International Trade Reporter*, "Mexico and Chile Sign Off on Expanded Trade Agreement," April 22, 1998.

[16] Reuters, "*Cumbre-México y Unión Europea Acuerdan Acelerar Libre Comercio*," May 17, 2008.

[17] Ibid.

[18] Global Agreement, Economic Partnership, Political Coordination and Cooperation Agreement between the European Community and its member States and the United Mexican States. See WTO Regional Trade Agreement Database, see http://www.wto.org.

[19] The Chinese University of Hong Kong, *The Mexico-EU Free Trade Agreement*, 2000, http://intl.econ.cuhk.edu.hk.

[20] Transnational Institute, Mexican Action Network on Free Trade (RMALC), *The EU-Mexico Free Trade Agreement Seven Years On*, June 2007.
[21] U.S.-Mexico Chamber of Commerce, The Free Trade Agreement Between Mexico and the European Union, August 2000.
[22] Free Trade Agreement Between the State of Israel and the United Mexican States. See WTO Regional Trade Agreement Database, see http://www.wto.org.
[23] U.S.-Mexico Chamber of Commerce, "History of Mexico-Israel Trade Relations," September 2000.
[24] Tratado de Libre Comercio México-El Salvador, Guatemala y Honduras (Triángulo del Norte). See http://www.sice.oas.org.
[25] Salazar-Xirinachs, José Manuel and Maryse Robert, editors, *Toward Free Trade in the Americas*, April 2001, p. 99-100.
[26] The European Free Trade Association (EFTA) Secretariat, *EFTA and Mexico to Amend Free Trade Agreement*, September 2008.
[27] Free Trade Agreement between the EFTA States the United Mexican States. . See WTO Regional Trade Agreement Database, see http://www.wto.org.
[28] *Mexico-EU Trade Links*, "Mexico-EFTA Free Trade Agreement: After Six Years," July 2007.
[29] *The Asahi Shumbun*, "Japan, Mexico Ink Landmark Accord," September 20, 2004.
[30] Press Center Japan, "Japan and Mexico Agree on Conclusion of Free-Trade Agreement," March 31, 2004.
[31] Agreement Between Japan the United Mexican States for the Strengthening of the Economic Partnership. See WTO Regional Trade Agreement Database, see http://www.wto.org.
[32] *Nikkei Weekly*, "FTA with Mexico Paves Way for Talks with Asian Nations," March 15, 2004.
[33] *The Asahi Shumbun*, "Japan, Mexico Ink Landmark Accord," September 20, 2004.
[34] The Group of 77 (G-77) was established on June 15, 1964 by seventy-seven developing countries, signatories of the "Joint Declaration of the Seventy-Seven Countries," issued at the end of the first session of the United Nations Conference on Trade and Development (UNCTAD) in Geneva.
[35] United Nations Conference on Trade and Development, Press Release, "Global System of Trade Preferences," June 16, 2004.
[36] Ibid.
[37] Latin American Integration Association (ALADI) website, see http://www.aladi.org.
[38] *Latin American Newsletters*, "Latin American Mexico and NAFTA Report," June 2009.
[39] *Miami Herald*, "The Left's Favorite U.S. Nobel May Surprise his Fans," by Andres Oppenheimer, August 16, 2009.
[40] Latin America/Caribbean and Asia/Pacific Economics and Business Association, *Economic Integration and Manufacturing Performance in Mexico: Is Chinese Competition to Blame*?, by Ernesto López-Córdova, Working Paper No. 23, December 2004.
[41] *Mexico Now*, "Mexico's and China's Programs to Attract Foreign Investment," by Ramiro Villega and Migual A. Díaz Marín, pp. 52-55.
[42] Santiago Levy, *Progress Against Poverty*, Brookings Institution, 2006.
[43] Levy, Santiago, *Good Intensions, Bad Outcomes: Social Policy, Informality, and Economic Growth in Mexico*, Brookings Institution Press, 2008, pp. 1-6.
[44] For more information, see CRS Report RL34733, *NAFTA and the Mexican Economy*, by M. Angeles Villarreal.
[45] See CRS Report RS22701, *Security and Prosperity Partnership of North America: An Overview and Selected Issues*, by M. Angeles Villarreal and Jennifer E. Lake.
[46] NADBank and its sister institution, the Border Environment Cooperation Commission (BECC), were created under a bilateral side agreement to NAFTA called the Border Environmental Cooperation Agreement (BECC) to address environmental infrastructure problems along the U.S.-Mexican border.

In: Mexico: Background and Issues
Editor: Richard C. Bradley

ISBN: 978-1-61728-498-4

Chapter 6

NAFTA AND THE MEXICAN ECONOMY*

M. Angeles Villarreal and Marisabel Cid

SUMMARY

The North American Free Trade Agreement (NAFTA), in effect since January 1994, plays a very strong role in the bilateral economic relationship between Mexico and the United States. The two countries are also closely tied in areas not directly related to trade and investment such as security, environmental, migration, and health issues. The effects of NAFTA on Mexico and the state of the Mexican economy have important impacts on U.S. economic and political interests. As NAFTA approaches its 15th anniversary, a number of policymakers have raised the issue of revisiting NAFTA and renegotiating parts of the agreement. Some important factors in evaluating NAFTA include the effects of the agreement on Mexico and how these relate to U.S.-Mexico economic relations. In the 110th Congress, major issues of concern have been related mostly to economic conditions in Mexico, the effect of NAFTA on the United States and Mexico, and Mexican migrant workers in the United States.

In 1990, then Mexican President Carlos Salinas de Gortari approached the United States with the idea of forming a free trade agreement (FTA). Mexico's main motivation in pursuing an FTA with the United States was to stabilize the Mexican economy by attracting foreign direct investment. The Mexican economy had experienced many difficulties throughout most of the 1980s with a significant deepening of poverty. The intention of Mexico in entering NAFTA was to increase export diversification by attracting foreign direct investment (FDI), which would help create jobs, increase wage rates, and reduce poverty.

At the time that NAFTA went into effect, the expectation among supporters was that the agreement would improve investor confidence in Mexico, attract investment, and narrow the income differentials between Mexico and the United States and Canada. Measuring the effects of NAFTA on the Mexican economy is difficult because the economy was also

* This is an edited, reformatted and augmented version of a CRS Report for Congress publication dated November 2008.

affected by other factors, such as economic cycles in the United States (Mexico's largest trading partner) and currency fluctuations. In addition, Mexico's unilateral trade liberalization measures of the 1980s and the currency crisis of 1995 both affected economic growth, per capita gross domestic product (GDP), and real wages.

While NAFTA may have brought economic and social benefits to the Mexican economy as a whole, the benefits have not been evenly distributed throughout the country. Wages and employment tend to be higher in states experiencing higher levels of FDI and trade. The agricultural sector experienced a higher amount of worker displacement after NAFTA because of increased competition from the United States and because of Mexican domestic agricultural reforms. In terms of regional effects, initial conditions in Mexico determined which Mexican states experienced stronger economic growth as a result of NAFTA. States with higher levels of telecommunications and transportation infrastructure gained more benefits than poorer states with lower levels of education, infrastructure, and institutional capacity. Some economists argue that while trade liberalization may narrow income disparities over the long run with other countries, it may indirectly lead to larger disparities in income levels within a country.

Introduction

The North American Free Trade Agreement (NAFTA), in effect since January 1994, plays a very strong role in the bilateral economic relationship between Mexico and the United States. The two countries are also closely tied in areas not directly related to trade and investment such as security, environmental, migration, and health issues. The effects of NAFTA on Mexico and the state of the Mexican economy have important impacts on U.S. economic and political interests. As NAFTA approaches its 15th anniversary, a number of policymakers have raised the issue of revisiting NAFTA and renegotiating some aspects of the agreement. In evaluating NAFTA, it is important to examine the effects of the agreement on Mexico and how these relate to the economic relationship of the United States with Mexico. In the 110th Congress, some of the issues of concern have been related mostly to economic conditions in Mexico, the effect of NAFTA on Mexico, and Mexican migrant workers in the United States. This chapter provides an overview of Mexico's motivations for entering NAFTA, the Mexican economy, the economic effects of NAFTA in Mexico, and the views of NAFTA within Mexico. It also provides information on NAFTA's effect on Mexico's agricultural sector because this has been one of the more controversial issues surrounding NAFTA in Mexico.

Mexico's Motivations for Entering NAFTA[1]

In 1990, the President of Mexico at the time, Carlos Salinas de Gortari, approached then U.S. President George H.W. Bush with the idea of forming a free trade agreement (FTA). President Salinas de Gortari's main motivation in pursuing an FTA with the United States was to stabilize the Mexican economy by attracting foreign direct investment (FDI). The Mexican economy had experienced many difficulties throughout most of the 1980s with a significant deepening of poverty. Mexico's intention in entering NAFTA was to increase export diversification by attracting FDI, which would help create jobs, increase wage rates, and reduce poverty. At the time NAFTA went into effect, many studies predicted that the agreement would cause an overall positive impact on the Mexican economy.

From the 1930s through part of the 1980s, Mexico maintained a strong protectionist trade policy in an effort to be independent of any foreign power and as a means to industrialization. Mexico established a policy of import substitution in the 1930s, consisting of a broad, general protection of the entire industrial sector. Mexico placed high restrictions on foreign investment and controlled the exchange rate to encourage domestic industrial growth. Mexico also nationalized the oil industry during this time. These protectionist economic policies remained in effect until the country began to experience a series of economic challenges caused by a number of factors.

The 1980s in Mexico were marked by inflation[2] and a declining standard of living. The 1982 debt crisis in which the Mexican government was unable to meet its foreign debt obligations was a primary cause of the economic challenges the country faced in the early to mid-1980's. Much of the government's efforts in addressing the challenges were placed on privatizing state industries and moving toward trade liberalization. In the late 1980s and early into the 1990s, the Mexican government implemented a series of measures to restructure the economy that included steps toward unilateral trade liberalization.

Mexican began to reverse its protectionist stance in the mid-1980s when the government was forced to declare that it was unable to repay its debts and to default on its loans. Then President Miguel de la Madrid took steps to open and liberalize the Mexican economy and initiated procedures to replace import substitution policies with policies aimed at attracting foreign investment, lowering trade barriers and making the country competitive in non-oil exports. In 1986, Mexico acceded to the General Agreement on Tariffs and Trade (GATT), assuring further trade liberalization measures and closer ties with the United States.

In November 1987, the United States and Mexico entered into a bilateral understanding on trade and investment called the *Framework of Principles and Procedures for Consultation Regarding Trade and Investment Relations.*[3] Prior to this agreement, there had been no legal framework to govern commercial relations between the two countries. There were two parts to the agreement, one served as a mechanism to address trade issues, and the other established an agenda for the removal or reduction of trade barriers. Seven topics were listed in the agenda for possible future discussions: textiles, agriculture, steel, investment, technology transfer and intellectual property, electronics, and information on the service sector. Under this framework understanding, two sectoral agreements were reached which liberalized trade in steel, textiles, and alcoholic beverages. In addition, working groups started meeting on agriculture, industry, services, tariffs, and intellectual property rights.

In October 1989, the two countries entered into a second trade and investment understanding called *The Understanding Regarding Trade and Investment Facilitation Talks.*[4] This agreement built on the work of the 1987 agreement, establishing a negotiating process for expanding trade and investment opportunities. These two agreements significantly improved trade relations between Mexico and the United States and other improvements in trade relations followed. Marking the advances in trade relations between the two countries, Mexico proposed negotiations for a free trade agreement with the United States. In June 1990, then President Carlos Salinas de Gortari of Mexico and then President George H.W. Bush issued a joint statement in support of negotiating a free trade agreement.

ECONOMIC CONDITIONS IN MEXICO BEFORE AND AFTER NAFTA

The Mexican economy is strongly tied to economic conditions in the United States, making it very sensitive to economic developments in the United States.[5] Mexico is highly reliant on exports and most of Mexico's exports go to the United States. In 2007, Mexico's exports as a percent of GDP equaled 33%, up from 10% twenty years ago, and over 80% of Mexico's exports went to the United States. The state of the Mexican economy is important to the United States because of the close trade and investment ties between the two countries, and because of other social and political issues that could be affected by economic conditions, particularly poverty and how it relates to migration issues.

Not all changes in economic growth or trade and investment patterns in Mexico since 1994 can be attributed to NAFTA. The economy has also been affected by other economic factors such as economic growth in the United States and currency fluctuations. Also, trade-related job gains and losses since NAFTA may have accelerated trends that were ongoing prior to NAFTA and may not be totally attributable to the trade agreement. It is difficult to isolate the economic effects of NAFTA from other economic or political factors. For example, Mexico has experienced at least two major events outside of NAFTA that had economic consequences. Mexico's unilateral trade liberalization measures prior to NAFTA and the currency crisis of 1995 both affected economic growth, per capita GDP, and real wages in Mexico.

In the mid-1990s, Mexico experienced a financial crisis caused by a number of complex financial, economic, and political factors. The early 1990s in Mexico were marked by a large increase in foreign investment as investor confidence in the Mexican economy grew due to the prospect of NAFTA. However, signs that Mexico's economy was not as fundamentally strong as it appeared began to surface after the assassination of Mexican presidential candidate Luis Donaldo Colosio in March 1994.[6] The shock of the assassination resulted in a subsequent outflow of foreign exchange reserves and growing concerns about a currency devaluation. In response to these concerns, the Mexican government issued short-term dollar-indexed notes to finance the growing current account deficit.[7]

The Mexican government expected investor confidence to be restored after the August 1994 presidential election. Foreign investment flows, however, did not recover to the level of expectation. In the months following the election, the current account deficit widened as imports surged due to an overvalued peso. The government began to experience a short-term liquidity crisis.[8] By December 1994, the continued decrease in the inflows of foreign direct investment and foreign exchange reserves put pressure on the government to abandon its previous fixed exchange rate policy and adopt a floating exchange rate regime. As a result, Mexico's currency plunged by around 50% within six months, sending the country into a deep recession.[9]

In the aftermath of the 1994 devaluation, the Mexican government took several steps to restructure the economy and lessen the impact of the currency crisis among the more disadvantaged sectors of the economy. The United States and the International Monetary Fund (IMF) assisted the Mexican government by putting together an emergency financial support package of up to $50 billion. Mexico adopted tight monetary and fiscal policies to reduce inflation and absorb some of the costs of the banking sector crisis. The austerity plan also included an increase in the value-added tax, budget cuts, and increases in electricity and gasoline prices.[10]

The peso steadily depreciated through the end of the 1990s, which led to greater exports and helped the country's exporting industries. However, the peso devaluation also resulted in a decline in real income, hurting mostly the poorest segments of the population, but also the newly emerging middle class. Yet, NAFTA and the change in the Mexican economy to an export-based economy may have helped to soften the impact of the currency devaluation.

GDP Growth

Between 1960 and 1980, the Mexican economy grew at an average annual rate of over 6.5%, resulting in significant improvements in per capita GDP and living standards. Between 1980 and 1987, however, average real GDP growth dropped to less than 1% and productivity growth fell to negative numbers. The economic reforms in the latter part of the 1980s helped Mexico to recover from the 1982 debt crisis, with GDP growth averaging 3.8% between 1990 and 1994 (see Figure 1).[11] In 1995, after the financial crisis, GDP growth declined by 6.2%, but the Mexican economy managed to grow 5%-6% the following three years. Real GDP growth dropped from 6.2% in 2000 to -0.2% in 2001. Improved economic conditions in the United States after 2001 helped Mexico's economy improve as well. Real GDP growth in 2004 was 4.4%, up from 1.4% in 2003 and 0.8% in 2002. In 2006, GDP growth was 4.8% but decreased to 3.3% in 2007.[12] Real GDP growth for 2008 is forecast at 2.3%, and 1.6% for 2009.[13]

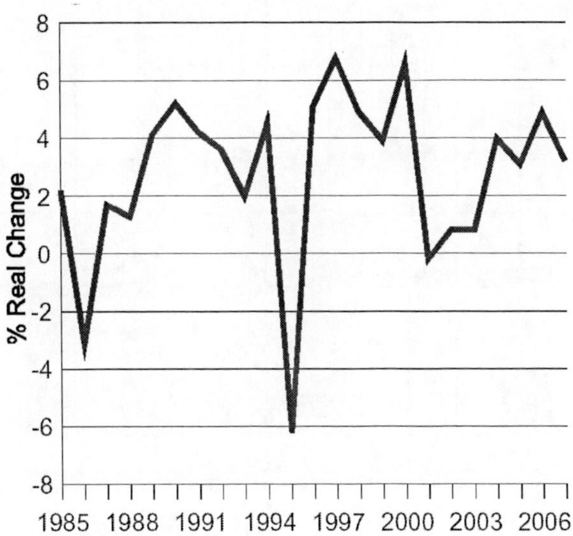

Source: Economist Intelligence Unit.

Figure 1. Real GDP Growth in Mexico

Poverty

Poverty is one of the more serious and pressing economic problems facing Mexico. President Felipe Calderon stated early in his administration that his top economic priorities were to reduce poverty and create jobs. Former President Fox also considered the problem of poverty as one of Mexico's principal challenges and stated that the highest priority of his administration was to combat poverty. According to a 2004 World Bank Study,[14] the Mexican government had made progress in its poverty reduction efforts, but poverty continues to be a basic challenge for the country's development. Poverty is often associated with social exclusion, especially of indigenous groups of people who comprise 20% of those who live in extreme poverty. The 1995 currency crisis was a major setback to Mexico's efforts in alleviating poverty levels, and though there was some improvement after the crisis, the poverty levels did not decline to their pre-crisis levels until 2002 (see Figure 2).[15]

The percentage of people living in extreme poverty as measured by the World Bank[16], fell from 24.2% of the population in 2000, to 20.3% in 2002, and 18.6% in 2005. Those living in moderate poverty fell from 53.7% of the population in 2000 to 51.7% in 2002 and 47.8% in 2005. Mexico's continuing problem of poverty is especially widespread in rural areas and remains at the Latin American average.[17] The government has made significant efforts to combat poverty, but it remains widespread and is closely linked to high levels of inequality in terms of unequal access to healthcare, education, and available work opportunities.[18]

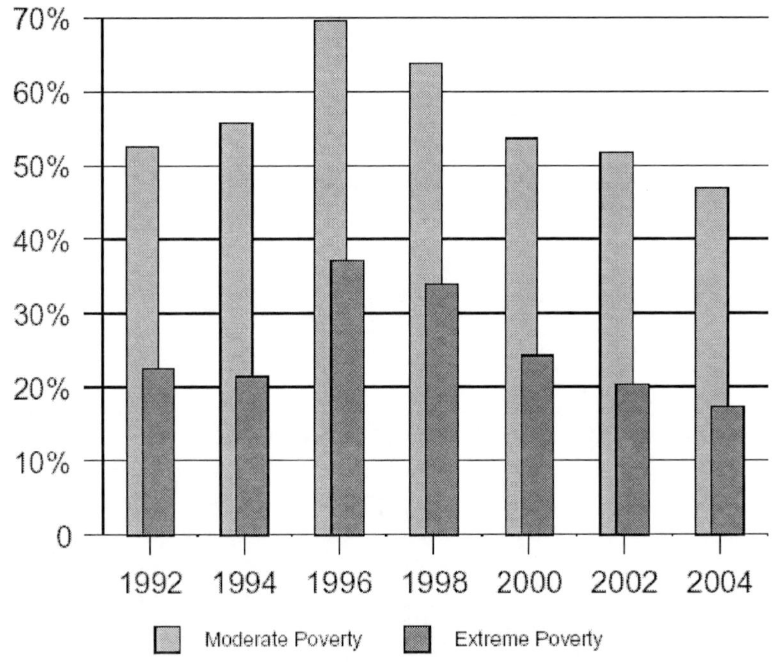

Sources: World Bank and the Woodrow Wilson International Center for Scholars, *Mexico Institute*.

Notes: Percentages of those living in moderate poverty, include those living in extreme poverty. The World Bank defines *extreme poverty* as living on less than U.S. $1 a day and *moderate poverty* as living on less than U.S. $2 a day.

Figure 2. Poverty Levels in Mexico

Mexico's main program to reduce poverty is the *Oportunidades* program. The program seeks to not only alleviate the immediate effects of poverty through cash and in-kind transfers, but also by improving nutrition and health standards among poor families and increasing educational attainment. This program provides cash transfers to families in poverty who demonstrate that they regularly attend medical appointments and can certify that children are attending school. Monthly benefits are a minimum of $15 with a cap of about $150. The majority of households receiving *Oportunidades* benefits are in Mexico's six poorest states: Chiapas, Mexico State, Puebla, Veracruz, Oaxaca, and Guerrero.[19]

EFFECTS OF NAFTA ON MEXICO

NAFTA is a free trade agreement that eliminated trade and investment barriers among NAFTA trading partners. Upon implementation, almost 70% of U.S. imports from Mexico and 50% of U.S. exports to Mexico received duty-free treatment. The remainder of duties were eliminated over a period of 15 years after the agreement was in effect. The agreement also contained provisions for market access to U.S. firms in most services sectors; protection of U.S. foreign direct investment in Mexico; and intellectual property rights protection for U.S. companies. At the time that NAFTA went into effect, a number of economic studies predicted that the trade agreement would have a positive overall effect on the Mexican economy, narrowing the U.S.-Mexico gap in prices of goods and services and the differential in real wages.

Economic Effects

While a number of studies have found that NAFTA has brought economic and social benefits to the Mexican economy as a whole, the benefits have not been evenly distributed throughout the country. Most studies after NAFTA have found that the effects on the Mexican economy tended to be modest at most.[20] While there have been periods of positive growth and negative growth in Mexico after the agreement was implemented, much of the increases in trade began in the late 1980s when the country began trade liberalization measures. Though its net economic effects may have been positive, NAFTA itself has not been enough to lower income disparities within Mexico, or between Mexico and the United States or Canada.

A 2005 World Bank study assessing some of the economic impacts from NAFTA on Mexico concluded that NAFTA helped Mexico get closer to the levels of development in the United States and Canada. The study states that NAFTA helped Mexican manufacturers to adopt to U.S. technological innovations more quickly and likely had positive impacts on the number and quality of jobs. Another finding was that since NAFTA went into effect, the overall macroeconomic volatility, or wide variations in the GDP growth rate, has declined in Mexico. Business cycles in Mexico, the United States, and Canada have had higher levels of synchronicity since NAFTA, and NAFTA has reinforced the high sensitivity of Mexican economic sectors to economic developments in the United States.[21]

Several economists have noted that it is likely that NAFTA contributed to Mexico's economic recovery directly and indirectly after the 1995 currency crisis. Mexico responded to the crisis by implementing a strong economic adjustment program but also by fully adhering to its NAFTA obligations to liberalize trade with the United States and Canada. NAFTA may have supported the resolve of the Mexican government to continue with the course of market-based economic reforms, resulting in increasing investor confidence in Mexico. The World Bank study estimates that FDI in Mexico would have been approximately 40% lower without NAFTA.[22]

One of the main arguments in favor of NAFTA at the time it was being proposed by policymakers was that the agreement would improve economic conditions in Mexico and narrow the income gap between Mexico and the United States. Studies that have addressed the issue of economic convergence[23] have noted that economic convergence in North America might not materialize under free trade as long as "fundamental differences" in initial conditions persist over time. One study argues that NAFTA is not enough to help narrow the disparities in economic conditions between Mexico and the United States and that Mexico needs to invest more in education; innovation and infrastructure; and in the quality of national institutions. The study states that income convergence between a Latin American country and the United States is limited by the wide differences in the quality of domestic institutions, in the innovation dynamics of domestic firms, and in the skills of the labor force.[24] Another study also notes that the ability of Mexico to improve economic conditions depends on its capacity to improve its national institutions, adding that Mexican institutions did not improve significantly more than those of other Latin American countries during the post-NAFTA period.[25]

Mexican Wages and Per Capita GDP

This section provides information on Mexican wages over a period of time, however any changes in Mexican wages since NAFTA implementation cannot be solely attributable to trade integration. Wages are reflective of a number of economic variables including GDP, productivity, exchange rates, and international trade. Mexican wages rose steadily from the early 1980s until the mid-1990s, when the currency crisis hit. After a drop in average real wages in 1996 of 15.5%, real wages increased steadily until 2000, when the average rate of growth was 11.8%. Since then the average rate of growth has only varied slightly (see **Table 1**).

Mexico's trade liberalization measures may have affected the ratio between skilled and non-skilled workers in Mexico. In 1988, the real average wage of skilled workers in Mexico's manufacturing industry was 2.25 times larger than that of nonskilled workers. This ratio increased until 1996, when it was about 2.9, but then remained stable until 2000.[26] The World Bank study found that NAFTA brought economic and social benefits to the Mexican economy, but that the agreement in itself was not sufficient to ensure a narrowing of the wage gap between Mexico and the United States. The study states that NAFTA had a positive effect on wages and employment in some Mexican states, but that the wage differential within the country increased as a result of trade liberalization.[27]

Table 1. Mexican Wages and Per Capita GDP: 1996-2008

	1996	1998	2000	2002	2004	2006	2008[a]
Average Real Wage Index[b] (LCU, 1995=100)	78	80	89	96	99	103	103
Average Real Wages[c] (% change from previous year)	-15.5	2.6	11.8	1.6	0.0	2.7	-0.1
Per Capita GDP ($ US)	3,527	4,328	5,819	6,334	6,512	7,820	8,910
Per Capita GDP ($ PPPs[d)])	7,649	8,543	9,551	9,769	10,550	11,820	12,920

Source: Economist Intelligence Unit

[a] Forecast.

[b] Average real wage index in local currency rebased to 1996=100.

[c] Percentage change in hourly wages in local currency adjusted for inflation over previous year.

[d] PPP refers to purchasing power parity, which reflects the purchasing power of foreign currencies in U.S. dollars.

According to a report published in the *Journal of Development Economics* that examines wage inequality in Mexico before and after NAFTA, studies on NAFTA have not always agreed on the effect of trade on wages or the reasons for the increasing wage differential between skilled and unskilled Mexican workers.[28] Some studies conclude that the reason for the rise in wages for more highly skilled workers is the technological change brought about by trade. Others link the rise in wage differentials to trade and the changes in prices of skill-intensive goods that result from trade liberalization. As prices for skill-intensive goods decline after trade liberalization, the demand for skilled workers rises and wages rise. The authors of the report conclude that the sharp increase in wage inequality in Mexico was caused by technological change. They argue that trade liberalization alone had almost no effect on the wage gap, but that the technological change that came about after NAFTA caused the wage gap to widen.[29]

U.S.-Mexico Trade

Mexico's trade with the United States has grown considerably since 1994. Mexico had a trade deficit of $1.3 billion with the United States in 1994, the year of NAFTA implementation (see Table 2). In subsequent years, the trade balance shifted to a surplus as exports to the United States increased. While imports from the United States also increased after NAFTA, the rate of growth was not as high. In 2007, Mexico had a trade surplus of $90.8 billion with the United States. U.S. imports from Mexico totaled $210.2 billion in 2007 while exports to Mexico totaled $119.4 billion. In 2007, the top U.S. imports from Mexico were crude petroleum oil, television apparatus, motor vehicles, and motor vehicle parts. The top U.S. exports to Mexico were motor vehicle parts, petroleum oil products (other than crude), motor vehicles, and insulated wire or cables.[30]

Table 2. U.S.-Mexico Trade: 1994-2007 (US $ billions)

	1994	1996	1998	2000	2002	2004	2006	2007	% Change 1994-2007
U.S. Exports	50.8	54.7	75.4	100.4	86.1	93.0	114.6	119.4	135%
U.S. Imports	49.5	74.2	93.0	134.7	134.1	155.0	197.1	210.2	325%
Trade Balance	1.3	-19.5	-17.6	-34.3	-48.0	-62.0	-82.5	-90.8	

Source: Compiled by CRS using trade data from the United States International Trade Commission.

Much of the increase in U.S.-Mexico trade could be attributable to NAFTA, but, as stated previously, exchange rates and economic conditions have also been a factor. The devaluation of the Mexican peso against the U.S. dollar in 1995 limited the purchasing power of the Mexican people and also made products from Mexico less expensive for the U.S. market. U.S. imports from Mexico increased from $49.5 billion in 1994 to $74.2 billion in 1996, while U.S. exports to Mexico also increased but at a slower rate. As economic conditions in Mexico improved in the late 1990s, trade with the United States rose steadily until 2001 when the downturn in the U.S. economy caused trade to slow down. In the years after 2001, Mexico's economy continued to follow U.S. economic trends and trade increased in the following years, though at a slower rate.

Regional Effects of NAFTA

While the overall effects of NAFTA on the Mexican economy might have been positive, the effects have been unequal across regions and sectors. Wages and employment tend to be higher in states experiencing higher levels of foreign direct investment and trade. The effects of trade liberalization have varied widely among regions, and while trade liberalization may narrow income disparities over the long run with other countries, it may indirectly lead to larger disparities in income levels within a country.

Studies have found that initial conditions in Mexico determined which Mexican states experienced stronger economic growth as a result of NAFTA.[31] States with less developed infrastructure (transportation and communications) did not receive the benefits from NAFTA as other states. Telecommunications infrastructure and human capital were especially important in determining the economic performance of individuals states. The states with more telephone service and a higher skilled labor force experienced more positive impacts. Northern and central states grew faster throughout the 1990s, modestly reducing the income differentials with those of the Mexico City area. Poorer southern states grew slower during the same time period due to low levels of education, infrastructure, and quality of local institutions, making them less prepared to gain from trade liberalization.[32]

MEXICO'S AGRICULTURAL SECTOR AND NAFTA

One of the more controversial aspects of NAFTA has been its effect on the agricultural sector in Mexico and the perception that NAFTA has caused a higher amount of worker displacement in the agricultural sector than in other sectors of the economy. While some of the changes in the agricultural sector are a direct result of NAFTA, as Mexico faced increasing import competition from the United States, many of the changes are also attributable to Mexico's unilateral agricultural reform measures. Mexico began to reform its agricultural sector in the 1980s; most domestic agricultural and trade policy reform measures included privatization and resulted in increased competition. Mexico's unilateral reform measures included eliminating state enterprises related to agriculture and removing staple price supports and subsidies.[33] With the reform of Mexico's Agrarian Law, lands that had been distributed to *ejidos* or community rural groups following the 1910 revolution gained the right to privatize. Another major reform was the abolishment of *CONASUPO*, Mexico's primary agency for government intervention in agriculture. The agency bought staples from farmers at guaranteed prices and processed the products or sold them at low prices to processors and consumers. By 1999, the company was abolished.[34] Many of Mexico's domestic reforms in agriculture coincided with NAFTA negotiations, beginning in 1991, and continued beyond the implementation of NAFTA in 1994. The unilateral reforms in the agricultural sector make it difficult to separate those effects from the effects of NAFTA.

Mexican Productivity, Exports and Prices

With Mexico's entry into NAFTA, the expectation was that relative prices for certain Mexican crops would decrease while prices for other crops would likely remain the same. This was based on the economic expectation that, by removing Mexico's price and trade interventions in basic crops such as grains and oilseeds, prices for the same goods in Mexico and the United States would equalize. Prices for crops that were exported such as fruits and vegetables were expected to stay the same because these had not been subject to major government intervention before or since NAFTA. NAFTA and Mexico's internal reforms were expected to lead to the "law of one price" for all agricultural goods produced in North America. This meant that prices for basic crops such as grains and oilseeds produced in Mexico, which previously had fixed prices by the government, would decline as these goods faced competition from U.S. goods. NAFTA and agriculture reform measures were also expected to increase efficiency in Mexico's agricultural production as farmers adjusted to competition from lower cost imports. Production in agricultural sectors that had prior price and trade interventions was expected to decrease as lower-priced imports from the United States entered the market, while production in export-oriented sectors, mainly fruits and vegetables, was expected to increase. As a result of these shifts, employment was expected to increase in some areas, but, according to one study, the increase was not expected to be large enough to absorb all the workers who would be displaced by reduced production in other sectors.[35]

After NAFTA, Mexican prices of basic crops such as maize dropped and, subsequently, Mexican imports of those crops increased. Mexican agricultural production, however, did not decrease after NAFTA. The Mexican government's unilateral liberalization of corn and NAFTA were both factors in declining prices of corn in Mexico. In 1993, the price of corn in Mexico was $4.84 per bushel; the price fell to $3.65 per bushel in 1997 and has remained at about the same level ever since.[36] Mexican corn production, however, increased despite the decline in prices (see Figure 3). Total production of maize increased from an annual average of 12.5 million metric tons during the 1983-1990 period to an annual average of 17.7 million metric tons, representing an increase of 41%, during the post-NAFTA period of 1994-2001.[37] Mexican corn production yields were a fraction of U.S. corn production yields in 2003, but in spite of the low yields, Mexican corn production increased after NAFTA. Between 1990 and 2003, Mexican corn production increased 44%, a faster rate of growth than U.S. corn production which increased by 27% during the same time period.[38]

Most of the effects from NAFTA likely took place within the first ten years of implementation. From 1993 to 2003, Mexican exports to the United States in agricultural products increased from $2.7 billion in 1993 to $6.3 billion in 2003, while Mexican exports to Canada increased from $136 million to $409 million over the same time period. Mexican imports from the United States also increased during this time period, from $3.6 billion in 1993 to $7.9 billion in 2003. Mexican exports to the United States sharply increased in the following categories: sugar and related products (595%), beverages excluding fruit juices (584%), and grains and feeds (328%). U.S. foreign direct investment in the Mexican food processing industry more than doubled from $2.3 billion in 1993 to $5.7 billion in 2000.[39]

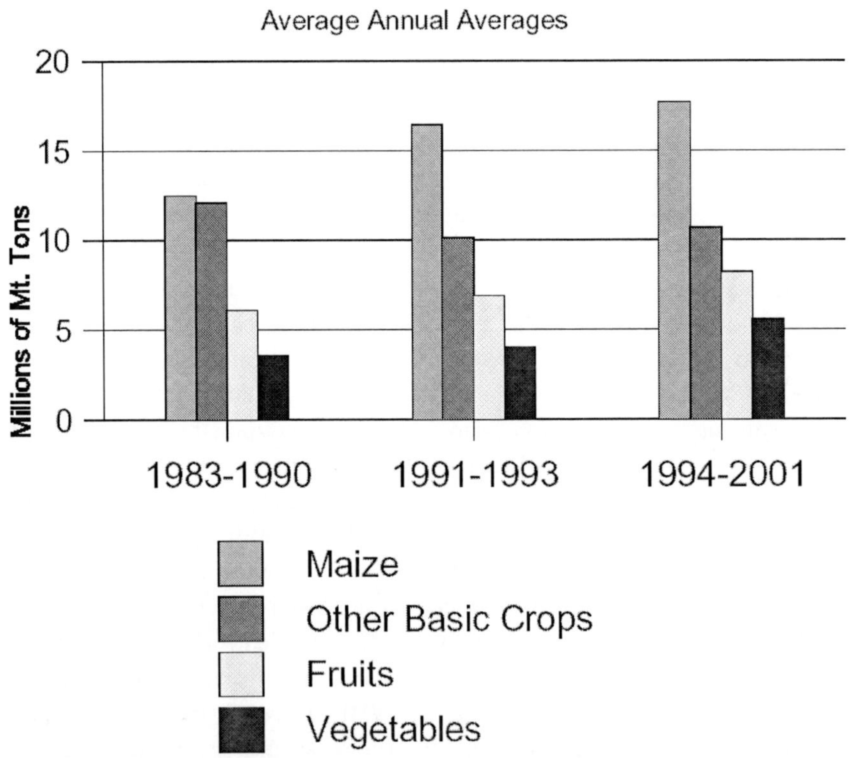

Source: Yunez Naude and Taylor, 2006.

Figure 3. Mexican Agricultural Production

Employment

Changes in agricultural employment in Mexico since NAFTA implementation cannot be attributed entirely to trade liberalization, not only because of Mexico's unilateral reform measures which coincided with NAFTA, but also because these changes may result from the industrialization process. Some economists argue that as countries become more industrialized, agriculture plays a smaller role in the economy and employs a smaller share of the workforce. One study covering 76 countries shows that a 1% increase in per capita GDP is associated with a reduction in agriculture value-added as a share of GDP by about 0.6 percentage points. In South Korea, for example, the agricultural share of GDP declined from about 25% in 1970 to 5% in 2000 due to rapid industrialization.[40]

A report by the Institute for International Economics (IIE) on the achievements and challenges of NAFTA discusses the effect of NAFTA on the agricultural sector. The report uses international comparisons that suggest that the Mexican agricultural labor force as a proportion of total labor was very high at the time of NAFTA and that many farmers were likely to lose their jobs as the country became more efficient in agricultural production. The study cites an estimate that, once all Mexican tariffs were eliminated, total farm employment in Mexico would decline by an estimated 800,000 workers.[41] Agricultural production in Mexico has been increasingly centered on large-scale farms, factory-type livestock lots, and capital-intensive food processing, which puts pressure on small-scale farms and household farmers in Mexico. Another study states that the number of Mexicans employed in rural agriculture declined from 8.1 million to 6.8 million and that the value added[42] by Mexican agriculture dropped from about $32 billion in 1993 to about $25 billion in 2003.[43]

Rural-Urban Migration

Several studies found that the composition of Mexico's agricultural supply did not change significantly after NAFTA, although there were shifts in production as the agricultural sector adjusted to trade liberalization. One study found that some commercial farmers shifted production from staple crops to crops for export purposes and that yields of basic crops increased after NAFTA, but only for those crops grown under irrigated conditions.[44] The study states that Mexico's productivity of irrigated lands increased after NAFTA, but non-export, non-irrigated agriculture did not increase. The study also cited a disparity in agricultural productivity between the northern and southern states due to the poor transportation and irrigation networks in the central and southern states of Mexico, making transportation costs very expensive. Another reason is access to credit. Those with small farms in the rural areas have difficulties finding access to credit. Without government guarantees, Mexican commercial banks often hesitate to provide loans because of the historically high default rate on agricultural loans. To help address this problem, the Mexican government created *Financiera Rural* in 2002, which helps provide access to microcredits for farmers to buy machinery, equipment, and technology.[45]

The effect of NAFTA on rural-urban migration within Mexico or on migration from Mexico to the United States is difficult to quantify because of the various factors affecting migration. Mexican migration after NAFTA was affected by a combination of higher efficiency in Mexican agricultural productivity, sectoral adjustments to trade as some sectors experienced higher growth than others, urban growth in Mexico, and demands for unskilled labor in the United States. A study by the Carnegie Endowment for International Peace discusses the experience of Mexico since the enactment of NAFTA. The study's analysis focuses on people, the communities they live in, and the choices they make in response to their social and economic environment. The study states that NAFTA accelerated the transition of Mexico to a liberalized economy but did not create the necessary conditions for the public and private sectors to respond to the economic, social, and environmental effects of increased trade with its NAFTA partners. One of the study's conclusion is that NAFTA's agricultural policies did not benefit subsistence farmers, while providing larger commercial farmers with substantial support.[46]

On the issue of Mexico's demographic patterns, one study found that NAFTA has had a minor role in Mexico's rural-urban migration. The study argues that the observed trend of migration from rural areas of Mexico to urban centers is directly the result of agricultural liberalization. However, the study also notes that these migration patterns have been in place since 1960.[47] Therefore, it is not clear how much of a role NAFTA has had in Mexico's rural-urban migration. While some observers believe that the trend of migration from rural areas of Mexico to urban centers is directly a result of NAFTA, many economists argue that rural-urban migration trends are common in the industrialization process of most countries. For this reason, some argue that the high concentration of poverty in rural areas makes it very important for Mexican policymakers to understand the nature of Mexico's farming structure when proposing development policies.[48]

Mexican Programs for Farmers

Anticipating the possible effects of NAFTA on farmers, the Mexican government established the Program of Direct Support for the Countryside, *Programa de Apoyos Directos Para el Campo (*PROCAMPO), in 1993. PROCAMPO provided income support to farmers over a 15-year transitional period through hectare-based direct payments to producers. However, budget austerity caused by Mexico's 1995 peso crisis resulted in budget cuts for the program. Another Mexican program, *Alianza para el Campo,* or Alianza, was created in 1995 to improve agricultural productivity with modern equipment and technology. A third program, *Produce Capitaliza*, provides infrastructure and extension-type assistance and support to livestock producers for upgrading pastures. While these three programs have provided support for Mexican farmers, there continues to be a huge disparity in subsidy levels between the United States and Mexico.[49] One study suggested that if the United States continued to subsidize corn production in the United States, Mexico should be permitted to impose some form of safeguard measures to protect farmers.[50]

VIEWS OF NAFTA IN MEXICO

Views of NAFTA within Mexico are mixed. Media reports tend to highlight the anti-NAFTA sentiment in the Mexican agricultural sector, but according to an extensive nonpartisan opinion survey conducted by two independent groups in Mexico, the majority of the Mexican population views NAFTA favorably. A public opinion survey conducted in 2006 showed that the majority of the Mexican population favors trade liberalization with the United States and Canada. The survey, conducted by the *Centro de Investigación y Docencia Económicas* (CIDE) and the *Consejo Mexicano de Asuntos* Internacionales (Mexican Council on Foreign Relations, COMEXI)[51], also showed that Mexicans have a very positive view of globalization, though there is some division on whether NAFTA should be renegotiated and whether Mexico should continue forming new trade agreements with other countries.[52]

The survey examined the views of the general public and another group of individuals, labeled as "leaders" in the study, which comprises 259 representatives from five sectors (government, politics, business, media and academic, and non-government organizations) with an interest in international affairs or professional ties with other countries. Both groups ranked export promotion among Mexico's two most important foreign-policy objectives and hold a largely favorable opinion of international trade. The poll showed that both the general public and the "leaders" considered international trade to be beneficial for the country's economy, job creation, Mexican businesses, poverty reduction, and their own living conditions. Ninety-six percent of the "leaders" and 79% of the general public favored increasing international trade (see Figure 4).[53]

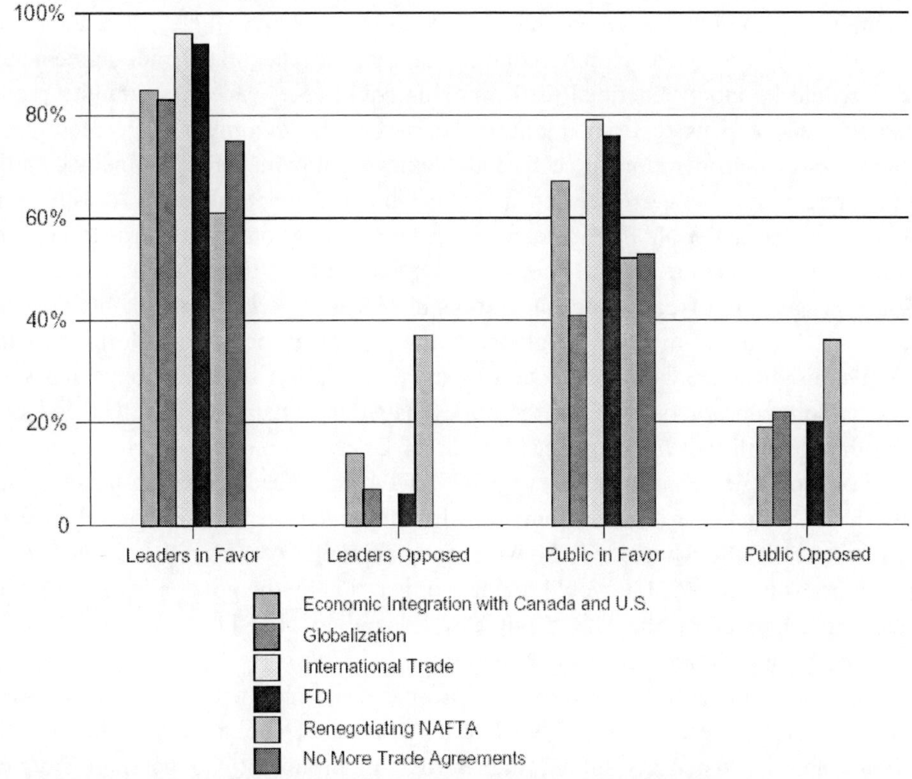

Source: *Mexico and the World 2006 - Leaders, public opinion and foreign policy in Mexico, the United States, and Asia: A Comparative Study*, CIDE and COMEXI, 2006.

Figure 4. Mexican Public Opinion of Trade Liberalization

The most vocal opponents of NAFTA in Mexico have criticized the agreement because of its negative effect on Mexico's agricultural sector. Labor and farmers' coalitions joined forces in early 2008 to protest the final tariff eliminations under NAFTA on corn. Tens of thousands marched on the streets of Mexico City in February 2008 to protest the agreement. Many of these were farmers or peasants with farm plots of less than 12 acres and criticized the Mexican government for not doing enough to help them adjust to increased competition from the United States. They stated that most of the government aid to help farmers has gone to large agricultural businesses in northern states. Groups representing the small farmers argue that, in the long run, small farmers in Mexico will not be able to compete with the "Americans' heavily subsidized and mechanized farms."[54]

DISCUSSION

Mexico's economic relationship with the United States is of mutual importance to both Mexico and the United States. As NAFTA approaches its fifteenth anniversary, policymakers in the United States and Mexico have mentioned the possibility of revisiting NAFTA. Economic studies on NAFTA's effects on Mexico and the Mexican views of NAFTA could provide a valuable perspective when evaluating the possibility of reopening parts of the agreement or alternative policy options. Some observers have suggested that one of the lessons from NAFTA for developing countries is that they negotiate trade agreements in a way that would be more beneficial to them. This could take place by including provisions such as financial assistance from trading partners or new minimum wage requirements.[55] Possible areas of consideration for U.S. and Mexican policymakers may include furthering economic integration between Mexico and the United States; enhancing or strengthening institutions created under NAFTA side agreements; or taking other measures to help resolve the issues related to income disparity between Mexico and the United States.

Some proponents of economic integration in North America have maintained that the emergence of China and India in the global marketplace may be putting North America at a competitive disadvantage with other countries and that NAFTA should go beyond a free trade agreement. Some observers have written policy papers proposing that the U.S. government consider the possibility of forming a customs union or common market.[56] However, critics of this level of economic integration believe that NAFTA has already gone too far and that it has harmed the U.S. and Mexican economies and undermined democratic control of domestic policymaking.[57] If the United States were to potentially consider the further economic integration in North America, it would require cooperation by the governments of Mexico and Canada, and approval by the U.S. Congress. Expanding NAFTA to a customs union or common market would likely be very controversial.

A possible option to address Mexico's income disparities with the United States is to consider expanding the mandate of the North American Development Bank (NADBank). NADBank and its sister institution, the Border Environment Cooperation Commission (BECC), were created under a bilateral side agreement to NAFTA called the Border Environmental Cooperation Agreement (BECA). The objective of NADBank and BECC is to help U.S.-Mexico border communities plan and finance environmental infrastructure projects. A number of Members of the U.S. Congress and elected officials from Mexico have discussed the possibility of expanding the mission of the NADBank to go beyond environmental and border issues. Some policymakers have proposed expanding NADBank projects to include transportation and other types of infrastructure projects. Others have suggested expanding eligible projects to the entire region of Mexico. An option that was mentioned at the June 2008 U.S.-Mexico Inter-parliamentary Group meeting in Mexico is for policymakers in the United States and Mexico is to consider creating an infrastructure fund that would be managed by NADBank to provide investment in infrastructure, communications, or education.

Another possible option for U.S. policymakers is to consider increased cooperation with Mexico in its efforts to address the continuing problem of poverty and the difficulties being faced by farmers in the southern Mexican states. The Mexican government has taken a number of measures to lessen the impact of NAFTA on farmers and to address on-going poverty issues, but the results of these programs has been mixed. Although the programs are not NAFTA-related, they do benefit segments of the population and regions of Mexico that have benefitted little from trade liberalization.

APPENDIX. MAP OF MEXICO

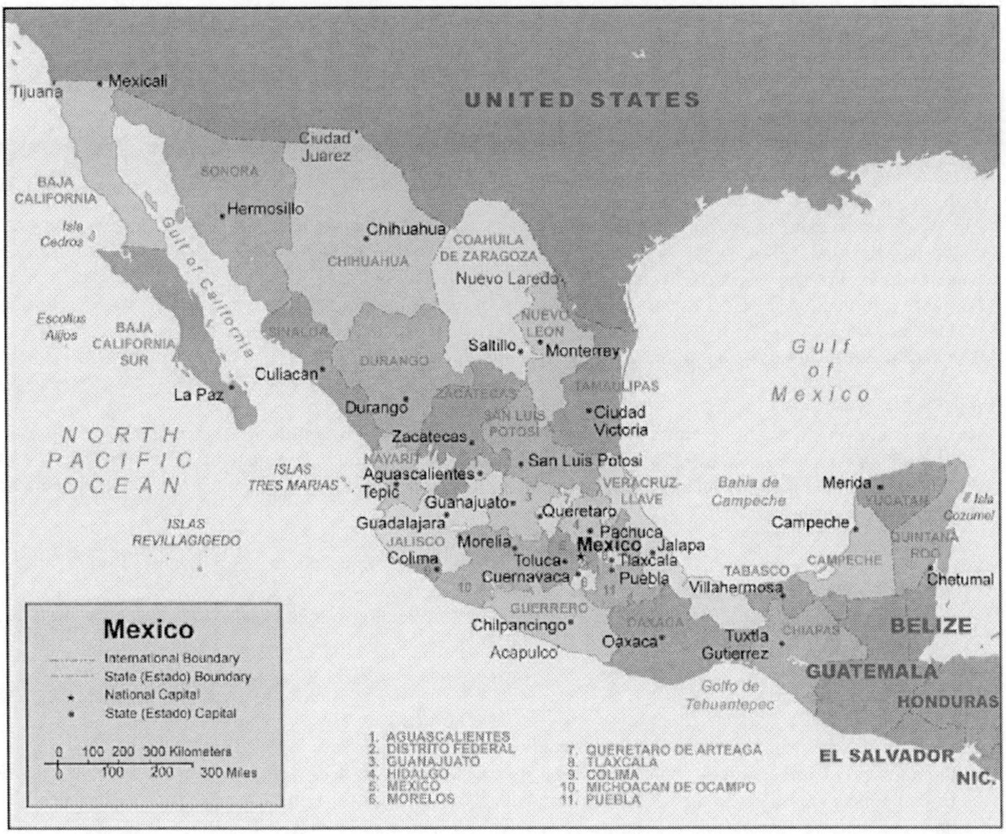

Figure 5. Map of Mexico

End Notes

[1] This section draws upon information from the following sources: CRS Report 93-668 E, *Mexico's Changing Policy Toward Foreign investment: NAFTA Implications,* by M. Angeles Villarreal, July 19, 1993. United Nations, Economic Development Unit, *Mexico: Economic Growth, Exports, and Industrial Performance after NAFTA,* by Juan Carlos Moreno-Brid, Juan Carlos Rivas Valdivia, and Jesús Santamaria, December 2005.

[2] High inflation causes interest rates and prices to go up and real wages to fall, thus decreasing consumption and investments due to the uncertainty in the market flow which contributes to a decline in the overall standard of living.

[3] Gary Hufbauer and Jeffrey Schott, *North American Free Trade: Issues and Recommendations,* Institute for International Economics, 1992.

[4] Ibid.

[5] For more information, see CRS Report RL32934, *U.S.-Mexico Economic Implications: Trends, Issues, and Implications,* by M. Angeles Villarreal.

[6] U.S. General Accounting Office, *Mexico's Financial Crisis: Origins, Awareness, Assistance, and Initial Efforts to Recover,* GAO Report GGD-96-56, February 1996, p. 9.

[7] Ibid., p. 10.

[8] GAO Report GGD-96-56, pp. 5-6.

[9] Economist Intelligence Unit (EIU), "Mexico Finance: The Peso Crisis, Ten Years On," January 3, 2005.

[10] Joachim Zietz, "Why Did the Peso Collapse? Implications for American Trade," *Global Commerce*, by , Volume 1, No. 1, Summer 1995.

[11] International Monetary Fund (IMF) Working Paper, *GDP Growth, Potential Output, and Output Gaps in Mexico,* by Ebrima Faal, May 2005.

[12] EIU, *Country Reports: Mexico*, various years.

[13] EIU, *Country Outlook,* September 2008.

[14] The World Bank Group, *Mexico Makes Progress and Faces Challenges in Poverty Reduction Efforts,* June 2004.

[15] The World Bank Group, *Poverty in Mexico - Fact Sheet,* 2008. Woodrow Wilson International Center for Scholars, *More than Neighbors: An Overview of Mexico and U.S.-Mexico Relations,* by Andrew Selee, undated.

[16] The World Bank defines *extreme poverty* as living on less than U.S. $1(purchasing power parity) a day and *moderate poverty* as living on less than U.S. $2 (purchasing power parity) a day.

[17] Ibid.

[18] The World Bank, *Poverty in Mexico: An Assessment of Conditions, Trends and Government Strategy,* Report No. 28612-ME, June 2004.

[19] Santiago Levy, *Progress Against Poverty,* Brookings Institution, 2006.

[20] For more information, see CRS Report RS21737, *NAFTA at Ten: Lessons from Recent Studies,* by J.F. Hornbeck, June 8, 2005.

[21] The World Bank, *Lessons from NAFTA for Latin America and the Caribbean,* by Daniel Lederman, William F. Maloney, and Luis Servén, 2005. (Hereinafter *Lessons from NAFTA,* 2005)

[22] Ibid.

[23] Economic convergence can be broadly defined as a narrowing of the disparities in the economic levels and the manufacturing performances of particular countries or their regions. The goal of the theory of economic convergence is to research and analyze the factors influencing the rates of economic growth and real per capita income in countries.

[24] *Lessons from NAFTA*, 2005.

[25] *Economia*, "NAFTA and Convergence in North America: High Expectations, Big Events, Little Time," by William Easterly, Norbert Fiess, and Daniel Lederman, Fall 2003.

[26] Esquivel, Gerardo, and José Antonio Rodríguez-López, "Technology, trade, and wage inequality in Mexico before and after NAFTA," *Journal of Development Economics,* 2003.

[27] *Lessons from NAFTA*, 2005.

[28] Esquivel and Rodríguez-López, p. 553.

[29] Ibid., pp. 551-552.

[30] Based on trade data from the United States International Trade Commission.

[31] William Easterly, Norbert Fiess, and Daniel Lederman, *Economia,* "NAFTA and Convergence in North America: High Expectations, Big Events, Little Time," Fall 2003. The World Bank, *Lessons from NAFTA for Latin America and the Caribbean,* by Daniel Lederman, William F. Maloney, and Luis Servén, 2005. Gerardo Esquivel and Miguel Messmacher, *Economic Integration and Sub-National Development: The Mexican Experience with NAFTA,* February 2003.

[32] Easterly, Fiess, and Lederman, "NAFTA and Convergence in North America: High Expectations, Big Events, Little Time," Fall 2003.

[33] Mexico's agricultural reform measures of the 1990s removed government subsidies and price controls in the agricultural sector that resulted in rising prices for tortillas. Tortillas are the basic staple for the Mexican diet and a necessity of the poor. For this reason, higher prices had a greater effect on the poor than on middle- and higher-income Mexicans.

[34] Yuñez Naude, Antonio, and J. Edward Taylor, *The Effects of NAFTA and Domestic Reforms in the Agriculture of Mexico: Predictions and Facts, Région et Développement No. 23-2006,* 2006, p. 163. (Hereinafter Yuñez Naude and Taylor)

[35] Yuñez Naude and Taylor, p. 165.

[36] Hufbauer, Gary Clyde, and Jeffrey J. Schott, *NAFTA Revisited: Achievements and Challenges,* pp. 333-334. (Hereinafter Hufbauer and Schott)

[37] Yuñez and Naude, p. 179.

[38] Hufbauer and Schott, p. 331-332.

[39] Hufbauer and Schott, p. 288.

[40] Ibid, p. 286.

[41] Hufbauer and Schott cite the study by Antonio Yuñez-Naude in the World Bank, *Lessons from NAFTA: The Case of Mexico's Agricultural Sector,* Washington, DC, 2002.

[42] Value added refers to the additional value created at a particular stage of production. The number is often used by economists to avoid double-counting the units of production in the final value of the product.

[43] Hufbauer and Schott, p. 289.

[44] Yuñez and Naude, p. 166.

[45] See [http://www.financierarural.gob.mx].

[46] Audley, John J., Demetrios G. Papademetriou, Sandra Polaski, Scott Vaughan, Carnegie Endowment for International Peace, *NAFTA's Promise and Reality: Lessons from Mexico for the Hemisphere,* 2004.

[47] Ibid.

[48] Yuñez and Naude, p. 176.

[49] Hufbauer and Schott, pp. 295-296.

[50] Ibid, pp. 343-344.

[51] The *Centro de Investigación y Docencia Económicas* (CIDE) is an academic non-government organization dedicated to research and education in Mexico. The *Consejo Mexicano de Asuntos Internacionales* (Mexican Council on Foreign Relations, COMEXI) is an independent, non-government organization in Mexico financed by membership dues and corporate support; members have a broad spectrum of professional experience from all over the world.

[52] *Mexico and the World 2006 - Leaders, public opinion and foreign policy in Mexico, the United States, and Asia: A Comparative Study,* CIDE and COMEXI, 2006.

[53] Ibid, pp. 20-21.

[54] *International Herald Tribune,* "Mexican Farmers Protest End of Corn-Import Taxes," by James C. McKinley Jr., February 1, 2008.

[55] Audley, John J., Demetrios G. Papademetriou, Sandra Polaski, Scott Vaughan, Carnegie Endowment for International Peace, *NAFTA's Promise and Reality: Lessons from Mexico for the Hemisphere,* 2004.

[56] U.S. Council of the Mexico-U.S. Business Committee, Council of the Americas, *ACompact for North American Competitiveness,* April 2005; Grubel, Herbert G., The Fraser Institute, *The Case for the Amero: The Economics and Politics of a North American Monetary Union,* September 1999.

[57] Public Citizen, Global Trade Watch, *North American Free Trade Agreement,* see [http://www.citizen.org].

In: Mexico: Background and Issues
Editor: Richard C. Bradley
ISBN: 978-1-61728-498-4

Chapter 7

COUNTRY PROFILE: MEXICO*

Library of Congress-Federal Research Division

Formal Name: United Mexican States (Estados Unidos Mexicanos).

Short Form: México.

Term for Citizen(s): Mexican(s).

Capital: Mexico City (Ciudad de México), located in the Federal District (Distrito Federal) with a population estimated at 8.8 million in 2008.

Major Cities: The Greater Mexico City metropolitan area encompasses Mexico City and several adjacent suburbs, including the populous cities of Ecatepec de Morelos (1.8 million residents in 2005) and Netzahualcóyotl (1.2 million). The total population of the Greater Mexico City metropolitan area is estimated at about 16 million. Other major cities include Guadalajara (1.6 million), Puebla (1.3 million), Ciudad Juárez (1.2 million), Tijuana (1.1 million), and Monterrey (1.1 million).

Independence: September 16, 1810 (from Spain).

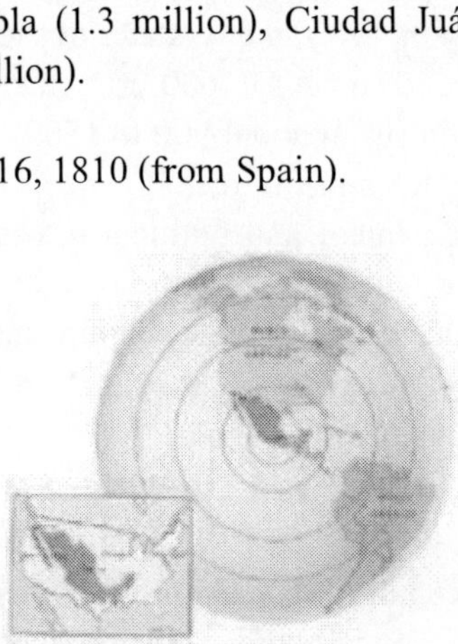

* This is an edited, reformatted and augmented version of a Library of Congress publication dated July 2008.

Public Holidays: New Year's Day (January 1); Constitution Day (February 5); Birthday of Benito Juárez (March 21); International Labor Day (May 1); Independence Day (September 16); Discovery of America (October 12); Anniversary of the Revolution (November 20); Christmas (December 25); and New Year's Eve (December 31).

Flag: Three equal vertical bands of green (hoist side), white, and red; the coat of arms (an eagle perched on a cactus with a snake in its beak) is centered in the white band.

Historical Background

Early Settlement and Pre-Columbian Civilizations

Nomadic paleo-Indian societies are widely believed to have migrated from North America into Mexico as early as 20,000 B.C. Permanent settlements based on intensive farming of native plants such as corn, squash, and beans were established by 1,500 B.C. Between 200 B.C. and A.D. 900, several advanced indigenous societies emerged. During this "Classic Period," urban centers were built at Teotihuacán (in central Mexico), Monte Albán (in the territory now making up the state of Oaxaca), and in the Mayan complexes (in the modern-day states of Chiapas, Tabasco, Campeche, Yucatán, and Quintana Roo, as well as at sites in the modern-day countries of Honduras, Guatemala, and Belize). These advanced societies developed written languages, displayed high levels of occupational specialization and social stratification, and produced elaborate art, architecture, and public works. After the unexplained collapse of the Teotihuacán society around A.D. 650, the early civilizations of central Mexico were eclipsed by the Mayan city-states of the Yucatan Peninsula. The lowland Mayan communities flourished from A.D. 600 to A.D. 900, when they, too, abruptly declined. The Post-Classic period (from about 900 to 1500) was characterized by widespread migration throughout Mesoamerica and the reemergence of the central valley of Mexico as the site of large-scale urban settlement and political power. By the 1300s, the Aztecs had established themselves on the site of present-day Mexico City. The militaristic and bureaucratic Aztec state ruled a far-flung tributary empire spanning much of Central Mexico.

Spanish Conquest, Colonization, and Christianization

During the early sixteenth century, Spanish military adventurers based in Cuba organized expeditions to the North American mainland. The first major military expedition to Mexico, led by Hernán Cortés, landed near present-day Veracruz in 1519 and advanced inland toward the Aztec capital of Tenochtitlán hoping to conquer central Mexico. By 1521 Spanish forces under Cortés, reinforced by rebellious Indian tribes, had overthrown the Aztec empire and executed the last Aztec king, Cuauhtémoc. The Spanish subsequently grafted their administrative and religious institutions onto the remnants of the Aztec empire. During the early years of colonial rule, the conquistadors and their descendants vied for royal land titles (*encomiendas*) and Indian labor allotments (*repartimientos*). The early colonial economic system was based largely on the ability of the *encomienda* holders (*encomenderos*) to divert Indian labor from agriculture to the mining of precious metals for export to Spain. The *encomienda* became the basis for a semi-autonomous feudal society that was only loosely accountable to the central authorities in Madrid.

New Spain and the Mercantile Economy

During the sixteenth and seventeenth centuries, Mexico experienced far-reaching demographic, cultural, and political change. New Spanish-style cities and towns were founded throughout central Mexico, serving as commercial, administrative, and religious centers that attracted an increasingly Hispanicized and Christianized mestizo population from the countryside. Mexico City, built on the ruins of Tenochtitlán, became the capital of Spain's North American empire. Colonial society was stratified by race and wealth into three main groups: whites (European- and American-born), *castas* (mestizos), and native peoples; each had specific rights or privileges (*fueros*) and obligations in colonial society. New Spain was ruled by a viceroy appointed by the Spanish crown but in practice enjoyed a large degree of autonomy from Madrid.

Throughout the colonial period, Mexico's economic relationship with Spain was based on the philosophy of mercantilism. Mexico was required to supply raw materials to Spain, which would then produce finished goods to be sold at a profit to the colonies. Trade duties that placed stringent restrictions on the colonial economies protected manufacturers and merchants in Spain from outside competition in the colonies. In the mid-eighteenth century, the third Bourbon king of Spain, Charles III, reorganized the political structure of Spain's overseas empire in an effort to bolster central authority, reinvigorate the mercantile economy, and increase tax revenues. New Spain was divided into 12 military departments (*intendencias*) under a single commandant general in Mexico City who was independent of the viceroy and reported directly to the king.

War of Independence

The spread of late eighteenth-century Enlightenment philosophy, together with the egalitarian example of the American and French revolutions, motivated Mexican-born whites (criollos) to seek greater autonomy and social status within the colonial system. Discrimination against criollos in the granting of high offices had long been a source of contention between Spain and Mexico City. In 1808 the invasion of the Iberian Peninsula by Napoleon Bonaparte and the forced abdication of the Spanish king, Charles IV, disrupted Spain's faltering authority over Mexico. Rejecting the puppet regime installed by France, the incumbent viceroy allied himself with the criollos and declared an independent junta ostensibly loyal to Charles IV. Allies of the Napoleonic regime responded by staging a coup and installing a new viceroy, an action that set the stage for war between criollos and Spanish loyalists.

On September 16, 1810, Miguel Hidalgo y Costilla, a criollo parish priest, issued the Grito de Dolores (Cry of Dolores), a call to arms against Spanish rule that mobilized the Indian and mestizo populations and launched the Mexican war of independence. After a brief siege of Mexico City by insurgents in 1814, Spanish forces waged a successful counteroffensive that had nearly annihilated the rebels by 1820. However, the tide turned in favor of the criollos in February 1821, when a loyalist officer, Augustín de Iturbide, spurned the newly established constitutional monarchy in Spain and defected with his army to the rebels. Under the conservative Plan of Iguala, the rebel army agreed to respect the rights of Spanish-born whites (*peninsulares*) and to preserve the traditional privileges (*fueros*) and land titles of the Roman Catholic Church. The Spanish, now outmaneuvered politically as well as militarily, lost the will to continue the war and recognized Mexican independence in September 1821.

Empire and Early Republic

Upon the withdrawal of Spain, Iturbide declared himself emperor of Mexico and Central America. Within months, however, his imperial regime was bankrupt and had lost the support of the criollo elite. In February 1823, Iturbide was overthrown by republican forces led by General Antonio López de Santa Anna. The Mexican empire was dissolved when the United Provinces of Central America declared their independence in July 1823.

Clashes between the conservative and liberal parties dominated politics during the early republic. Conservatives, who advocated a centralized republic governed from Mexico City and the maintenance of clerical and military *fueros*, had the support of the Roman Catholic Church and much of the army. Liberals, on the other hand, advocated federalism, secularism, and the elimination of *fueros*. Under the federal republic in effect from 1824 to 1836, Mexico was ruled by a series of weak and perennially bankrupt liberal governments. General Santa Anna and his allies fashioned a centralized republic that held power from 1836 to 1855. Although nominally a liberal, Santa Anna was primarily a nationalist who dominated Mexico's politics for two decades. Santa Anna's efforts to assert Mexican government authority over Anglo-American settlements in Texas spurred that region's secession from Mexico in 1835. Excesses committed by a punitive Mexican expedition against Texan garrisons at the Alamo and Goliad provoked strong anti-Mexican sentiment in the United States and galvanized U.S. public support for Texan independence. In April 1836, Texan forces defeated and captured Santa Anna at San Jacinto. During a brief captivity, the Mexican general signed a treaty recognizing Texan independence from Mexico.

Mexican-American War, Civil War, and French Intervention

A dispute with the United States over the boundaries of Texas led to war between the United States and Mexico in April 1846. Two U.S. Army columns advancing southward from

Texas quickly captured northern Mexico, California, and New Mexico, repelling Santa Anna's forces at Buena Vista. An amphibious expeditionary force led by General Winfield Scott captured the Gulf Coast city of Veracruz after a brief siege and naval blockade. Scott's forces subdued Mexico City in September 1847, following a series of pitched battles along the route inland to the Mexican capital and its surrounding bastions. In the ensuing Treaty of Guadalupe Hidalgo, U.S. withdrawal was contingent on Mexico's ceding of the territories of New Mexico and Upper California (the present-day states of California, Nevada, Utah, and parts of Arizona, New Mexico, Colorado, and Wyoming) and its acceptance of the incorporation of Texas into the United States.

In 1855 Santa Anna was ousted and forced into exile by a revolt of liberal army officers. A liberal government under President Ignacio Comonfort oversaw a constitutional convention that drafted the progressive constitution of 1857. The new constitution contained a bill of rights that included habeas corpus protection and religious freedom and mandated the secularization of education and the confiscation of Catholic Church lands. It was strongly opposed by conservatives and church officials who objected to its anticlerical provisions. Seeking to avoid armed conflict, President Comonfort delayed its promulgation and instead decreed his own moderate reform agenda known as the Three Laws. However, in January 1858, after unsuccessful efforts by Comonfort to craft a political compromise, the factions took up arms, and the government was forced from office. A three-year civil war between conservative and liberal armies, known as the War of the Reform, engulfed the country. After initial setbacks, the liberals, led by the prominent Zapotec Indian politician and former vice president Benito Juárez, gained the upper hand. In January 1861, the liberals regained control of Mexico City and elected Juárez president.

In January 1862, the navies of Spain, Britain, and France jointly occupied the Mexican Gulf coast in an attempt to compel the repayment of public debts. Britain and Spain quickly withdrew, but the French remained and, in May 1863, occupied Mexico City. Drawing on the support of the Mexican conservatives, Napoleon III installed Austrian prince Ferdinand Maximilian von Habsburg as Mexican Emperor Maximilian I. By February 1867, a growing liberal insurgency under Juárez and the threat of war with Prussia had compelled France's withdrawal from Mexico. Maximilian was captured and executed by Juárez's forces shortly thereafter. Juárez was restored to the presidency and remained in office until his death in 1872.

Porfirio Díaz Era

From 1876 until 1910, governments controlled by the liberal caudillo Porfirio Díaz pursued economic modernization while maintaining authoritarian political control. In contrast to his liberal predecessors, Díaz established cordial relations with the Catholic Church, an institution he considered central to Mexican national identity. The Díaz years, known as the "Porfiriato" saw heavy state investment in urban public works, railroads, and ports—all of which contributed to sustained, export-led economic growth. The Porfiriato governments encouraged foreign investment in export agriculture and the concentration of arable land in the form of haciendas. Although the urban middle class experienced substantial improvements in quality of life, Mexico's peasant majority found its livelihood threatened by the loss of communal lands to the haciendas. In response to growing unrest in the countryside, Díaz created the Rural Guard, a paramilitary force that became notorious for its repressive tactics.

Mexican Revolution and Aftermath

By the turn of the century, opposition to Díaz had spread among dissident liberals who sought a return to the principles of the constitution of 1857. Following Díaz's fraudulent re-election in 1910, several isolated rural revolts coalesced into a nationwide insurrection. Unable to regain control of several rebellious state capitals, Díaz resigned the presidency in May 1911 and fled to France. A provisional government under the liberal reformer Francisco I. Madero was installed but failed to maintain the support of radical peasants led by Emiliano Zapata, who was conducting a rural insurgency in southern Mexico. Amid general unrest, a counterrevolutionary government under Victoriano Huerta assumed power in February 1913. Huerta's authority was undermined when U.S. Marines occupied Veracruz in response to a minor incident. Following Huerta's resignation in July 1914, fighting continued among rival bands loosely allied with Venustiano Carranza and Francisco "Pancho" Villa. U.S. support for Carranza prompted Villa to retaliate by raiding several U.S. border towns. In response, the United States dispatched troops under General John J. Pershing on an unsuccessful expedition into northern Mexico to either kill or capture Villa. Carranza negotiated a cease-fire among several of the warring Mexican factions in December 1916 and restored order to most of the country by accepting the radical constitution of 1917. Rural violence continued in the south, however, until the assassination of Zapata by Carranza's forces in November 1920. The Mexican Revolution exacted a heavy human and economic toll; more than 1 million deaths were attributed to the violence.

Consolidation of the Revolution

From the 1920s through the 1940s, a series of strong central governments led by former generals of the revolutionary armies governed Mexico. Most Mexican presidents complied with the constitutional provision mandating a single six-year term *(sexenio)* with no re-election. During the late 1920s, President Plutarco Elías Calles established many of the institutions that would define the Mexican political system throughout the twentieth century. This system was based on an authoritarian state controlled by a hegemonic "revolutionary" party headed by a powerful president, economic nationalism, limited land collectivization, military subordination to civilian authority, anticlericalism, and the peaceful resolution of social conflict through corporatist representation of group interests. Tactics such as extensive use of state patronage, manipulation of electoral laws and electoral fraud, government propaganda and restrictions on the press, and intimidation of the opposition helped ensure the decades-long domination of government at all levels by the Institutional Revolutionary Party (Partido Revolucionario Institucional—PRI). Through their top-down control of the PRI, presidents acquired the power to handpick their successors, decree laws, and amend the constitution virtually at will.

The ideology of the revolutionary regime took a leftward turn during the *sexenio* of Lázaro Cárdenas (1934–40). Cárdenas nationalized Mexico's oil industry and vastly expanded the acreage of nontransferable collectivized farms (*ejidos*) set aside for peasant communities. During World War II and the early years of the Cold War, the governments of Miguel Avila Camacho (1940–46) and Miguel Alemán Valdés (1946–52) repaired strained relations with the United States and returned to more conservative policies. In the postwar years, Mexico pursued an economic development strategy of "stabilizing development" that relied on heavy public-sector investment to modernize the national economy. Concurrently, Mexican governments followed conservative policies on interest and exchange rates that helped maintain low rates of inflation and attracted external capital to support industrialization. This dual strategy helped maintain steady economic growth and low rates of inflation through the 1960s.

Crisis and Recovery

During the presidencies of Luis Echeverría (1970–76) and José López Portilllo (1976–82), the public sector grew dramatically, and state-owned enterprises became a mainstay of the national economy. Massive government spending was sustained in part by revenues from the export of newly discovered offshore oil deposits. By the late 1970s, oil and petrochemicals had become the economy's most dynamic sectors. However, the windfall from high world demand for oil would be temporary. In mid-1981, Mexico was beset by falling oil prices, higher world interest rates, rising inflation, a chronically overvalued peso, and a deteriorating balance of payments that spurred massive capital flight. In August 1982, the Mexican government defaulted on scheduled debt repayments—an event that heralded a regionwide debt crisis. President López Portillo responded to the crisis by nationalizing the banking industry, further undermining investor confidence. His successor, Miguel de la Madrid Hurtado (1982–88), implemented economic austerity measures that laid the groundwork for economic recovery. In September 1985, the country suffered another blow when two major earthquakes struck central Mexico. Between 5,000 and 10,000 people are believed to have died and 300,000 left homeless in the worst natural disaster in Mexico's modern history. Many victims lost their lives in modern high-rise buildings constructed in violation of safety codes. The high death toll and the government's inadequate response to the disaster further undermined public confidence in the PRI-dominated political system.

In the run-up to the 1988 presidential and congressional elections, a splinter faction of left-wing former PRI members opposed to market reforms rallied behind the independent presidential candidacy of Cuahtemoc Cárdenas. In the first competitive presidential election in decades, the PRI candidate, Carlos Salinas de Gortari, was declared the winner with a bare majority of the vote. Numerous irregularities in the vote tally, including an unexplained shutdown of the electoral commission's computer system, led to widespread charges of fraud. Overcoming a weak mandate and strong opposition from organized labor, President Salinas undertook a sweeping liberalization of the economy. Reforms included the privatization of hundreds of state- owned enterprises, liberalization of foreign investment laws, deregulation of the financial services sector, and across-the-board reductions in tariffs and nontariff trade barriers. Economic liberalization culminated in the negotiation of the North American Free

Trade Agreement (NAFTA) with Canada and the United States in 1992. Salinas's reforms were overshadowed by subsequent revelations of corruption within the top echelons of the PRI, as well as by the unexpected emergence of a rural insurgency in the southern state of Chiapas.

Despite the assassination of the original PRI candidate, Luis Donaldo Colosio, the presidential election proceeded as scheduled in the fall of 1994. The replacement PRI candidate, Ernesto Zedillo Ponce de León, managed to stave off a serious challenge from the center-right National Action Party (Partido de Acción Nacional—PAN) to win the presidency.

Transition to Democracy

During the mid-1990s, an economic crisis stemming from an unsustainable current account deficit and mismanagement of the government bond market plunged Mexico into a severe recession. President Zedillo spent much of his *sexenio* restoring macroeconomic balance and responding to demands for greater accountability and transparency of public institutions. Zedillo also had to contend with the Zapatista rebellion in Chiapas, which highlighted the poverty and marginalization that characterized many of Mexico's indigenous communities. In the political realm, the Zedillo administration advanced electoral system reforms that leveled the playing field for opposition parties and set the stage for a genuine transition to democracy. The July 1997 midterm elections left the PRI with a minority of seats in the Chamber of Deputies (the lower house of Congress), expanded opposition control of state governorships, and gave the left-wing Party of the Democratic Revolution (Partido de la Revolución Democrática—PRD) control of Mexico City's government.

The opposition's momentum carried over into the September 2000 general elections. The PAN candidate, Vicente Fox Quesada, won the historic presidential race, becoming the first opposition head of state since the consolidation of the revolution. President Fox promised a deepening of Mexico's economic and political reforms, declared "war" on organized crime, and planned to negotiate an immigrant "guest worker" program with the United States. Despite strong public support early in its term, the Fox administration was weakened by the PAN's loss of congressional seats during the 2003 midterm elections and the government's failure to craft a legislative coalition in support of its reform agenda. By the end of his term in 2006, much of President Fox's structural reform program remained unfulfilled.

On July 2, 2006, Mexico held general elections for president, all seats in Congress, and several state governorships. The presidential race was closely contested between the PAN candidate, former Fox administration energy minister Felipe Calderón Hinojosa, and the PRD candidate, populist former mayor of Mexico City Andrés Manuel López Obrador. The PRI candidate, former Tabasco governor Roberto Madrazo Pintado, trailed in the race, as voters appeared wary of returning the PRI to the presidency. Opinion polls indicated that the election was largely a referendum on Mexico's two decades of market-oriented economic reforms. Calderón promised to continue the reform agenda by promoting greater foreign investment and increasing the competitiveness of Mexico's economy through structural reforms of the pension and labor laws. He also pledged to continue the government's fight against the drug cartels and to improve public safety. By contrast, López Obrador vowed to focus on Mexico's domestic problems, such as poverty and social inequality, and to halt so-called "neo-liberal" reforms. He promised to create thousands of jobs by funding massive public works projects and affirmed that he would seek to renegotiate NAFTA in order to protect Mexican farmers from an influx of imported U.S. corn. Further, López Obrador vowed to break up the unpopular commercial oligopolies that emerged from the privatization of state assets during the 1 990s.

Official tallies showed the results of the presidential election to be extremely close. Initial uncertainty about the accuracy of the preliminary vote count led both of the leading candidates to claim victory. However, subsequent official tabulations by the independent Federal Electoral Institute (Instituto Federal Electoral—IFE) confirmed that Calderón had indeed won the election by a slim plurality of 35.89 percent versus López Obrador's 35.31 percent of the vote (a margin of victory of 244,000 votes out of 41.8 million cast).

The results of the 2006 congressional races saw both the PAN and the PRD gain seats at the expense of the formerly dominant PRI. For the first time in its history, the PRI lost its plurality of seats in both houses of Congress, an event observers interpreted as a further sign of the party's decline. Nonetheless, the PRI retained a sufficiently large bloc of seats to remain an influential congressional force and was well positioned to become a coalition partner of any future Mexican government. The PRD retained control of the powerful mayoralty of Mexico City. All three major parties held state governorships.

During 2007, the Calderón administration made public safety and the fight against drug cartels its highest domestic priorities. In response to escalating drug violence, the federal government deployed 24,000 troops to various states and removed hundreds of corrupt police officials. Mexican public opinion strongly backed Calderón's aggressive tactics against the drug gangs. Under Calderón's leadership, the center-right PAN government courted the center-left PRI in an effort to advance the president's legislative agenda. During the 2007 legislative session, Congress passed far-reaching fiscal and pension system reforms that had stalled during the Fox administration.

By mid-2008 successive Mexican governments had made progress in reforming the economy and reducing extreme poverty. However, significant disparities in wealth, high levels of crime, and corruption persisted. The less-developed states in the south continued to lag economically behind the more prosperous north and center, fueling illegal migration to the United States. Mexico's economy was also lagging behind those of other middle-income countries, such as China, in terms of overall competitiveness. In addition to further consolidating Mexico's transition to democracy, the 2006 general elections presented an opportunity to overcome executive-legislative stalemate and move toward consensus on economic and public-sector reforms.

GEOGRAPHY

Location: Mexico is located in the southern portion of North America, bordering the southwestern United States from California to Texas. The southernmost Mexican states of Quintana Roo, Campeche, and Chiapas define the northern border of the isthmus of Central America.

Size: Mexico has an area of 1,964,375 square kilometers—making it the third largest nation in Latin America (after Brazil and Argentina).

Land Boundaries: Mexico has 4,301 kilometers of international land borders: 3,152 kilometers with the United States, 956 kilometers with Guatemala, and 193 kilometers with Belize.

Disputed Territory: Mexico has no outstanding international territorial disputes.

Length of Coastline: Mexico has a 10,143-kilometer coastline: 7,338 kilometers on the Pacific Ocean and Gulf of California and 2,805 kilometers on the Gulf of Mexico and Caribbean Sea.

Maritime Claims: Mexico claims a territorial sea of 12 nautical miles, a contiguous zone of 24 nautical miles, an exclusive economic zone that extends 200 nautical miles off each coast and covers approximately 2.7 million square kilometers, and a continental shelf of 200 nautical miles or to the edge of the continental margin.

Topography

Mexico has a varied topography consisting mainly of plateaus in the eastern two-thirds of the national territory and a mountainous spine running through the western third of the country. The interior north of the Mexico City metropolitan area is mainly high plateau—known as the Mesa Central and Mesa del Norte. The average elevation in the plateaus ranges from about 900 meters in the north to 2,400 meters in the southern portion of the Mesa Central. In the far northwest, the Baja Peninsula stretches southeast from the U.S. border for 1,300 kilometers. The peninsula is extremely dry and rugged, with a very narrow coastal plain. The southern highlands, located south of the Mesa Central, contain a number of steep mountain ranges, deep valleys, and dry plateaus. The Yucatan Peninsula extends northeast from the Isthmus of Tehuantepec into the Gulf of Mexico. It is a flat, low-lying limestone plateau lacking in major rivers. Mexico has several massive mountain ranges, most of which extend from northwest to southeast: the Sierra Madre Occidental in the west, the Sierra Madre Oriental in the east, and the Sierra Madre del Sur in the south. Lesser ranges include the Sierra Madre de Chiapas and the Cordillera Neovolcánica—an east-to-west volcanic range spanning the breadth of the country just south of Mexico City. The country's highest point, the Pico de Orizaba (5,636 meters), is located within the Cordillera Neovolcánica about 193 kilometers southeast of Mexico City. Mexico has extensive lowlands largely along the Gulf coast and in the Yucatan Peninsula.

Principal Rivers

Mexico has nearly 150 rivers, two-thirds of which empty into the Pacific Ocean and the remainder into the Gulf of Mexico or the Caribbean Sea. Most rivers are short and non-navigable, running from coastal mountain ranges to the coast. Water volume is unevenly distributed throughout the country. Five rivers—the Usumacinta, Grijalva, Papaloapán, Coatzacoalcos, and Pánuco—account for 52 percent of the average annual surface water volume. Most of the larger rivers are located in the southeastern part of the country and flow into the Gulf of Mexico. Northern Mexico contains less than 10 percent of the country's water resources. The Río Bravo del Norte (known as the Rio Grande in the United States) defines Mexico's northern border from Ciudad Juárez east to the Gulf of Mexico.

Climate

Mexico experiences great climatic variation owing to its considerable north-south extension and variations in elevation. The climate of much of northern and central Mexico is characterized by high temperatures and moderate to low rainfall. The highlands of the central plateau generally have a moderate climate with few extremes of hot or cold. Temperatures in Mexico City, for example, range from an average of 17° C in July to 12° C in January. The northern and central areas of the plateau are arid to semiarid; the drier regions receive about 300 millimeters of rainfall annually. Annual rainfall increases to about 600 millimeters in the southern part of the plateau, including the Mexico City area. The northern coastal areas, including Baja California, are arid. Rainfall along the Pacific Coast averages just 130 millimeters, as compared with 250 to 600 millimeters along the northern Gulf coast. Much of southern Mexico has a tropical climate with distinct rainy and dry seasons. Temperatures in the coastal regions range from 21° C to 27° C. Annual rainfall, which ranges from 1,500 millimeters to 2,000 millimeters, occurs mainly during the rainy season of May to October. The Gulf coast is subject to hurricanes.

Natural Resources

Mexico has abundant natural resources. In addition to extensive subsoil resources (including large reserves of oil and silver), the country has a rich biodiversity and varied wildlife. As of 2003, about 5 percent of Mexico's land area was under a protected status. Protected sites included six wetlands of international importance (Ramsar sites) totaling 1.1 million hectares and 12 biosphere reserves totaling 6.8 million hectares.

Land Use

Although nearly half of Mexico's total land area is officially classified as agricultural, only 12 percent of the total area is cultivated. Extensive irrigation projects carried out in the 1940s and 1950s greatly expanded Mexico's cropland, especially in the north. One- third of Mexican territory is officially designated as grazing land. These lands are located mainly in the north. Some 9 percent of Mexico's territory consists of forest or woodland, 59 percent of which is in the tropics, 15 percent in the subtropical zone, and 26 percent in the temperate and cool zones. Temperate forests cover some 49 million hectares, almost one-third of which are open to logging, mainly in the states of Chihuahua, Durango, and Michoacán.

Environmental Factors

Mexico faces significant environmental challenges affecting almost every section of the country. Vast expanses of tropical and subtropical forests in the south have been denuded for cattle raising and agriculture. Deforestation has contributed to serious levels of soil erosion nationwide. Soil destruction is particularly pronounced in the north and northwest. More than 60 percent of land is considered in a total or accelerated state of erosion. The result is a mounting problem of desertification throughout the region. Mexico's coastline is threatened by inadequately protected petroleum extraction in the Gulf of Mexico, which has damaged marine ecosystems. Mexico City is one of the world's most polluted urban areas. Vehicle emissions and other airborne contaminants have been blamed for a wide range of respiratory illnesses. Polluted water from Mexico City has been linked to congenital birth defects and high levels of gastrointestinal illnesses in the neighboring state of Hidalgo. Government antipollution measures have met with limited success.

Time Zones

Most of Mexico, including Mexico City, is in the Central Time zone (Coordinated Universal Time (UTC)/Greenwich Mean Time (GMT) –6 hours). The state of Northern Baja California is on Pacific Time (UTC/GMT –8 hours). The states of Baja California Sur, Sonora, Sinaloa, Chihuahua, and Nayarit are on Mountain Time (UTC/GMT –7 hours). In Mexico, however, Mountain Time is usually referred to as "Pacific Time" because most of these states border the Pacific Ocean. The state of Quintana Roo is on Eastern Time

(UTC/GMT –5 hours). Mexico uses daylight saving time (DST). During 2008 DST was scheduled for April 6 to October 26.

SOCIETY

Population

In mid-2008 Mexico had an estimated population of 106.7 million. The population growth rate has been falling since the 1 970s, declining from an average of 3.4 percent annually during the 1960s to 1.8 percent annually in the 1990s. The decrease is largely attributable to declining fertility. Emigration to the United States has increased significantly since the 1970s. The number of Mexican-born residents in the United States grew from an estimated 760,000 in 1970 to 8.5 million in 2000 (8.7 percent of Mexico's population in the 2000 census).

Immigration has not been a significant factor in population growth since the 1920s. Nationwide, population density was 52 residents per square kilometer according to the 2000 census. Density varied widely among the 31 states and Federal District from a high of 5,975 residents per square kilometer in the Federal District to a low of 12 residents per square kilometer in Baja California Sur. Mexico experienced heavy urbanization during the latter half of the twentieth century. In 1950 less than half the population (42.6 percent) lived in communities of 2,500 or more inhabitants. By 2005 more than three-quarters (76.2 percent) of Mexicans lived in such communities. The national population is heavily concentrated in central Mexico along a roughly northwest to southeast axis from Guadalajara to Veracruz. This area includes the heavily populated contiguous states of Jalisco, Guanajuato, Michoacán, Hidalgo, México, Distrito Federal, Morelos, Puebla, and Veracruz–Llave—which together are home to about half the national population. Major urban agglomerations are also found in the north, centered on the cities of Ciudad Juárez, Tijuana, and Monterrey—with more than 1 million residents each. In the south, the largely Amerindian populations in the states of Chiapas and Oaxaca live mainly in small- to medium-sized towns and villages.

Demography

Mexico's birthrate has been declining since the 1960s. During the 1990s, the rate of natural increase was 1.6 percent, half the rate observed during the 1960s (3.1 percent). In 2008 there were an estimated 20.0 live births and 4.8 deaths per 1,000 population. Life expectancy at birth was estimated at 75.8 years overall (73.1 years for men and 78.8 years for women). The total fertility rate (children born per woman) was 2.4. Infant mortality stood at 19.0 per 1,000 live births in 2008, compared to 79.3 deaths per 1,000 live births in 1970. The 2008 age structure of the population was as follows: 0–14 years, 30 percent; 15–29 years, 27 percent; 30–49 years, 27 percent; 50–64 years, 10 percent; 65 years and older, 6 percent. The median age was 26 years, and females slightly outnumbered males by a ratio of 1.04:1. As a result of declining fertility and rising life expectancy, by 2025 Mexico's population is predicted to age overall; the share of the youngest cohort (0–14) will decline to 24 percent, and that of the oldest will rise to 10 percent.

Ethnic Groups

The two main ethnic categories of mestizo and Indian/Amerindian are defined broadly along cultural rather than racial lines. The term "mestizo" describes persons with a solely European background, those with a mixed European–indigenous ancestry, and indigenous people who have adopted the dominant Hispanic societal values. According to anthropologists, the terms "Indian" or "indigenous" describe persons who identify themselves as such, use an indigenous language in daily speech, remain actively involved in indigenous communal affairs, or participate in religious ceremonies rooted in native American traditions. Approximately 60 percent of the population is mestizo, 30 percent Amerindian or predominantly Amerindian, 9 percent white or European, and 1 percent "other."

Languages

Spanish is the dominant language for both the mestizo and Indian populations. Approximately 6 million Mexicans spoke an indigenous language as a first language in 2000. The number of indigenous language speakers rose slightly in absolute terms from 1990 to 2000 but declined slightly as a percentage of the total Mexican population (7.2 percent in 2000 versus 7.8 percent in 1990). Indigenous speakers are highly concentrated in the southern states of Guerrero, Oaxaca, Quintana Roo, Chiapas, and Yucatán. Among indigenous language speakers, 83 percent also speak Spanish, while about 1 million are monolingual. Linguistically isolated communities are most prevalent in the states of Chiapas and Guerrero. Specialists have identified 12 distinct Mexican indigenous linguistic families, more than 40 subgroups, and at least 90 individual languages. According to the 2000 census, nearly 24 percent of all native speakers spoke Náhuatl, the language of the Aztec people and the most geographically dispersed native language. Other major indigenous languages include Maya, Zapotec, Mixtec, Otomí, Tzeltal, and Tzotzil.

Religion

Roman Catholicism is the main religion; 88 percent of the population five years of age and older identified themselves as Roman Catholic in the 2000 census. Protestants and Evangelicals were the second largest religious group, accounting for approximately 5 percent of the population. The rapid growth in Protestant and Evangelical membership slowed during the 1990s, averaging a 3.7 percent annual rise from 1990 to 2000 (versus 10 percent during the 1970s and 5 percent during the 1980s).

Education and Literacy

During the past several decades, Mexico has made significant advances in literacy and the provision of public education. In 2004 the adult literacy rate stood at 91 percent (92 percent among men and 90 percent among women). Mexican law mandates universal preschool, primary, and secondary education. Eleven years of education are compulsory, but in practice the average number of years of schooling for the population 15 and over was around eight years during 2005. That year, Mexico had 27.1 million students in primary, secondary, and postsecondary educational institutions. Enrollment rates in primary education are high (97 percent of girls and 98 percent of boys); however, many students— especially those from poor families—do not complete high school, opting instead to enter the workforce. Seventy percent of eligible students were enrolled in secondary education in 2006. Education accounts for a quarter of public spending—the highest share of public spending on education among Organisation for Economic Co-operation and Development (OECD) countries. Notwithstanding the proportionally large education budget, spending per student is low by international standards—about a quarter of the OECD average for primary education and a third of the OECD average for secondary education. Most current spending at the primary and secondary levels goes to the compensation of staff, leaving few resources for infrastructure, supplies, and training. The performance of Mexican secondary school students in math, reading, and science is the lowest of all OECD countries and ranks well below the OECD average.

Health

Aggregate health statistics have improved greatly since the 1 970s. However, Mexico lags well behind other OECD countries in health status and health care availability. Total health care spending accounted for 6.4 percent of gross domestic product (GDP) in 2005; per capita spending on health care was US$675 (adjusted for purchasing power parity)—about a quarter of the OECD average. During 2005, 45.5 percent of health spending was paid from public sources—comparable to the share of public spending in the United States but significantly below the OECD average. Private financing in Mexico is almost entirely in the form of out-of-pocket payments, as only 3.1 percent of total expenditures on health are funded through private health insurance. In 2005 Mexico had 1.8 doctors and 2.2 nurses per 1,000 population, a significant increase in health care personnel over the previous decade but again below the OECD averages for these indicators. The mortality rate for children younger than five years was 27 per 1,000 live births in 2005. Ninety-seven percent of the population had direct access to potable water and 79 percent to sanitation. In 2005 the incidence of human immunodeficiency virus/acquired immune deficiency syndrome (HIV/AIDS) among persons aged 15 to 49 was 0.3 percent.

Welfare

Mexico has made progress in reducing poverty since the late 1990s, performing above the Latin American average. However, nearly half the population continues to live in poverty; about 15 percent of the total population subsists in extreme poverty, with limited access to food and basic services. Residents of southern Mexico consistently trail the rest of the country in quality-of-life indicators. Urban workers in the informal sector of the economy do not have access to the same level of health care as their counterparts in the formal sector, nor do they qualify for retirement or pension benefits. About half the workforce is registered with the Mexican Social Security Institute.

ECONOMY

Overview

Mexico is a middle-income country with a developing market economy that is closely linked to the much larger economy of the United States. Mexico's economy ranks as "moderately free" in the *2008 Index of Economic Freedom* (a joint publication of the *Wall Street Journal* and the Heritage Foundation). From the 1940s through the late 1960s, successive governments followed an economic strategy of import substitution and fiscal and monetary restraint intended to promote growth while holding inflation in check. During the 1970s, populist governments abandoned fiscal discipline and oversaw a massive expansion of consumer subsidies and state ownership of productive sectors. Unsustainable public-sector spending backed by over-reliance on oil export revenues and abundant international credit contributed to chronically high inflation and wild fluctuations in economic performance. As a result, the economy experienced spurts of rapid growth followed by sharp recessions in 1976 and 1982. The mid- to late 1980s were years of economic austerity and stagnant growth during which Mexico was able to balance its national accounts while combating high inflation. Gross domestic product (GDP) grew at an average rate of just 0.1 percent per year between 1983 and 1988. During these years, monetary policy was severely restricted and public-sector spending sharply curtailed.

The late 1980s and early 1990s saw far-reaching market-oriented structural reforms, including privatization of hundreds of state-owned enterprises, liberalization of foreign investment laws, deregulation of the financial services sector, and across-the-board reductions in tariffs and nontariff trade barriers. These reforms, which culminated in the ratification of the North American Free Trade Agreement (NAFTA) in 1994, attracted an influx of US$148 billion in foreign direct investment (FDI) during the next decade. From 1988 to 1994, GDP growth averaged 2.6 percent annually, sustained by exports and an influx of foreign capital. However, the collapse of the peso in December 1994 and the ensuing economic crisis erased most of the real wage gains from the previous years. In response to the 1994 crisis, Mexico passed legislation granting greater independence to its central bank. Growth resumed in the late 1 990s, but the recovery was cut short by the spillover effects of the 2001 recession in the United States. Since 2002, a worldwide commodity price boom, a U.S. economic recovery, and sound macroeconomic policies have helped boost economic growth while allowing inflation to remain in the single digits.

The economy is hampered by structural weaknesses that limit Mexico's potential for future growth and job creation. Mexico's workers are generally low skilled and have less schooling than workers in advanced industrial economies. This deficit in human capital manifests itself in stagnant labor productivity and real wages, as well through the existence of a large "informal" labor sector that deprives the education, health care, and social security systems of crucial tax revenues. Income distribution remains highly unequal; about half of Mexico's population lives in poverty.

Despite recent reforms, some public policies continue to hold back the economy's competitiveness and growth potential: rigid labor and commercial codes discourage hiring and inhibit informal workers from transitioning into the formal economy; the important energy sector, which remains state-owned, suffers from numerous inefficiencies and undercapitalization; and the federal government relies heavily on the oil industry for revenues, which consequently renders public budgets vulnerable to cyclical fluctuations in hydrocarbon prices. Whereas the liberalizing reforms associated with NAFTA have been a boon to northern and central Mexico's manufacturing centers, few new jobs have materialized for the predominantly agricultural states in the south and southwest. This uneven development pattern has failed to slow large-scale wage migration to the United States. As global competition for capital investment has increased— particularly from low-cost manufacturing in Asia—Mexico's status as a premier export hub for the North American market has eroded.

Gross Domestic Product (GDP)

Nominal GDP stood at US$879.2 billion dollars in 2007 (US$1.23 trillion in terms of purchasing power parity, or PPP), representing a per capita GDP of approximately US$8,088 (US$11,337 in terms of PPP)—the highest in Latin America. In 2008 Mexico was entering its fifth consecutive year of economic expansion. Annualized real GDP growth slowed from of a peak rate of 4.8 percent in 2006 to 3 percent in 2007, partly as a result of a slowdown in the U.S. economy. Economic output in 2007 was divided among the sectors as follows: services, 70 percent; industry, 26 percent; and agriculture, 4 percent.

Government Budget and Public Finance

During 2007, Mexico's public-sector budget was balanced, with expenditures matching revenues of US$209 billion (equivalent to 24 percent of gross domestic product). The public sector typically relies on profits from the state-owned hydrocarbons sector for a quarter of its revenues. Federal tax revenue is derived from several sources: corporate and individual income taxes, a nationwide value-added tax, and excise taxes on the mining industry. State and local governments rely heavily on federal government revenue transfers for their budgets.

Inflation

Inflation has trended generally downward since the late 1980s (when it exceeded 150 percent), thanks to a commitment by successive governments and the independent central bank to anti-inflationary fiscal and monetary policies. During 2007, annual inflation was approximately 4 percent.

Agriculture, Forestry, and Fishing

In 2007 agriculture accounted for only 4 percent of gross domestic product but employed 18 percent of the labor force. Agricultural practices range from traditional techniques, such as slash-and-burn cultivation of indigenous plants for family subsistence, to the use of advanced technology and marketing in large-scale, capital-intensive export agriculture. The staple food crops are maize, wheat, sorghum, barley, rice, beans, and potatoes. The principal cash crops are coffee, cotton, sugarcane, fruit, and vegetables. Other important agricultural goods include beef, poultry, dairy products, and wood products.

Agricultural exports, valued at US$7 billion in 2006, are destined primarily for the United States. Forestry production is geared toward the exploitation of domestic fuelwood, sawlogs for construction, and pulpwood for processing in domestic paper mills. Mexico's coastal fishing grounds offer a rich variety of fish and other seafood. The Pacific coast accounts for nearly three-quarters of Mexico's total catch, producing mainly lobster, shrimp, croaker, albacore, skipjack, and anchovies. Mexico's Gulf and Caribbean waters produce shrimp, jewfish, croaker, snapper, mackerel, snook, and mullet. In 2005 the total catch exceeded 1.4 million metric tons.

Non-fuel Mining and Minerals

Mexico has abundant mineral resources and is the world's second-largest producer of silver. During 2007 silver production was approximately 2.3 million metric tons. Other significant mining products in 2007 were iron (7.3 million metric tons), sulphur (1.0 million metric tons), fluorite (0.92 million tons), zinc (0.42 million metric tons), copper (0.32 million metric tons), and manganese (0.16 million metric tons). Mexico also possesses substantial deposits of mercury, bismuth, antimony, cadmium, phosphates, and uranium.

Industry and Manufacturing

Manufacturing is the economy's leading export sector, accounting for 81 percent of total export revenues in 2007 and about a quarter of gross domestic product. About a quarter of Mexico's labor force is engaged in some type of industrial or manufacturing activity. The manufacturing sector was transformed by the liberalizing reforms of the late 1980s and early 1990s, which privatized hundreds of state enterprises and greatly expanded opportunities for foreign direct and portfolio investment. Manufacturing attracts about half of all foreign direct investment in Mexico, two-thirds of which is concentrated in the *maquiladora* sector, comprising more than 2,000 businesses employing 1.13 million workers in 2004. Overall manufacturing output is dominated by three activities: machinery and equipment (primarily the automotive sector); food, beverages, and tobacco; and chemicals, petrochemicals, rubber, and plastics. Together, these three sectors account for three-quarters of manufacturing output. Other components of manufacturing output include textiles, clothing, and leather goods; metals; and paper products. Principal industrial centers are located in and around the Mexico City metropolitan area, Monterrey, and Guadalajara.

Energy

The state oil corporation, Petróleos de Mexico (Pemex), holds a constitutionally established monopoly on the exploration, production, transportation, and marketing of the nation's oil and natural gas. In 2006 Mexico was the sixth-largest producer of oil in the world, and the second largest in the Western Hemisphere. About half of Mexico's crude oil production is consumed domestically, while the other half is exported—mainly to the United States. The country extracted an average of 3.1 million barrels per day of crude oil in 2007. Over the past two decades, the oil sector's share of total export revenues has fallen sharply as the economy has diversified and as an increasing share of production has been dedicated to meeting domestic demand. Crude oil exports accounted for 15.6 percent of total export revenues in 2006 versus 61 percent in 1985. Mexico's proven oil reserves have declined substantially since 2000, from 26.9 billion barrels to less than half that amount by 2007. Barring new oil discoveries, Mexico is expected to curtail its oil exports within the next few years.

In addition to crude oil, Mexico had 434 billion cubic meters of proven natural gas reserves in 2006. Since the late 1980s, Mexican demand for natural gas has outpaced production. As a result, Mexico imported 9.7 billion cubic meters of natural gas in 2005, representing about one- fifth of national consumption. Pemex retains sole control of natural gas exploration and production and operates an extensive pipeline network consisting of approximately 453 pipelines spanning 4,700 kilometers.

Mexico has 1.3 billion tons of recoverable coal reserves. During 2006 it produced 13 million short tons of coal while consuming 21 million short tons. Most coal consumption is for electricity generation, while the remainder is for steelmaking.

Mexico has a single nuclear power plant. The 1,400-megawatt Laguna Verde plant is located near Veracruz.

Mexico generated 240 billion kilowatt-hours of electric power in 2006: 79 percent from conventional thermal sources, 13 percent from hydroelectricity, 4 percent from nuclear power, and 3 percent from geothermal, wind, or solar energy. The bulk of conventional thermal capacity in the national electricity grid consumes fuel oil, followed by coal and natural gas. Electricity demand is projected to grow by 6 percent per year during the next decade.

Services

Services (including financial services) make up the largest segment of the Mexican economy, accounting for 70 percent of gross domestic product (GDP) in 2007 and employing about 60 percent of the national workforce. In recent years, major transnational retailers have expanded their presence in the country. Merchandise counterfeiting and intellectual property rights crimes are pervasive within the informal retail sector, threatening the profitability of the formal retail sector. Tourism, which caters primarily to U.S. and Canadian travelers, accounts for about 1 percent of GDP.

Banking and Finance

Financial services represent the most advanced component of the services sector, accounting for about a quarter of all foreign investment. In 2006 more than 80 percent of banking sector assets were foreign-owned. Mexico has a central bank (Banco de México) and six types of banking institutions: public development banks, public credit institutions, private commercial banks, private investment banks, savings and loans associations, and mortgage banks. Other components of the financial system include securities market institutions, development trust funds, insurance companies, credit unions, factoring companies, mutual funds, and bonded warehouses. Since 1994, Banco de México has been largely autonomous. The bank is governed by a five-member board composed of a chairperson or "governor" and four "subdirectors." The governor serves a six-year term; subdirectors serve eight-year terms and are appointed on a staggered basis. All members are appointed by the president but once confirmed may not be removed except in cases of gross misconduct or incapacitation as outlined in the Central Bank Law.

Labor

In 2006 the labor force was estimated at 44.5 million (out of a total population of 107 million). Approximately 1 million new workers enter the labor force annually; however, the Mexican economy typically creates only about half as many new jobs. The Mexican labor market is characterized by the existence of an informal sector, in which workers are mostly unskilled, do not pay taxes, and do not receive benefits, and a formal sector, in which jobs generally require more skills, and working conditions and benefits are regulated by strict labor laws. The informal sector is estimated to make up between 40 and 65 percent of the total labor force. During 2007 Mexico reported a low unemployment rate of approximately 4 percent; however, real wages have stagnated during the past decade, and 25 percent of the workforce is believed to be underemployed. In 2007 the labor force was distributed by occupation as follows: services, about 60 percent; industry, about 25 percent; and agriculture, about 18 percent.

Foreign Economic Relations

Mexico's extensive trade linkages to the United States dominate its foreign economic relations. In 2006 the leading markets for Mexican products in terms of percentage of total exports were the United States, 84.7 percent; Canada, 2.1 percent; Germany, 1.3 percent; and Spain, 1.2 percent. Mexico's leading suppliers in terms of percentage of total imports were the United States, 50.9 percent; China, 9.5 percent; Japan, 5.9 percent; and South Korea, 4.2 percent. Since the early 1 990s, Mexico's foreign economic relations have emphasized active participation in the World Trade Organization (WTO) and the negotiation of free-trade agreements (FTAs)—most notably the North American Free Trade Agreement (NAFTA) with Canada and the United States. Mexico has entered into regional and bilateral FTAs involving more than 40 countries.

Trade Balance

Since the late 1990s, the overall merchandise trade balance has been slightly negative, largely as a result of growing deficits with the European Union and Asia (mainly China). During 2007 Mexico's total merchandise imports were valued at US$280.1 billion versus US$269.1 billion in exports. Mexico's trade deficit with the rest of the world is largely offset by a trade surplus with the United States. This surplus has grown steadily since the late 1 990s, driven initially by the boom in manufacturing exports and, more recently, by high world oil prices. In 2006 Mexico's trade surplus with the United States stood at US$81.4 billion.

Balance of Payments

In recent years, Mexico has overcome a historical pattern of unsustainable high current account deficits. Since the late 1990s, the current account deficit has shrunk to sustainable levels of generally less than 3 percent of gross domestic product (GDP). Current transfers—made up largely of wage remittances from Mexicans living in the United States—have become an important contributor to Mexico's external accounts, providing capital inflows estimated to be as much as 2.5 percent of GDP. In 2006 Mexico's current account deficit was estimated at US$1.7 billion.

External Debt

Total external debt was US$165 billion in 2006. At 19 percent of gross domestic product (GDP), Mexico's external debt-to-GDP ratio is one of the lowest in Latin America. The debt-service ratio (the ratio of debt service to export earnings) has declined from 25.5 percent in 2001 to an estimated 15.8 percent in 2005.

Foreign Investment

Mexico is the largest host of foreign direct investment (FDI) in Latin America. During 2006 the stock of FDI in Mexico was US$236.2 billion. During the 10-year period following the ratification of the North American Free Trade Agreement (1994–2004), Mexico attracted a cumulative US$148 billion in FDI, about 50 percent of which was invested in manufacturing and another 25 percent directed toward the financial services sector. Net portfolio investment has been rising since 2002; by mid-2005, foreign holdings of government bonds totaled approximately US$10 billion, while foreign investment in the Mexican stock market exceeded US$85 billion.

Foreign Aid

The World Bank is the leading provider of foreign expertise and financial support to Mexico. Presently, the bank is financing 32 projects in the country, with an average annual commitment of up to US$1.7 billion. The World Bank's 2005–2008 Country Assistance Strategy (CAS) for Mexico projects loans totaling about US$4.8 billion during the strategy's four-year timeline and is designed to support the government's commitment to fighting poverty and inequality.

Currency and Exchange Rate

Mexico's currency is the peso (MXN). In early July 2008, the exchange rate was approximately US$1=MXN10.

Fiscal Year

Calendar year.

TRANSPORTATION AND TELECOMMUNICATIONS

Overview

Mexico's economy relies heavily on the country's road network and maritime ports for the transportation of cargo. The extensive road system handles the bulk of domestic passenger and cargo surface transportation, while airports are struggling to keep up with the growth in international passenger travel. In recent years, the privatization of railroads and ports and the granting of toll road concessions have attracted substantial foreign investment and encouraged modernization of facilities.

Roads

Mexico has one of the most extensive road networks in Latin America, linking nearly all areas of the national territory. In 2005 the country had 235,670 kilometers of roads, 122,677 kilometers of which were paved. The network includes 6,336 kilometers of modern toll highways. Although extensive, much of Mexico's public road system is in poor condition as a result of insufficient investment in maintenance and an overreliance on heavy trucks to haul overland cargo. Roads handle 59 percent of total cargo transportation and 99 percent of domestic passenger journeys.

Railroads

Railroads transport 10 percent of total cargo and play only a minor role in passenger travel. The rail system consists of 26,662 kilometers of track, nearly all of which is made up of 1.435-meter, standard-gauge line. The largest rail line historically has been the state-owned Mexican National Railways (Ferrocarriles Nacionales Mexicanos—FNM), which owns about 70 percent of total track. During the late 1990s, the FNM was broken up into regional rail lines and privatized. The newly privatized entities were granted 50-year leases to operate on the rail system's main routes. By 2004, 81 percent of total rail traffic was handled by private companies. Mexico City maintains a subway system comprising eight lines with 135 stations and a total route length of 158 kilometers.

Ports

The maritime port system has grown rapidly from about 75 ports in the mid-1990s to 108 ports in 2008 with the expansion of international trade. The system has experienced an influx of foreign capital as a result of the comprehensive privatization of port facilities begun during the 1990s. The largest ports, located on the Pacific coast, include Manzanillo, Lázaro Cárdenas, Salina Cruz, Guaymas, and Mazatlán. Important ports on the Gulf Coast include Veracruz, Tampico, and Coatzacoalcos. During 2007 Mexican ports handled 240 million tons of cargo (mostly petroleum and derivatives, followed by bulk mineral and agricultural products). Container ports moved about 2.7 million twenty-foot equivalent units (TEUs) in 2006. Cruise ship passenger arrivals nearly tripled from 2.3 million in 1997 to 6.4 million in 2007, corresponding to 3,082 cruise ship arrivals in 2007.

Inland Waterways

Mexico's 2,900 kilometers of navigable rivers and coastal canals play only a minor role in the transportation system.

Civil Aviation and Airports

Mexico's civil aviation system is extensive and includes 227 airports—35 of which are international airports—and approximately 1,800 airfields and airstrips nationwide. During 2006 Mexican airports handled approximately 45.4 million passenger journeys, 29.0 million of which were conducted on domestic airlines and 16.4 million on international airlines. The busiest airports are Mexico City (Benito Juárez—MEX), Guadalajara (Miguel Hidalgo y Costilla—GDL), Monterrey (General Mariano Escobedo—MTY), and Cancún (CUN). Despite recent capital expenditures on terminals and runways, the largest airports are struggling to meet rising demand for air transportation services.

Telecommunications

Since the 1990s, telecommunications services have been transformed by privatization of the national telephone company and the advent of wireless technologies. Following the privatization of Teléfonos de México (Telmex) and the opening of the sector to other private carriers in the 1990s, fixed-line density rose from 6.4 lines per 100 in 1990 to 18 lines per 100 in 2006. The latter figure corresponds to approximately 20 million fixed telephone lines in use. Availability of residential fixed-line service varies greatly by region; Mexico City and the more developed northern states experience much higher service densities than the eight poorest southern states. The continued high cost of fixed-line services, together with an incomplete build-out of the fixed-line network, has contributed to a proliferation of mobile telephone use. The number of mobile cellular telephone accounts rose from 14 million in 2000 to more than 57 million in 2006. That year, approximately 22 million Mexicans were classified as Internet users. Major telecommunications infrastructure includes 120 domestic satellite earth stations, 52 international stations, and an extensive microwave radio relay network.

Government and Politics

Political System

Mexico is a federal republic consisting of 31 states and a Federal District. During much of the twentieth century, Mexico was ruled by authoritarian governments under the control of the Institutional Revolutionary Party (Partido Revolucionaro Institucional—PRI). The PRI exercised hegemony over the political system while observing formal democratic procedures, such as regular elections, tolerance of opposition parties, and political campaigning. Mexico's political system historically has concentrated power in the executive branch. By exercising strong leadership over the PRI party apparatus as well as their extensive constitutional prerogatives, Mexican presidents wielded formidable influence over public policy. Since 1997, however, when the first opposition-controlled Congress in Mexico's modern history was voted into office, a more balanced relationship among the branches has developed. Following a series of political and electoral system reforms, the PRI lost its seven-decade monopoly on the presidency in the 2000 elections. The development of a three-party system at the national level has led to a more even distribution of power and has given rise to coalition-style politics. Mexican federalism has historically been weak. State and local governments rely heavily on the federal government for revenues.

Constitution

Mexico's formal government institutions are defined by the constitution of 1917, which is widely regarded as an expression of popular will that guarantees labor and civil rights, electoral democracy, and national independence. Inspired by both socialist and classical liberal political philosophy, as well as by earlier Mexican constitutions, the drafters prescribed a federal republic with separation of powers, recognized a broad range of political and social rights, and treated many matters of public policy explicitly. Key provisions include Article 27, which, before being amended in 1992, imposed stringent restrictions on the ownership of property by foreigners and the Catholic Church and declared national ownership of the country's natural resources; and Article 123, which affirms a variety of labor rights, including the right to organize and an eight-hour workday, and provides for the protection of women and minors in the workplace. Constitutional amendments may be passed with a two-thirds vote of both chambers of the federal Congress and ratification by a majority of the state legislatures. The constitution has been amended extensively since 1917. Major amendments include the granting of women's suffrage in 1953, the easing of nationalist restrictions on foreign investment in 1992, and numerous electoral system reforms during the 1980s and 1990s.

Branches of Government

The federal executive branch is headed by the president and 18 cabinet-level ministers (secretaries). The president holds the formal titles of chief of state, head of government, and commander in chief of the armed forces. Presidents are elected directly by a simple majority of registered voters in the 31 states and the Federal District. Presidents serve a six-year term (*sexenio*) with no possibility of re-election; there is no vice president. If the presidential office falls vacant during the first two years of a *sexenio*, the Congress designates an interim president, who, in turn, must call a special presidential election to complete the term. If the vacancy occurs during the latter four years of a *sexenio*, the Congress designates a provisional president for the remainder of the term. The president has sole authority to appoint and dismiss cabinet secretaries—except for the attorney general, who must receive the consent of the Senate.

The bicameral Congress is composed of a Senate and a Chamber of Deputies. The Senate's 128 seats are filled by a mixture of direct election and proportional representation (96 by direct election and 32 by proportional representation from party lists). In the lower chamber, 300 deputies are directly elected to represent single-member districts, and 200 are selected by a modified form of proportional representation from five electoral regions. Senators are elected to six-year terms, and deputies serve three-year terms. All members of Congress are barred from immediate re-election but may serve nonconsecutive terms. The powers of Congress include the right to pass laws, impose taxes, declare war, approve the national budget, approve or reject treaties and conventions made with foreign countries, and ratify diplomatic appointments. The Senate addresses all matters concerning foreign policy, approves international agreements, and confirms presidential appointments. The Chamber of Deputies oversees all matters pertaining to the government's budget and public expenditures. Each legislative chamber has a number of committees that study and recommend bills. If there is disagreement between the chambers, a joint committee is appointed to draft a compromise version.

The judicial branch is divided into federal and state systems. Additionally, justice of the peace courts are available at the municipal level. Federal district courts exercise broad jurisdiction over federal crimes and writ of injunction (*amparo*) suits and civil controversies regarding the enforcement or application of federal laws or international treaties, among others. The rulings of federal district courts may be reviewed by collegiate and unitary circuit courts and by the Supreme Court. The federal judicial system is organized into 29 circuits, encompassing 172 collegiate circuit courts, 62 unitary circuit courts, and 285 district courts. The Supreme Court is made up of 11 justices (including the chief justice). The court holds biennial sessions in which it is divided into two chambers: Civil and Criminal Affairs and Administrative and Labor Affairs.

Supreme Court justices are appointed by a two-thirds vote of the Senate from among a list of candidates submitted by the president. In the event that two-thirds of the Senate cannot agree on an appointee, the president may fill the vacancy without Senate approval. Justices serve a single 15-year term without the possibility of reappointment. The chief justice is elected from among the sitting justices by a collegial vote of the membership. He or she presides over the court for a term of four years. Chief justices may not serve consecutive terms but may be reelected by their colleagues during their 15-year tenure on the court. District and circuit judges are appointed by the Federal Judicial Council, a quasi-independent judicial branch agency chaired by the chief justice of the Supreme Court. The seven-member council is in charge of carrying out judicial career laws, overseeing judicial functioning, and selecting judges at all levels below the Supreme Court. In addition to the chairmanship, three seats are occupied by judges appointed by the Supreme Court, two seats by notable judicial scholars appointed by the Senate, and one seat by a presidential appointee. Except for the chief justice, all council members serve a single five-year term.

Administrative Divisions

Mexico is a federal republic with 31 states and a Federal District encompassing Mexico City and its immediate environs. Approximately 2,000 municipalities are legally recognized.

State and Local Government

Each of Mexico's 31 states has its own constitution modeled on the national charter and has the right to legislate and levy taxes other than interstate customs duties. Following the federal organization at the national level, state and local governments also have executive, legislative, and judicial branches. The state executive branch is headed by a governor, who is directly elected for a six-year term and may not be reelected. State legislatures are unicameral, consisting of a single Chamber of Deputies that meets in two ordinary sessions per year, with extended periods and extraordinary sessions when needed. Deputies serve three- year terms and may not be immediately reelected. Legislative bills may be introduced by the deputies, the state governor, the state Superior Court of Justice, or a municipality within a given state. Governors appoint the justices of the Superior Court of Justice with the approval of state legislatures. These magistrates, in turn, appoint all lower state court judges. Municipal governments, headed by a mayor or municipal president (*regente*) and a municipal council (*ayuntamiento*), are popularly elected for three-year terms.

Judicial and Legal System

Mexico's judicial system is largely derived from Spanish and Napoleonic civil and criminal codes. The most powerful juridical instrument is the writ of *amparo* (literally, "refuge"), a writ of injunction that can be invoked against acts by any government official. The trial system consists of a series of fact-gathering hearings during which the court receives documentary evidence or testimony, after which a judge in chambers reviews the case file and issues a final written ruling. The record of the proceeding is not available to the general public; only the parties involved have access to the official file and then only by special motion. The law provides for the right of the accused to attend the hearings and to challenge the evidence or testimony presented. The law also guarantees the right to an attorney, although in actual practice the understaffed public defender system is characterized by low professional standards, and, as a result, most indigent defendants are inadequately represented.

In June 2008, the president signed into law legislation reforming the federal legal system to introduce public, oral trials and guaranteeing to defendants the presumption of innocence. Following its passage by both legislative chambers, a constitutional amendment was approved by a majority of Mexico's 31 state legislatures. (Approval by 17 state legislatures is required for the amendment to become law.) Implementation of the reform is to be completed by 2016.

Electoral System

Article 41 of the constitution of 1917 and subsequent amendments regulate electoral politics in Mexico. Suffrage is universal for all citizens 18 or older, and voting is compulsory, although this provision is rarely enforced. The constitution enshrines the principle of direct election by popular vote of the president and most other elected officials. Executive officeholders may not be reelected, and legislators may not serve consecutive terms. Ordinary elections are held every six years for the president and members of the Senate and every three years for deputies. Gubernatorial elections are distributed throughout a six-year presidential term (*sexenio*), so that no more than six governorships are contested in any given year. Elections at the federal, state, and local levels are administered by the Federal Electoral Institute (Instituto Federal Electoral—IFE). The IFE is a semi-autonomous organization established by the 1990 electoral code, consisting of representatives from government and the major political parties. During the 1990s, reforms of the IFE strengthened its capacity to serve as a nonpartisan electoral commission. These reforms included the introduction of majority nonpartisan representation (six out of 11 seats) on the IFE governing board, a legal framework for Mexican and foreign observers to monitor elections, and an independent audit of the national voter list. Voting procedures and requirements incorporate numerous safeguards against fraud, including mandatory voter registration cards bearing photo identification and fingerprints. An autonomous, seven-member Electoral Tribunal adjudicates election disputes.

Politics and Political Parties

The Institutional Revolutionary Party (Partido Revolucionario Institucional—PRI) was the country's preeminent political organization from 1929 until the early 1990s. Historically, the PRI has been ideologically a center-left party, blending nationalism with mildly redistributionist public policies. Since its founding, the PRI has portrayed itself as a champion of workers and landless peasants. However, during the mid-1980s the "technocratic" wing of the party, which favored market-oriented reform, became dominant over its populist wing. Over the course of three general election cycles (1982, 1988, and 1994), the PRI's leadership selected presidential candidates primarily based on their ability to implement market- oriented reforms. This trend alienated much of the PRI's populist "*político*" wing, prompting many party members to defect to organizations farther to the left.

Until the early 1 980s, the PRI's position in the Mexican political system was hegemonic, and opposition parties posed little or no threat to its power base or its near monopoly of public office. This situation changed during the mid-1980s as opposition parties of the left and right began to seriously challenge PRI candidates for local, state, and national offices. On the right, the National Action Party (Partido de Acción Nacional—PAN) has made the greatest inroads into national politics—most notably by attaining the presidency in 2000 and ending seven decades of PRI control over the executive branch. The PAN emerged as a conservative reaction to the nationalizations and land confiscations undertaken by PRI governments in the 1930s. Its power base is heavily concentrated in the wealthier states of the north and center of the country. The PAN resembles a standard Christian Democratic party, deriving its early support primarily from the Roman Catholic Church, the business sector, and other groups alienated by the left-wing populist policies of past PRI governments. On the left, the Democratic Revolutionary Party (Partido Revolucionario Democrático—PRD) emphasizes social welfare concerns and opposes most economic reforms implemented since the mid-1980s. Although it encompasses much of the rank and file of the former communist and socialist parties, the PRD is controlled by former PRI leaders. Several minor parties also are represented in the Congress and in state and local governments: the Labor Party (Partido del Trabajo—PT), Mexican Green Ecologist Party (Partido Verde Ecologista Mexicano—PVEM), New Alliance Party (Partido Nueva Alianza), and Social Democratic and Rural Alternative Party (Partido Democracia Social y Alternativa Rural).

Mass Media

Mexico is considered the media capital of Spanish-speaking Latin America. The country has approximately 300 daily newspapers, 1,300 radio stations, and 460 television stations, most under private ownership. Television is the most influential medium; a majority of stations are affiliated with either the Televisa or Tele Azteca national networks. The press is largely free; however, liberal defamation and libel laws have been widely cited as a constraint on press freedoms. Violence against journalists by drug smuggling gangs poses a growing threat to freedom of expression, especially in northern Mexico.

Foreign Relations

Historically, Mexico has sought to advance its interests abroad and to project its influence largely through moral persuasion. In particular, Mexico has been a champion of the principles of nonintervention and self-determination. However, during the administration of President Vicente Fox Quesada (2000–2006), Mexico took a more active stance on Western Hemisphere regional issues such as trade promotion, economic development in Central America, migration, combating organized crime, and human rights. Mexican foreign policy has also shifted away from economic nationalism to embrace globalization and participation in international commerce. During its first year, the Felipe Calderón Hinojosa administration (2006–) signaled that it would retreat somewhat from its predecessor's activist approach to international affairs, while continuing to promote domestic economic and political reforms.

The bilateral relationship with the United States is at the forefront of Mexican foreign policy. Since 1981, the management of the broad array of U.S.–Mexico issues has been formalized in the U.S.–Mexico Binational Commission, composed of numerous U.S. cabinet members and their Mexican counterparts. The commission holds annual plenary meetings, and many subgroups meet during the course of the year. The most important U.S.–Mexico bilateral issues are illegal immigration, drug trafficking and border crime, and the promotion of trade and investment. Mexico has urged the United States to enact an expanded guest worker program that would increase opportunities for legal migration of Mexican nationals. Mexico also advocates the granting of amnesty to Mexican illegal immigrants already in the United States and opposes the deployment of fencing across the U.S.–Mexico border. Since the early 1990s, Mexico and the United States have collaborated closely in combating the illegal drug trade.

Membership in International Organizations

Mexico is a member of numerous international organizations, including the following: Agency for the Prohibition of Nuclear Weapons in Latin America and the Caribbean (OPANAL), Asia Pacific Economic Cooperation (APEC) forum, Bank for International Settlements (BIS), Caribbean Development Bank (CDB), Central American Bank for Economic Integration (BCIE), Council of Europe (CE) (observer), European Bank for Reconstruction and Development (EBRD), Food and Agriculture Organization (FAO), Group of Three (Colombia, Mexico, Venezuela—G–3), Group of Six (G–6), Group of Fifteen (G–1 5), Group of Twenty-four (G–24), Inter-American Development Bank (IADB), International Atomic Energy Agency (IAEA), International Bank for Reconstruction and Development (IBRD), International Civil Aviation Administration (ICAO), International Confederation of Free Trade Unions (ICFTU), International Criminal Court (ICC), International Criminal Police Organization (Interpol), International Development Association (IDA), International Federation of Red Cross and Red Crescent Societies (IFRCS), International Finance Corporation (IFC), International Fund for Agricultural development (IFAD), International Hydrographic Organization (IHO), International Labor Organization (ILO), International Maritime Organization (IMO), International Monetary Fund (IMF), International Olympic Committee (IOC), International Organization for Migration (IOM), International Organization for Standardization (ISO), International Red Cross Movement (ICRM), International Telecommunication Union (ITU), Inter-Parliamentary Union (IPU), Latin American Economic System (LAES), Latin American Integration Association (LAIA), North American Free Trade Agreement (NAFTA), Non-Aligned Movement (NAM) (observer), Nuclear Energy Agency (NEA), Organisation for Economic Co-operation and Development (OECD), Organization for the Prohibition of Chemical Weapons (OPCW), Organization of American States (OAS), Permanent Court of Arbitration (PCA), Rio Group (RG), United Nations (UN), United Nations Conference on Trade and Development (UNCTAD), United Nations Educational, Scientific and Cultural Organization (UNESCO), United Nations High Commissioner for Refugees (UNHCR) executive committee, United Nations Industrial Development Organization (UNIDO), United Nations Institute for Training and Research (UNITAR), United Nations Monitoring, Verification, and Inspection Commission (UNMOVIC), Universal Postal Union (UPU), World Confederation of Labor (WCL), World Customs Organization (WCO), World Federation of Trade Unions (WFTU), World Health Organization (WHO), World Intellectual Property Organization (WIPO), World Meteorological Organization (WMO), World Tourism Organization (WToO), and World Trade Organization (WTO).

Major International Treaties

Mexico is a party to numerous arms control, commercial, and environmental treaties, as well as several regional and bilateral free-trade agreements: Act of Chapultepec, Basel Convention on the Trans-boundary Movement of Hazardous Wastes, Biological Weapons Convention, Chemical Weapons Convention, Convention on Biological Diversity, Convention on International Trade in Endangered Species, Convention on the International

Maritime Organization, Convention to Combat Desertification, Framework Convention on Climate Change (UNFCCC), General Agreement on Tariffs and Trade (GATT), Geneva Protocol, Hague Conventions, Inter-American Democratic Charter, Kyoto Protocol to the UNFCCC, Law of the Sea Treaty, Limited Test Ban Treaty, Mexico–Bolivia Free Trade Agreement (FTA), Mexico–Chile FTA, Mexico–Colombia–Venezuela (Group of Three) FTA, Mexico–Costa Rica FTA, Mexico–European Union FTA, Mexico–Israel FTA, Mexico–Nicaragua FTA, Mexico–Northern Triangle (Guatemala, El Salvador, Honduras) FTA, North American Agreement on Environmental Cooperation, North American Free Trade Agreement (NAFTA), Nuclear Non-Proliferation Treaty (NPT), Renunciation of War Treaty, Rio Declaration on Environment and Development, Terrorism Prevention Convention, Treaty for the Prohibition of Nuclear Weapons in Latin America (Treaty of Tlatelolco), United Nations Conference on Disarmament, United Nations Convention on the Law of the Sea, Rome Statute of the International Criminal Court, Vienna Convention for the Protection of the Ozone Layer, and World Trade Organization (WTO) Agreement.

National Security

Armed Forces Overview

Mexico maintains one of the smallest militaries in the Western Hemisphere in per-capita terms. In 2007 Mexico had 237,800 active armed forces personnel and 39,899 reservists. Active-duty personnel are assigned to the various services as follows: army, 183,700; navy, 42,400 (including 12,600 marines); and air force, 11,700. The armed forces' primary missions are domestic antidrug operations, rural counterinsurgency, and disaster relief.

Foreign Military Relations

Historically, relations between the military establishments of Mexico and the United States have not been close. Cooperation peaked for a brief period during and after World War II. In the Cold War atmosphere that followed, however, Mexico opposed U.S. concepts of regional security. During the late 1980s, relations between the Mexican and U.S. military establishments improved as cooperative efforts expanded in the fight against illicit drugs. Numerous Mexican officers receive training in the United States and are well acquainted with U.S. military doctrine, but on the whole, the Mexican armed forces are less influenced by the U.S. military than are the armed forces of other countries in Latin America.

External Threat

Mexico has no foreign nation-state adversaries and little ambition to impose itself upon other nations. It repudiates the use of force to settle disputes and rejects interference by one nation in the affairs of another. Although it has not suffered a major terrorist incident, Mexico considers itself a potential target for international terrorism.

Defense Budget

In 2007 Mexico's defense budget was US$3.3 billion or about 0.4 percent of gross domestic product.

Major Military Units

The principal units of the Mexican army are nine infantry brigades and a number of independent regiments and infantry battalions. The main maneuver elements of the army are organized in three corps, each consisting of three infantry brigades, all based in and around the Federal District. Distinct from the brigade formations, independent regiments and battalions are assigned to zonal garrisons (45 in total) in each of the country's 12 military regions. Infantry battalions, composed of approximately 300 troops, generally are deployed in each zone, and certain zones are assigned an additional motorized cavalry regiment or an artillery regiment. The air force is organized into two wings and 10 air groups, as well as an airborne brigade. The air force's principal base is located at Santa Lucía in the state of México. Other major air bases are located in the states of Baja California Sur, Oaxaca, Quintana Roo, Veracruz, and Yucatán. The navy's operational command is divided between the nation's two coasts. The Pacific fleet is headquartered at Acapulco; the Gulf of Mexico coast command is located at Veracruz. Each command has three naval regions. There are 17 naval zones, one for each coastal state; some are subdivided into sectors. In addition to the surface fleet, the navy maintains an aviation arm and a marine force.

Major Military Equipment

The army is equipped with 272 reconnaissance vehicles, approximately 757 armored personnel carriers, 114 towed artillery, six self-propelled artillery, 1,955 mortars, 30 antitank guns, eight antitank guided weapons, 80 air defense guns, and an unspecified number of surface-to-air missiles. The navy inventory includes one destroyer, six frigates, 180 patrol and coastal combatants, three amphibious landing ships, and 19 logistics and support vessels. Naval aviation maintains 150 unarmed helicopters and eight combat aircraft. The navy's marine component is equipped with 16 towed howitzers, six multiple rocket launchers, 100 mortars, 25 assault amphibious vehicles, and 60 coastal assault craft. The air force has 84 combat aircraft and 123 helicopters.

Military Service

The navy and air force are all-volunteer services, while the 183,700-strong army includes 60,000 conscripts. Army conscripts are selected by lottery and are obligated to serve for one year. All male natural-born Mexican citizens are required to register for the selective service in January of the year in which they reach 18 years of age.

Paramilitary Forces

The Federal Preventive Police (Policía Federal Preventiva—PFP) under the Public Security Secretariat (Secretaría de Seguridad Pública—SSP) combats organized crime and domestic insurgencies. The PFP, which relies heavily on reassigned military police and intelligence personnel, includes several specialized tactical and investigative elements, an independent intelligence arm, the federal highway police, a border and port security branch, and an internal affairs component. In 2007 Mexico had 30,700 paramilitary forces, of which 12,700 were PFP and 18,000, Rural Defense Militia.

Foreign Military Forces

None present.

Military Forces Abroad

Consistent with its foreign policy of non-intervention in the affairs of other states, Mexico has declined United Nations (UN) requests for peacekeeping troops. However, in 2004 the Mexican Foreign Ministry stated that Mexico would be willing to contribute non-combat personnel to UN peacekeeping missions. Mexico has dispatched unarmed troops to Central America and Indonesia to provide humanitarian relief in the aftermath of major natural disasters. In September 2005, a Mexican army convoy delivered humanitarian supplies to survivors of Hurricane Katrina in Texas. Mexico maintains military attachés in several friendly foreign capitals.

Police

Police forces number aproximately 500,000 federal, state, and municipal officers. The paramilitary Federal Preventive Police (Policía Federal Preventiva—PFP) is the main enforcement arm of the federal government. The Federal Investigation Agency (Agencia Federal de Investigación—AFI) under the Office of the Attorney General is a multiskilled investigative agency comparable to the U.S. Federal Bureau of Investigation (FBI). The Special Unit Against Organized Crime (Unidad Especializada Contra la Delicuencia Organizada—UEDO), an investigative arm of the Office of the Attorney General, was specially created to combat organized crime.

Internal Threat

Mexico faces numerous internal threats to public safety, most notably from established domestic drug trafficking networks that transport and distribute South American cocaine and other illicit substances destined for the United States. The country's heavily armed, territorially organized drug trafficking networks regularly launch sophisticated, lethal attacks on police, rival drug gangs, journalists, and elected officials. During 2007 President Calderón committed his government to dismantling the country's narcotics trafficking cartels and mobilized more than 20,000 army troops and federal police against drug traffickers in 10 states. According to media reports, drug cartels killed approximately 2,470 persons, including 300 police officers and 27 soldiers, during 2007. Violence against police officials was particularly severe in the states of Monterrey, Guerrero, Michoacan, and Sinaloa. Street crime and targeted crimes such as kidnapping for ransom are common in major cities. Demonstrations and labor disputes occasionally turn violent. In 2006 the city of Oaxaca experienced a prolonged series of civil disturbances that resulted in approximately 20 civilian deaths. Politically inspired domestic insurgencies pose a minor, but persistent threat to public safety, mainly in the remote, mountainous zones of western and southern Mexico.

Terrorism

Several violent left-wing guerrilla groups have been active in Mexico since the late 1 960s. These groups engage in kidnappings for ransom as well as sporadic terrorist attacks against police, military personnel, and the nation's economic infrastructure. Mexico's government officially recognizes the existence of three insurgent organizations. The best known is the Zapatista National Liberation Army (Ejército Zapatista de Liberación Nacional—EZLN), with which the government has had an uneasy truce since the insurgents staged a violent, short- lived 1994 revolt in the southern state of Chiapas. The other two are the People's Revolutionary Army (Ejército Popular Revolucionario—EPR), which operates mainly in Guerrero and Oaxaca states, and an EPR offshoot formed in 1998 called the Revolutionary Army of the Insurgent People (Ejército Revolucionario del Pueblo Insurgente—ERPI). In July 2007, the EPR bombed a major gas pipeline from Mexico City to Guadalajara in western Mexico, causing the temporary shutdown of several foreign-owned factories. The EPR struck again in September, when it bombed six oil and gas pipelines in the state of Veracruz.

Mexico's drug trafficking gangs have begun to use improvised explosive devices (IEDs) and high-powered military-grade weapons in their attacks against rival gangs and police personnel. In February 2008, drug traffickers were suspected of setting off an IED near Mexico City's police headquarters in an attack that killed one person and wounded two others.

Mexico historically has been a haven for Latin American and Spanish militant groups, including the Basque Fatherland and Liberty (ETA) and Revolutionary Armed Forces of Colombia (FARC) terrorist organizations. Increased intelligence and law enforcement cooperation between Mexico and the governments of Colombia and Spain in recent years has helped reduce the presence of these groups in Mexico. Given its status as a major U.S. commercial partner and ally against terrorism, Mexico considers itself a potential target for attacks by the al Qaeda terrorist network. Since the 2001 terrorist attacks on the United States, Mexico has upgraded border security and deployed its armed forces at critical infrastructure sites throughout the country.

Human Rights

According to the U.S. Department of State, during 2007 the government of Mexico generally respected and promoted human rights at the national level; however, violations persisted at the state and local levels. Government efforts to improve respect for human rights were offset by a deeply entrenched culture of impunity and corruption, particularly among elements of the law enforcement community. As in much of Latin America, prison conditions generally are poor. The law prohibits discrimination based on race, gender, disability, or religion. Although the government continued to make progress in enforcing these provisions, significant problems, particularly violence against women, persisted. There was a marked increase during the year in narcotics trafficking-related violence, especially in the northern border region.

In: Mexico: Background and Issues
Editor: Richard C. Bradley
ISBN: 978-1-61728-498-4

Chapter 8

COUNTRY ANALYSIS BRIEFS: MEXICO*

Energy Information Administration

Mexico is a major non-OPEC oil producer, with one of the world's largest oil companies, Pemex.

BACKGROUND

In 2008, Mexico was the seventh-largest oil producer in the world, and the third-largest in the Western Hemisphere. State-owned Petroleos Mexicanos (Pemex) holds a monopoly on oil production in the country and is one of the largest oil companies in the world. However, oil production in the country has begun to decrease, as production at the giant Cantarell field declines. The oil sector is a crucial component of Mexico's economy: while its relative importance to the general Mexican economy has declined, the oil sector still generates over 15 percent of the country's export earnings. More importantly, the government relies upon earnings from the oil industry (including taxes and direct payments from Pemex) for about 40 percent of total government revenues. Therefore, any decline in production at Pemex has a direct effect upon the country's overall fiscal balance.

* This is an edited, reformatted and augmented version of an Energy Information Administration publication dated March 2009.

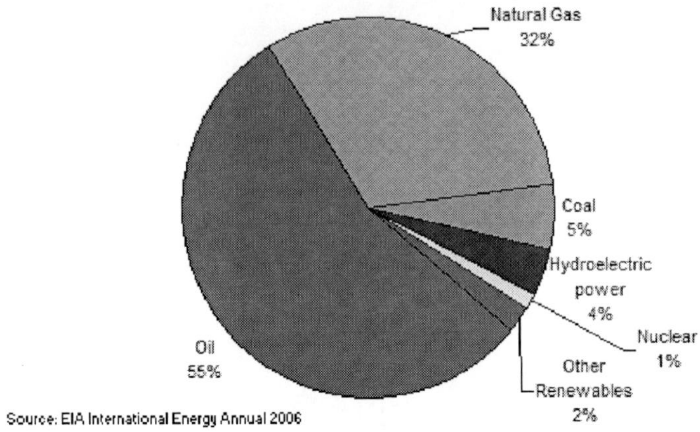

Total Energy Consumption in Mexico, by Type (2006)

Mexico's total energy consumption in 2006 consisted mostly of oil (55 percent), followed by natural gas (32 percent). All other fuel types contribute smaller amounts to Mexico's overall energy mix. Natural gas is increasingly replacing oil as a feedstock in power generation. However, Mexico is a net importer of natural gas, so higher levels of natural gas consumption will likely depend upon higher imports from either the United States or via liquefied natural gas (LNG).

OIL

Mexico is one of thetop three sources of U.S. oil imports.

According to the *Oil and Gas Journal* (*OGJ*), Mexico had 10.5 billion barrels of proven oil reserves as of January 1, 2009. Most reserves consist of heavy crude oil varieties, with a specific gravity of less than 25° API. The largest concentration of reserves occurs offshore in the southern part of the country, especially in the CampecheBasin. There are also sizable reserves in Mexico's onshore basins in the northern parts of the country.

In 2008, Mexico was the seventh-largest producer of oil in the world. The country produced an average of 3.19 million barrels per day (bbl/d) of total oil liquids during 2008, down from 3.50 million bbl/d in 2007. Of Mexico's oil production, about 88 percent was crude oil and condensate, the rest consisting of natural gas liquids (NGL) and refinery gain. Many analysts believe that Mexican oil production has peaked, and that the country's production will continue to decline in the coming years. Based on the March 2009 Short-Term Energy Outlook, EIA forecasts that Mexico will produce 2.9 million bbl/d of oil in 2009 and 2.7 million bbl/d in 2010. The decline is driven mainly by falling production at the super-giant Cantarell field, which has only been partially offset by higher production from other areas.

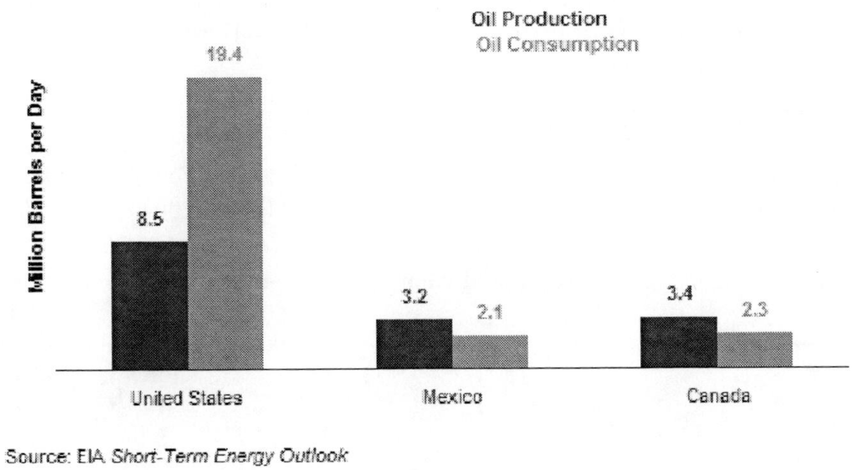

North America Oil Production and Consumption, 2008

Sector Organization

The Mexican constitution provides that the Mexican nation owns all hydrocarbon resources in the country. In 1938, Mexico nationalized its oil sector, creating Pemex as the sole oil operator in the country. Pemex has four operating subsidiaries: Exploration and Production, Gas and Basic Petrochemicals, Petrochemicals, and Refining. Pemex is the largest company in Mexico and one of the largest oil and natural gas companies in the world: in 2008, Pemex earned pre-tax profits of $43 billion, while it paid $50 billion to the government in the form of taxes and other transfers.

In 2008, Mexico enacted new legislation that sought to reform the country's oil sector. The goal of these reforms was to enable Pemex to curb the slide in oil production experienced over the past several years. The measures included several administrative changes, such as adding new seats to Pemex's administrative board for outside industry experts, creating a new advisory board designed to provide independent coordination of long-term energy strategy, and establishing a new hydrocarbons agency to regulate the sector. The reforms would also permit Pemex to create incentive-based service contracts with private companies. Pemex received greater autonomy under the reforms, including the ability to issue its own debt and establish more flexible mechanisms for procurement and investment.

Exploration and Production

Most of Mexico's oil production occurs in the Gulf of Campeche, located off the south-eastern coast of the country in the Gulf of Mexico. The two main production centers in the area include Cantarell and Ku-Maloop-Zaap (KMZ), with smaller volumes also coming from the fields off the coast of Tabasco state. In 2008, the Gulf of Campeche accounted for 80 percent of Mexico's total crude oil production. Due to the concentration of Mexico's oil production in the Gulf of Campeche, any tropical storms or hurricanes passing through the area can disrupt oil operations. In 2007, Hurricane Dean forced the evacuation of all offshore platforms and shut-in all production for several days. In 2005, Hurricane Emily also impacted Pemex's operations in the Gulf.

The Cantarell oil field is one of the largest oil fields in the world, but production there has declined dramatically in the past several years. In 2008, Cantarell produced 1.0 million bbl/d of crude oil, down over 30 percent from the 2007 level of 1.47 million bbl/d and down nearly 50 percent from the peak production level of 2.12 million bbl/d in 2004. As production at the field has declined, so has its relative importance to Mexico's oil sector: Cantarell contributed 36 percent of Mexico's total crude oil production in 2008, versus 62 percent in 2004.

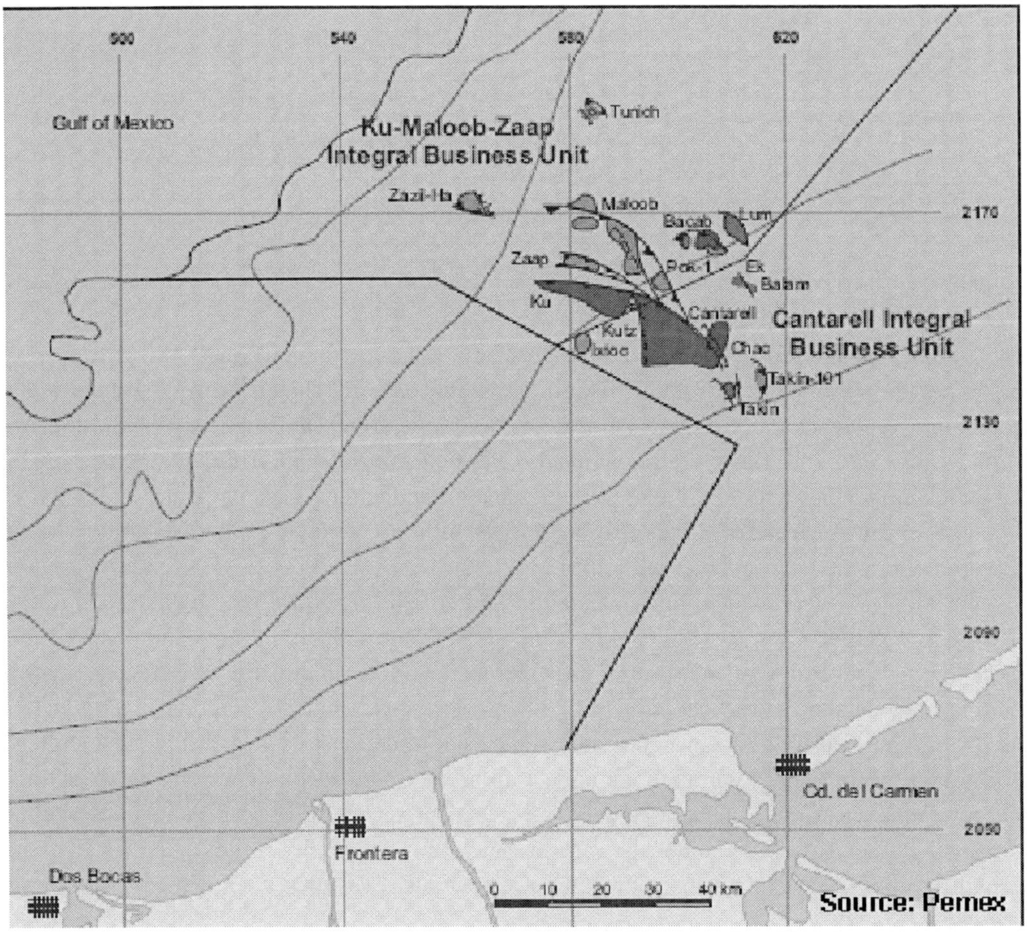

Cantarell consists of four major complexes: Akal, Nohoch, Chac, and Kutz. Production at Cantarell began in 1979, but it soon began to decline due to falling reservoir pressure. In 1997, Pemex developed a plan to reverse the field's decline by injecting nitrogen into the reservoir to maintain pressure. The plan was a success, with production at Cantarell in 2004 double the level seen in 1995. However, production at Cantarell soon began to decline again, with the rate of decline accelerating in recent years.

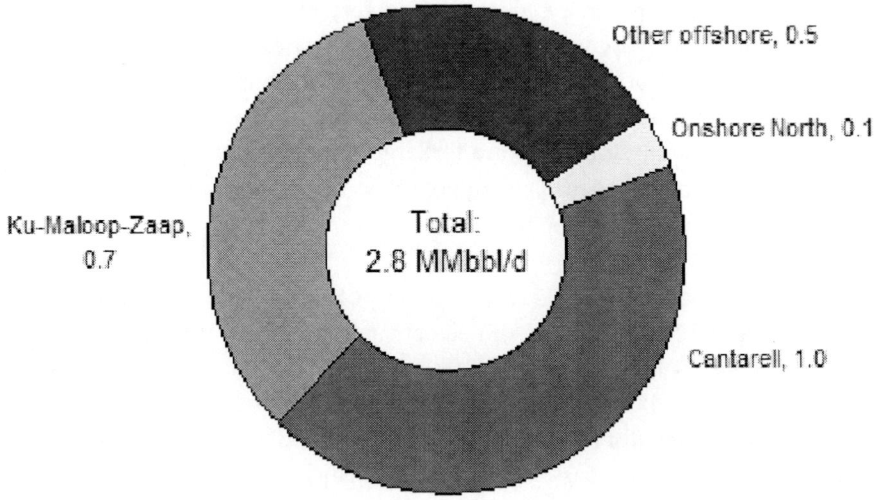

Source: Pemex

Mexico's Crude Oil Production, by Area, 2008 (millon barrels per day)

The KMZ project has been the largest source of new production growth in the past few years. Located adjacent to Cantarell, the KMZ complex produced 740,000 bbl/d of crude oil in 2008, up from 550,700 bbl/d in 2007. In just the last three years, production at KMZ has doubled, as Pemex employs a nitrogen re-injection program similar to that used at Cantarell. Production growth at KMZ has partially offset declines seen at Cantarell, and Pemex hopes to increase production further over the next few years. However, industry experts expect production at KMZ to also peak in the medium-term, perhaps as a soon as three years.

The offshore area adjacent to Tabasco state contains the Abkatun-Pol-Chuc and Litoral de Tabasco projects. Each project consists of several smaller fields, with combined crude oil production from the area standing at 500,000 bbl/d in 2008. Production from this area has stabilized in recent years, but it is about one-third lower than levels seen a decade ago.

Onshore fields only represent around 20 percent of Mexico's total crude oil production. Most of this production is in the southern part of the country, which contains 80 percent of total onshore production. The largest oilfield in the south is Puerto Ceiba, which produced about 50,000 bbl/d in 2008, while the largest oilfield in the north is Arenque (10,000 bbl/d in 2008).

Chicontepec

Pemex sees the onshore Chicontepec project, located northeast of Mexico City, as a potentially large source of future production growth. Chicontepec contains 29 distinct fields spread over an area of 2,400 square miles. The project currently produces about 30,000 bbl/d, but Pemex hopes to increase production to 700,000 bbl/d by 2017. In early 2009, Pemex announced a tender for the drilling of 170 development wells at Chicontepec, following earlier tenders in 2008 for the drilling of 1,000 wells. According to Pemex, Chicontepec contains an estimated 17.7 billion barrels of oil equivalent of possible (3P) hydrocarbon reserves.

According to industry reports, Chicontepec is very challenging technically. Most of the crude oil at Chicontepec is very heavy, with an API gravity of as little as 18°. The reservoir is also highly fractured and at low pressure, meaning that recovery rates could be low and Pemex will need a large number of wells to fully exploit the area. The region does not yet have much of the necessarily infrastructure for large-scale oil development, such as pipelines, which must be built amongst a dense, urban population.

Crude Varieties

Most of Mexico's crude oil production consists of heavy crude varieties. Maya, a heavy crude which averages 22° API and 3.5-4.0 percent sulfur content, generally represents around two- thirds of Mexico's total crude oil production. The country also produces two lighter crude streams, Isthmus (34° API) and Olmeca (39° API). In general, Mexico retains most of the lighter crude streams for domestic consumption and exports the bulk of its Maya production to the U.S. Gulf Coast, which has sophisticated refining capacity necessary to process these heavy crudes.

Pipelines

Pemex operates an extensive pipeline network in Mexico that connects major production centers with domestic refineries and export terminals. This network consists of over 453 pipelines spanning 2,900 miles, with the largest concentration occurring in the southern part of the country. Mexico does not have any international pipeline connections, with most exports leaving the country via tanker from three export terminals in the southern part of the country: Cayo Arcas, Dos Bocas, and Coatzacoalcos.

Oil Trade

Oil Exports

In 2008, Mexico exported 1.4 million bbl/d of crude oil. The United States receives the vast majority of Mexico's crude oil exports, which mostly arrive via tanker at the GulfCoast; in 2008, the U.S. imported 1.2 million bbl/d of crude oil from Mexico, of which 97 percent went to the GulfCoast. The U.S. also imported about 100,000 bbl/d of refined products from Mexico in 2008, mostly residual fuel oil, naphtha, and gasoline blending components.

Mexico is consistently one of the top three exporters of oil to the U.S., along with Canada and Saudi Arabia. The close proximity of the U.S. market and the sophisticated level of refineries in the United Stateswill continue to attract the bulk of Mexico's oil exports. Mexico's crude oil exports to the United States rose steadily through the 1 980s and 1 990s, before peaking in 2004 at 1.6 million bbl/d. The combination of Mexico's falling oil production and rising domestic demand have led to a reduction in exports to the United States since that peak. From 2004-2007, Mexico was the second-largest source of U.S. oil imports, but fell to third-largest in 2008.

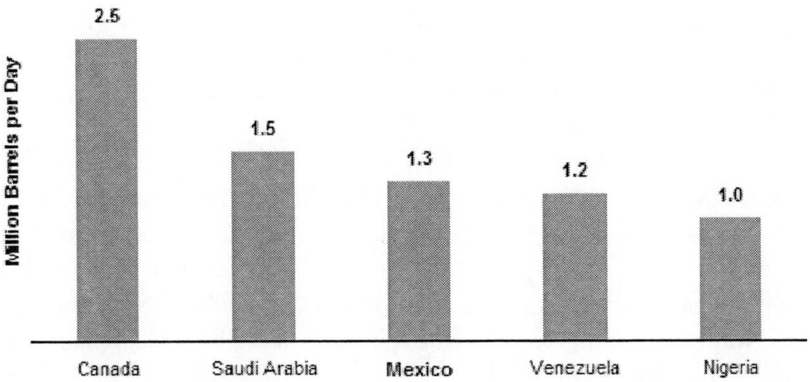

Source: EIA Petroleum Supply Monthly

Top 5 Sources of U.S. Petroleum Imports, 2008

Oil Imports

Despite its status as one of the world's largest crude oil exporters, Mexico is a net importer of refined petroleum products. In 2008, Mexico imported 550,000 bbl/d of refined petroleum products, while exporting 192,000 bbl/d. Gasoline represented over 60 percent of product imports. A resumption of brisk economic growth is one cause for the increase in refined product imports, along with fixed domestic product prices that are below international market levels.

Long-Term Developments in Mexico's Oil Trade

The *International Energy Outlook (IEO) 2009* forecasts that Mexico could become a net oil importer by 2020, with net imports reaching 300,000 bbl/d in 2030. As one of the largest oil exporters to the United States, this has important implications for future U.S. energy supplies. On the other hand, the *Annual Energy Outlook (AEO) 2009 Early Release* projects that U.S. crude oil imports could fall from 9.78 million in 2008 to 6.95 million bbl/d in 2030. As a result, the long-term fall in U.S. crude oil imports could be larger than the fall in Mexico's crude oil exports. From Mexico's perspective, changing into a net oil importer would have important repercussions upon the economy, due to the dependence of the federal government on Pemex for a sizable share of its revenues.

Downstream

Mexico's oil consumption averaged 2.1 million bbl/d in 2008. According to *OGJ*, Mexico has six refineries, all operated by Pemex, with a total refining capacity of 1.5 million bbl/d. The largest facility in the country is the 330,000-bbl/d Salina Cruz facility. Outside of Mexico, Pemex controls 50 percent of the 334,000-bbl/d Deer Park refinery in Texas. In order to reduce its imports of refined products, Pemex plans to build at least one additional refinery in Mexico. The company announced in early 2009 that the cost of its plans to build a new, 300,000-bbld refinery had increased to $10 billion. Pemex planned to start construction on the facility, which would have facilities to better process the country's heavy crude oil production, by the end of 2009.

NATURAL GAS

Mexico's natural gas consumption is rising primarily due to great use in power generation.

According to *OGJ*, Mexico had 11.8 trillion cubic feet (Tcf) of proven natural gas reserves as of January 2009. According to Pemex, the Southern Region of the country contains the largest share of proven reserves. However, the Northern Region will likely be the center of future reserves growth, as it contains almost ten times as much probable and possible natural gas reserves as the Southern Region. In 2007, Mexico produced 1.98 Tcf of natural gas, while consuming 2.4 Tcf, with imports coming both via pipeline from the United States and liquefied natural gas.

Mexico's natural gas production has grown in recent years, following steady declines during the late 1990s. During that time, natural gas consumption has grown steadily, driven mostly by the electricity sector, whose share of total natural gas consumption increased from 16 percent in 1997 to 33 percent in 2007. Pemex itself is the single largest consumer of natural gas, representing around 40 percent of domestic consumption in 2007.

Sector Organization

Pemex holds a monopoly on natural gas exploration and production in Mexico. The Mexican government opened the downstream natural gas sector to private operators in 1995, though no single company may participate in more than one industry function (transportation, storage, or distribution). It also created the Energy Regulatory Commission (CRE) to monitor the sector.

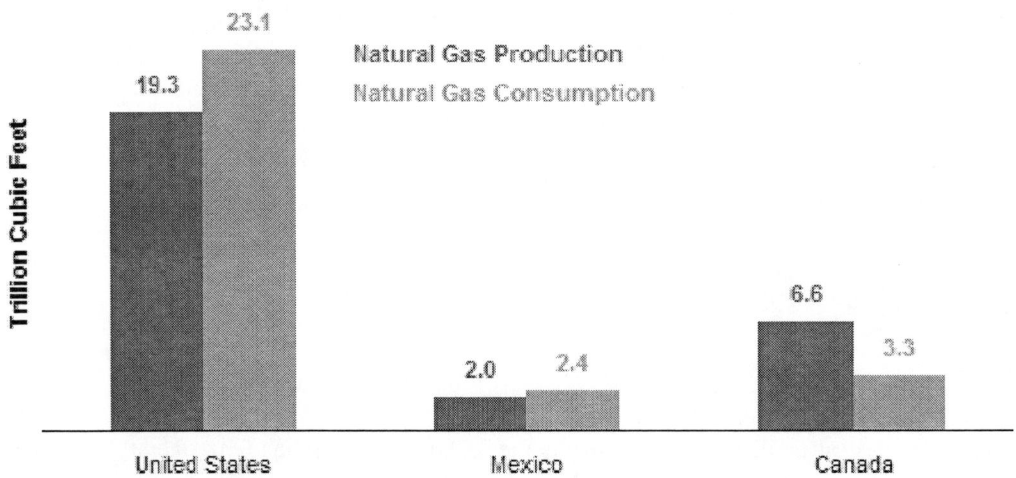

Source: EIA Country Energy Profile

North America Natural Gas Production and Consumption, 2007

Mexico's natural gas production is spread throughout the country. Onshore fields in the northern part of the country represented 42 percent of Mexico's natural gas production in 2007, while onshore fields in the south contributed 22 percent, and offshore fields in the Gulf of Campeche represented the remainder. Mexico's natural gas production is relatively-evenly split between associated and non-associated fields.

Pipelines and Storage

Pemex operates over 5,700 miles of natural gas pipelines in Mexico. The company has twelve natural gas processing centers, which produced 400,000 bbl/d of natural gas liquids (NGLs) and 200,000 bbl/d of liquefied petroleum gas (LPG) in 2007. Pemex also operates most of the country's natural gas distribution network, which supplies processed natural gas to consumption centers. The natural gas pipeline network includes ten active import connections with the United States. In 2008, Mexico imported 363.3 billion cubic feet (Bcf) of natural gas from the United States, while it also exported 42.9 Bcf.

Liquefied Natural Gas (LNG)

There are two operating LNG terminals in Mexico and one other currently under construction. In addition, there are other plants in various stages of the planning process. According to industry reports, the largest suppliers of LNG to Mexico in 2007 were Egypt, Nigeria, and Trinidad and Tobago.

East Coast

Altamira, a joint venture of Royal Dutch Shell (50 percent), Total (25 percent), and Mitsui (25 percent) received its first LNG cargo in August 2006. The plant, located in Tamaulipas state, has an initial capacity of 500 million cubic feet per day (MMcf/d), with plans to increase the project to a peak capacity of 1.3 Bcf/d. CFE has signed a 15-year contract to purchase the entire output of the terminal.

West Coast

The Costa Azul terminal near Ensenada, operated by Sempra, began receiving LNG in 2008. The current send-out capacity of the plant is about 1 Bcf/d. Most of the natural gas will supply domestic customers in northwest Mexico, but some natural gas could also be exported to California or Arizona.

Construction of a new LNG terminal at the port of Manzanillo began in 2008. The plant will have an initial capacity of 500 MMcf/d. A consortium of Mitsui, KOGAS, and Samsung is building the plant. The plant would be the second LNG terminal on the Pacific Coast.

In May 2004, DKRW signed an agreement with the state government of Sonora to build a 1.0- Bcf/d LNG receiving terminal at Puerto Libertad, on the Gulf of California. El Paso later joined the project as well, and the project will reportedly connect with the El Paso natural gas pipeline system in the United States. According to project sponsors, the plant could begin operations by 2011.

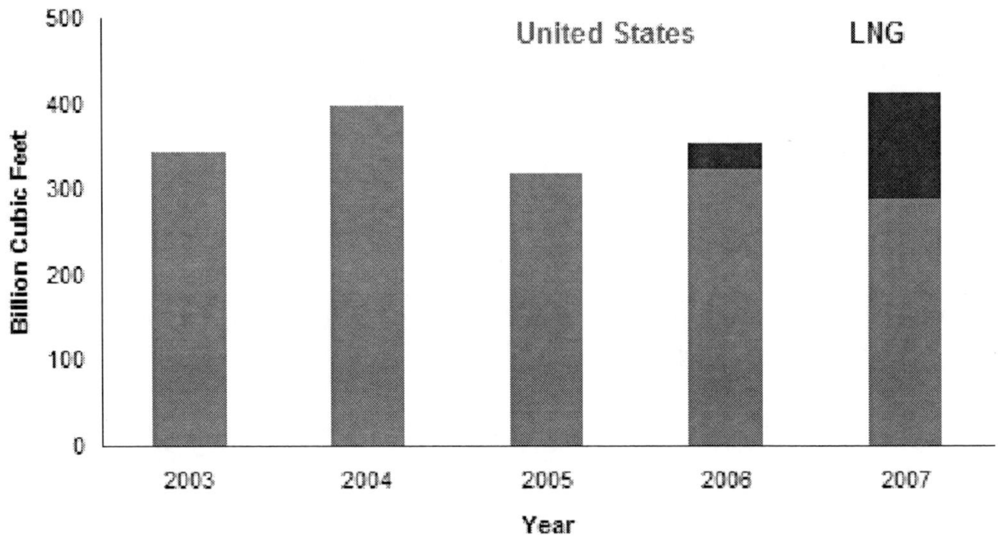

Source: International Energy Agency

Mexico's Natural Gas Imports, by Source

ELECTRICITY

Most of Mexico's electricity generation comes from conventional thermal sources, chiefly natural gas.

Mexico had 53.8 gigawatts of installed electricity generating capacity in 2007. The country generated 243 billion kilowatthours (Bkwh) of electric power in 2007. Conventional thermal generation represents the overwhelming majority of Mexico's electricity generation, though the mix from these sources is gradually shifting from oil products to natural gas. Mexico consumed 202 Bkwh of electric power in 2007.

Sector Organization

State-owned Comision Federal de Electricidad (CFE) is the dominant player in the generation sector, controlling about two-thirds of installed generating capacity. CFE also holds a monopoly on electricity transmission and distribution outside of Mexico City and some other municipalities; within those areas, state-owned Luz y Fuerza Centro (LFC) holds a monopoly on distribution activities. The Comision Reguladora de Energia (CRE) has principle regulatory oversight of the electricity sector.

Changes to Mexican law in 1992 opened the generation sector to private participation. Any company seeking to establish private electricity generating capacity or begin importing/exporting electric power must attain a permit from CRE. As of the end of 2008, private generators held about 22,700 megawatts (MW) of generating capacity, mostly consisting of combined-cycle, gas- fired turbines (CCGFT). CFE also operates Mexico's national transmission grid, which consists of 27,000 miles of high voltage lines, 28,000 miles of medium voltage lines, and 370,000 miles of low voltage distribution lines.

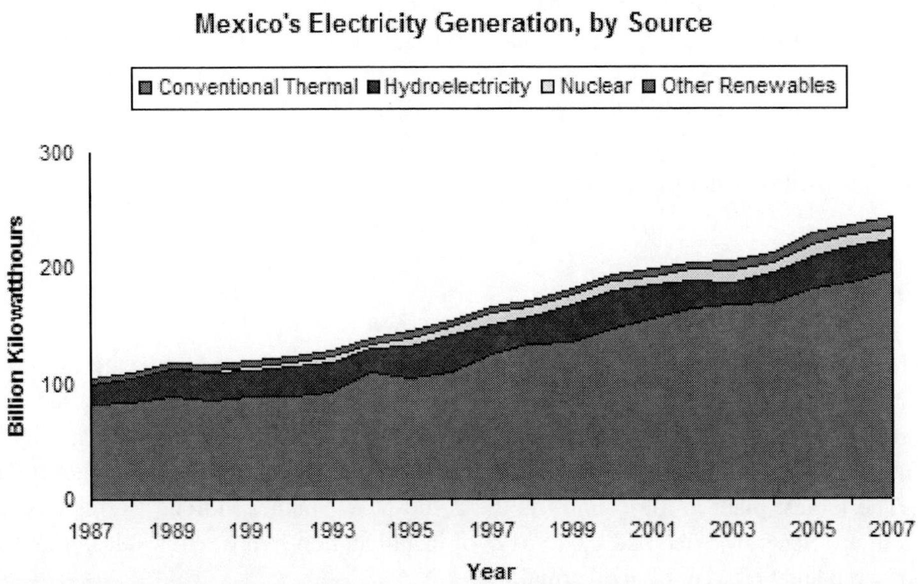

Source: ELA International Energy Annual

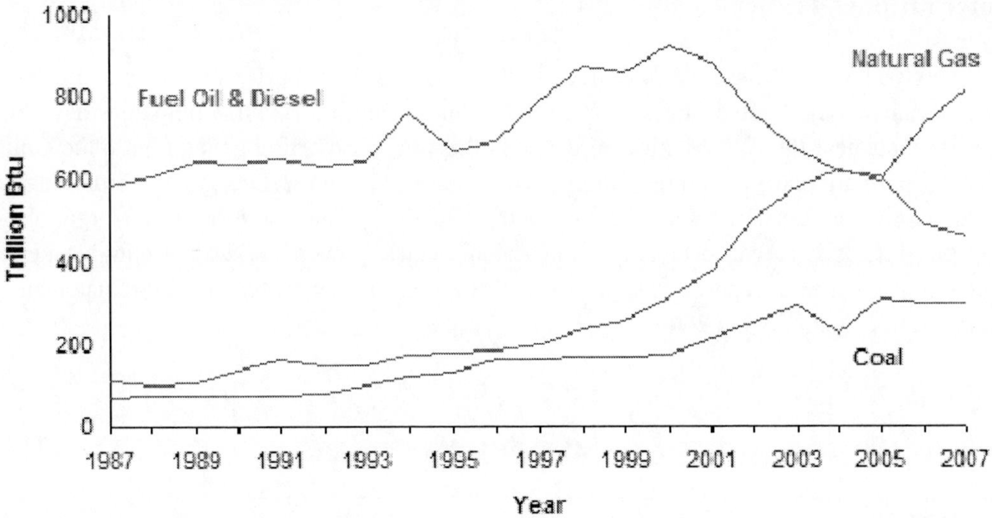

Source: Sener Balance National Energia

Consumption of Hydrocarbons for Electricity Generation in Mexico

Conventional Thermal

In the past, fuel oil and diesel fuel represented the largest share of the feedstock in Mexico's conventional thermal generation mix. However, natural gas consumption for electricity generation has risen dramatically in recent years, and natural gas is now the dominant feedstock: according to Mexico's Energy Secretariat (Sener), Mexico consumed 820 trillion Btu of natural gas for electricity generation in 2007, versus 460 trillion Btu of petroleum products. This shift has been the principle driver behind Mexico's rising natural gas consumption. Coal consumption by the electricity sector has also risen in recent years, reaching 300 trillion Btu in 2007.

Other Sources

Mexico has a single nuclear power plant, the 1,400-MW Laguna Verde nuclear reactor in Veracruz, operated by CFE. In April 2007, CFE awarded a contract to an international consortium headed by Alstom to modernize the plant and increase generating capacity by 20 percent. Hydroelectricity supplied about 10 percent of Mexico's electricity generation in 2007. The largest plant in the country is the 2,400-MW Manuel Moreno Torres in Chiapas. According to Sener, Mexico had 1,045 MW of installed, non-hydro renewables, including 85 MW of wind and 960 MW of geothermal.

International Trade

Mexico has an active electricity trade with the United States. Mexico exported 1.3 Bkwh of electricity to the United States in 2007, while importing 0.6 Bkwh. Companies have built power plants near the U.S.-Mexico border with the aim of exporting generation to the United States. There are plans to connect Mexico with Guatemala and Belize as part of the Sistema de Interconexion Electrica para America Central (SIEPAC). The plan is part of a larger effort, the Plan Puebla-Panama, to create an integrated electric power market in Central America. According to media reports, the section of SIEPAC linking Mexico and Guatemala is expected to come online in 2009.

QUICK FACTS

Energy Overview	
Proven Oil Reserves (January 1, 2009E)	10.5 billion barrels
Oil Production (2008E)	3,190 thousand barrels per day, of which 88% was crude oil.
Oil Consumption (2008E)	2,100 thousand barrels per day
Crude Oil Distillation Capacity (2008E)	1,540 thousand barrels per day

(Continued)

Proven Natural Gas Reserves (January 1, 2009E)	11.8 trillion cubic feet
Natural Gas Production (2007E)	1.98 trillion cubic feet
Natural Gas Consumption (2007E)	2.4 trillion cubic feet
Recoverable Coal Reserves (2005E)	1,335 million short tons
Coal Production (2007E)	11.6 million short tons
Coal Consumption (2006E)	18.6 million short tons
Electricity Installed Capacity (2007E)	53.8 gigawatts
Electricity Production (2007E)	243 billion kilowatt hours
Electricity Consumption (2007E)	202 billion kilowatt hours
Total Energy Consumption (2006E)	7.4 quadrillion Btus*
Total Per Capita Energy Consumption (2006E)	68.5 million Btus
Energy Intensity (2006E)	6,116 Btu per $2000-PPP**
Environmental Overview	
Energy-Related Carbon Dioxide Emissions (2006E)	436 million metric tons
Per-Capita, Energy-Related Carbon Dioxide Emissions (2006E)	4.1 metric tons
Carbon Dioxide Intensity (2006E)	0.36 metric tons per thousand $2000-PPP**
Oil and Gas Industry	
Organization	Petroleos Mexicanos (Pemex), state-owned oil and natural gas monopoly
Major Oil/Gas Ports	Cayo Arcas, Dos Bocas, and Coatzacoalcos
Foreign Company Involvement	Some service contracts. Foreign companies are also involved in the midstream natural gas sector.
Major Oil Fields	Cantarell, Ku-Maloop Zaap, Abkatun-Pol-Chuc
Major Natural Gas Fields	Cantarell, Caan, Culebra, Muspac
Major Refineries (capacity, bbl/d)	Salina Cruz (330,000), Ciudad Madero (190,000), Tula Hidalgo (315 ,000), Cadereyta (275,000), Salamanca (245,000), Minatitlan (185 ,000)

* The total energy consumption statistic includes petroleum, dry natural gas, coal, net hydro, nuclear, geothermal, solar, wind, wood and waste electric power.

**GDP figures from Global Insight estimates based on purchasing power parity (PPP) exchange rates.

LINKS

EIA Links

EIA - Mexico Country Energy Profile

U.S. Government
CIA World Factbook - Mexico
U.S. State Department's Consular Information Sheet - Mexico

Foreign Government Agencies
Comisión Reguladora de Energía (CRE)
Secretaría de Comunicaciones y Transportes (SCT)
Secretaría de Energía
Secretaría de Medio Ambiente y Recursos Naturales (Semarnat)

Oil and Natural Gas
PEMEX, the state-owned oil company of Mexico

Electricity
Comisión Federal de Electricidad
Luz y Fuerza del Centro

SOURCES

Business Latin America Select
Business News Americas
Cambridge Energy Research Associates
ChevronTexaco
Chicago Tribune
CIA World Factbook
Comisión Federal de Electricidad
Dallas Morning News
Deutsche Bank
Dow Jones
Economist Intelligence Unit ViewsWire
Electric Utility Week
Energy Compass
Financial Times
Foreign Policy in Focus
Foster Electric Report
Gas Matters Today
Global Insight
Global Power Report
Houston Chronicle
Inside Energy
Inside F.E.R.C.
International Energy Agency
International Oil Daily
International Petroleum Finance

Journal of American Academy of Business
Los Angeles Times
Marathon Oil Corporation
Mexico 's Ministry of Energy
Natural Gas Week
New York Times
Oil and Gas Investor
Oil and Gas Journal
Oil Daily
Offshore
Pemex
Petrobras
Petroleum Economist
Petroleum Intelligence Weekly
Pipeline and Gas Journal
Platts Oilgram News
PR News
Repsol -YPF
Reuters
San Diego Union-Tribune
Securities and Exchanges Commission
Sempra Energy
Sener
Shell
Tractebel
Transalta
Union Fenosa
Upstream
U.S. Department of State
U.S. Energy Information Administration
Voice of America
World Gas Intelligence
Wood Mack enzie
World Markets Analysis Online
World Wide Projects

INDEX

D

E

F

G

H

I

N

O

T